Raffi Bedrosyan

TRAUMA AND RESILIENCE
ARMENIANS IN TURKEY

Hidden, not hidden and no longer hidden

ԿԻ

Gomidas Institute
London

This book is a record of Raffi Bedrosyan's activities between 2011 and 2018 championing the rights of Armenians, especially "hidden" or Islamized Armenians, living in Turkey. It is a compilation of 49 newspaper articles written by Bedrosyan, as well as 10 new essays. All materials are insightful and well-written, and contribute to a growing awareness of the traumatic experience of Armenians in Turkey following the Armenian Genocide. We have reproduced Bedrosyan's work with fidelity to the original materials.

Gomidas Institute is an independent academic institution dedicated to modern Armenian and regional studies. Its activities include research, publications, and outreach programs.

ISBN 978-1-909382-46-6

Gomidas Institute
42 Blythe Rd.
London W14 0HA
United Kingdom

www.gomidas.org
info@gomidas.org

To my friends Hrant Dink, Fethiye Çetin,
Vartkes Ergün Ayık, and Cem Özdemir

Contents

Contents

Foreword by Fethiye Çetin

Ever since my childhood days, I often dream of a gently flowing stream in the shadow of green trees. The images in this dream are so clear that I can almost touch the stones at the bottom of the stream, I can almost jump in with my bare feet, and I can clearly hear the rhythmic sounds of the water.

Where is this stream of my frequent dreams which does not look like any real stream that I know? I kept wondering about this question – until I travelled to Havav, near Elazig, in present day Turkey. Havav is the name of the village where my grandmother Heranoush was born, where she ran in the streets, jumped on the stones of the stream, drank the crystal-clear water from the fountain, sang the Armenian song 'Hingala' on the way to school. And Havav is the village where she witnessed, at nine years old, such savagery and terror that she wouldn't forget until the end of her life.

My grandmother could never return to her village after the age of nine, but she completely transferred to me her longing and love for the village and its dreamy stream.

How can a person keep on having frequent dreams about a location never seen, never visited in real life? How can a person start feeling another person's love and longing for a certain location?

Freud interprets the secret links in family trees as follows: "People inherit not only characteristics from the past generation, but also memories." The link between generations must be the passage of subconscious memories.

The trips to Armenia organized by Raffi Bedrosyan for many, many hidden Armenians reminded me of the images and longing of the village stream passed on to me from my grandmother. The common thread between me and the hidden Armenians on these trips was the shared legacy as the grandchildren of forcefully Islamized Armenians. I thought the strong impulse for these hidden Armenians travelling from Diyarbakir, Dersim, Sasun or Hemshin to Armenia would be the longing to return home, to their nest and roots.

I know this from my own feelings.

The horror and savagery of 1915 was so immense that hundreds of thousands of Armenian women and children had to choose between Islamization and the sword, in order to survive. The Armenian men were mostly murdered en masse, and therefore, the forceful conversion to Islam was applied mainly to Armenian women and children. Some women converted in ordered to save their children, or their brothers and sisters, others were forcefully kidnapped. But what choice did the children have, like my grandmother Heranoush? These little kids were suddenly torn away from a loving and trusting environment, to be dropped into a hostile new world. They witnessed unimaginable horrors and violence, and then, they had to continue living with the perpetrators of the horrors and violence, in the very same location where the horrors and violence occurred.

They carried the psychological scars of the horrors they witnessed until the end of their lives, constantly in fear. Years passed, but the degradation, alienation and discrimination against them never ceased. Neither they nor their perpetrators forgot the horrors of the 1915 events. One by one, these hidden Armenians passed away quietly, without having the opportunity to talk about what they had witnessed, without having a chance to grieve. But they passed on to the next generations their memories, the longing, the trauma, the loneliness, the exclusion…

The Turkish state implemented a policy of forced amnesia of the 1915 events, but at the same time, continued to track the Islamized Armenians, their children and grandchildren as potentially untrustworthy troublemakers. These people lived, and continue to live, as rootless individuals, under constant threat and fear of persecution.

Raffi Bedrosyan's activities in helping the hidden Armenians return to their roots is very significant because it is a cure to relieve their wounds of rootlessness, loneliness and the great stress of hiding their past. One must also remember that the discrimination and exclusion toward these people has not only been from the Muslim Turks and Kurds surrounding them, but also from many Christian Armenians who still do not see them as real Armenians.

In recent years, many journalists and filmmakers have interviewed and produced stories of the hidden Armenians. Most of the hidden Armenians have reflected that these interviewers came, observed them with great curiosity and interest like a newly discovered species, and then left. Raffi

Bedrosyan's approach to the hidden Armenians is quite different. He has helped create environments where the hidden Armenians could gather, talk and listen to one another, share stories, troubles and happy moments. Lifelong friendships have been established with one another and with Raffi.

The Surp Giragos Church in Diyarbakir is one of these meeting places. Long tables are set in the church courtyard for Sunday breakfasts. Hidden Armenians come from near and far, sharing food, stories. Talking, touching. Raffi participated as a civil engineer and global fundraiser for the reconstruction of the church, from the early planning phases until completion. But the more important contribution was the long series of articles he wrote, patiently and persistently, explaining the significance of this church reconstruction to the Diaspora Armenians living in all corners of the world.

After the completion of the church reconstruction, he gave the first piano concert, introducing Armenian culture and music to the hidden Armenians. Other activities followed, Armenian language classes in Diyarbakir and Dersim, and then the organized trips to Armenia from various regions, Diyarbakir, Dersim, Sason, Urfa, Mush, Van and Hemshin. His concert in the Diyarbakir Church on the centennial of the Armenian Genocide attracted 1,000 hidden Armenians. They paid their respects to the victims, but also re-awakened their memories, roots, identities.

Although the conditions in Turkey have grown worse recently, preventing the continuation of these activities, Raffi has continued his support for the hidden Armenians in troubled times, earning a place in their hearts.

Beside his engineering and musical talents, Raffi is a skillful writer. He has written incredible stories about keeping the memory alive, challenging the forces which attempt to erase memory. His stories about individuals, buildings, locations, sometimes stories within stories, are written in an intimate, frank, gripping and fluent style, making the reader grasp the historic events much better.

Born and raised in Istanbul, Raffi understands Turkey and its people very well. But he is also a Diasporan Armenian living in Canada. These two perspectives and his multi-dimensional professions have enabled him to analyze events deeply and thoroughly. I always read his writings and political analysis with great interest, taking notes. He is one of those people who have made me feel like a close friends from the first glance, gracious as an artist, illuminating as a thinker and writer.

Raffi Bedrosyan's book is a precious piece of work which helps us face the history, holding a mirror to the peoples of Turkey, linking past events with the current ones.

—Fethiye Çetin, Hrant Dink's lawyer and author of
My Grandmother, Istanbul, Turkey

Foreword by Taner Akçam

It is often said that the Armenians were the first people to officially adopt Christianity. The lands upon which this ancient Middle Eastern and Caucasian people live were conquered and occupied, first by Muslim Arab armies and later by a succession of Turkish tribes and peoples, who followed one after the other. The Armenians, it may be said, have for centuries engaged in a struggle to "stay alive" amid a Muslim sea. Throughout history they have been forced to contend with the problem of "voluntary" or forced conversion to Islam.

The question of forcible conversion to Islam only began to be seen as a significant problem within the borders of the Ottoman Empire with the 1839 "Tanzimat" Reform Legislation. There were three separate reasons for this. The first is that the Ottoman State began, as part of its attempt to "modernize" the empire, to guarantee the right of its citizens to worship freely, regardless of religion. The second was the ideological repercussions of the French Revolution, which had inspired the birth of a number of movements of national awakening on Ottoman soil. Various Christian ethnicities were the ones most strongly affected, and chief among these were the Armenians, who began to press for social and political reforms. One of their principal complaints was forced conversions to Islam, and freedom of religion soon took on a central importance in the debate over reforms. The third reason was that the issue of forcible conversion or religious freedom was seen by the Great Powers as an opportunity to intervene in the internal affairs of the Ottoman State.

Although numerous similar instances of forcible conversion occurred in the past, one that took place in 1889—the abduction, rape, and forcible conversion to Islam of an Armenian girl named Gülizar by the Kurdish Musa Bey—would have repercussions beyond the borders of the Ottoman Empire, from London to even New Zealand.

With the 1878 Treaty of Berlin in particular, the "Armenian question" would enter a new stage, as the question of reforms in the Armenian areas of the Ottoman Empire and the "Armenian Question" in general would become one of the principal topics of late 19th century diplomacy. It would not be incorrect to characterize this period as one of a gradual genocidal process, one that would continue until 1923. During this period, the forcible conversion of Armenians to Islam would emerge from being a "normal" everyday activity to becoming an indispensible component of large-scale massacres directed at the Armenian population. During the massacres that occurred between 1894 and 1897 thousands of Armenians converted to Islam in order to avoid death at the hands of their Muslim assailants.

But there is an important difference between the practice of forced conversion during the 1915-1918 genocide and that of the earlier period. Up to that point, the practice—albeit, widespread—had been largely winked at or ignored by Ottoman leaders, but never officially sanctioned, out of fear of provoking the intervention of the Great Powers. In 1915, however, it was adopted as the policy of the regime. The policy itself fluctuated in intensity. At first, permission was given for Armenians who had converted "voluntarily" to Islam, to be exempted from the deportations, and when it became understood that the end goal of "deportation" was annihilation, the number of converts increased significantly. However, as the numbers began to grow inestimably large and unmanageable, the Ottoman government outlawed conversion and decided that those Armenians who had converted to Islam would be subjected to deportation as well. During the years 1916-18, which is considered the "second stage" of the genocidal operation, Armenians were once again allowed to convert to Islam. Those who did not were deported and overwhelmingly perished in the wastelands of Der-i Zor.

To this day, for political reasons, we do not know how many Armenians may have been forcibly converted. The research on this subject is sparse, as the forcible conversion of Armenians remains one of the more neglected subjects in our field. Indeed, the amount of thought and writing devoted to this matter can hardly be considered adequate.

In this sense, this book by Raffi Bedrosyan, which you now hold in your hands, is of the utmost significance, but this significance does not merely derive from the things that he has written, but also from the things that he has done as a person of action.

Since the beginning of the 21st century, the question of Armenians who were forcibly converted to Islam has been on the public agenda in Turkey. Within a great many families, individuals have come to terms with the fact that they had originally been Armenians, and, taking advantage of the more liberal atmosphere of this period, have embraced their Armenian identity and even converted back to Christianity. The significant portion who have continued to preserve their Muslim identity have unfortunately begun to be seen and identified by the Turkish general public as "crypto-Armenians".

A number of interested researchers have traveled to Anatolia in an effort to locate "hidden" Armenians, and in a very brief period some books have emerged on this topic. The great majority of these works consist of interviews and conversations with such persons. But Raffi Bedrosyan has gone beyond this in his work. Not being satisfied with merely "discovering" such persons, the author has become a part of their life stories and has labored in order to create the conditions for them to become reacquainted with their Armenian roots.

Raffi has participated in the task of repairing and restoring the historical Armenian church in Diyarbakır. Then, by organizing and holding cultural activities within the restored church, he has helped hundreds of "hidden" Armenians to find one another. He has organized trips to Armenia for "hidden" Armenians from Diyarbakır, Dersim, Urfa, Sason, Mush, Van and Hemshin (Artvin, Hopa) and has given these persons the chance to rediscover their own histories and Armenian culture in general. Through his writings and his activities,
Raffi Bedrosyan has shown the Armenians of the Diaspora the importance of the subject of "hidden" Armenians in Turkey, and through his efforts, he has secured both spiritual and material support toward restoring the identities of such persons.

It is precisely this activism in which Raffi has been engaged that gives so much greater meaning to his writings. His years of direct action on the subject of "hidden" Armenians is what separates Raffi Bedrosyan from the great number of persons whose writings on the subject have been limited to interviews and observations. In his book Bedrosyan doesn't simply give his stories as a detached narrator; instead, he gives directly of himself. Armed with this quality, Raffi performs the important task of "bridging" two worlds. In his writings we have the opportunity to learn first-hand and follow the life odysseys of numerous "hidden" Armenians. The stories are not only about present "hidden" Armenians but also past hidden ones, some of whom may be very well known in Turkey, but known as Turks, not as Armenians.

If one wishes to learn something about these "hidden" Armenians, there is no better source available on the topic than the book you now hold. I can only hope that you will find Raffi Bedrosyan's writings of as great a value and interest as I have.

—Taner Akçam, Department of History, Armenian Genocide Studies, Clark University, Massachusetts, USA

Author's Note

This book is a collection of articles and essays. I am not a historian, I am definitely not a man of letters, and I am most definitely not a prominent person to justify writing an autobiography to pass on to future generations. But I decided to compile all these articles together in a book, written over a span of ten years, to give the reader my viewpoint and perspective about events in Turkey which have profoundly affected the lives of Armenians, hidden Armenians and no longer hidden Armenians who have returned to their roots. I am proud to say I have had a role in participating or initiating some of these events, and therefore, some of the articles are not just about describing or observing the events and the players, but also reflecting the thoughts and feelings of someone who actively triggered or contributed to these events. Some articles are about history of Armenians including hidden ones, Armenian culture, heritage and architecture in Turkey, with historic facts still denied by the state or unknown by the general population of Turkey. Some articles are about current events in Turkey, about the hidden Armenians re-awakening and returning to their roots, and the reaction of Turks, Kurds, Armenians in Istanbul, Armenia and Diaspora to them. And there are some articles about me as an Armenian growing up in Turkey, living in Canada, returning to Turkey to bring hidden Armenians to Armenia.

In all of the articles, there is a common trait: Trauma, which may be resulting from discrimination, fear, danger, risk to one's own life or livelihood, and above all, a nagging negative emotion combining anger, sadness and defiance in the face of continuing denial and injustice. I feel this trauma on a daily basis. Over and above the usual challenges of maintaining a career or livelihood, caring and providing for my family, I have had to deal with these recurring questions that come to my mind every day, or several times every day: Why did 1915 happen? What could have been done to prevent it? What could have been done to reverse it after it happened? What could, or should, be done now and in the future? What can I do, or what can other Armenians, other Turks do to undo the denial or injustice? I am sure every Armenian, hidden, not hidden or no longer hidden, has felt or continues feeling this trauma in various degrees.

My life as an Armenian activist went through three main phases. As described in more detail in one of the articles, My Roots, growing up in Istanbul, Turkey, I didn't even know about the 1915 Armenian Genocide until I was seventeen. It was not taught in schools, never mentioned in any history books nor the media and never discussed at our home, perhaps an intentional decision of my Armenian parents to shield me from any unwanted attention or discrimination resulting from a reactionary outburst I might not control in my Turkish surroundings. But my grandmother opened up when I was seventeen after a strange situation arose at my high school. She explained her 1915 ordeal, being deported from Bursa while pregnant, giving birth to a baby boy (my uncle) while walking along the deportation route somewhere near Konya, the death of the baby after ten days due to lack of milk from my hungry and thirsty grandmother, who had to place the dead baby under a rock and continue walking while being prodded by the bayonets of the Ottoman gendarmes, and walk she did, all the way to Damascus, how she survived the war, returned to Bursa in 1919 and tried to enter her house, how she was assaulted and beaten up by Moslem Turkish refugees who had already settled in her house, how she had to find her way to Istanbul and start a new life. Upon hearing all these tragic events, I decided I cannot continue living in Turkey, and came to Canada to start my university education.

This is when the first phase of my 'Armenianness' started in the mid 1970s. As a pianist, I started giving concerts to benefit the Toronto Armenian community, with proceeds and donations to the local Armenian schools. The second phase of activism started in the late 1980s triggered by the events in Armenia, the 1988 earthquake, the Karabagh/Artsakh war and the 1991 independence of Armenia. All my efforts were channeled to help Armenia, combining proceeds from my concerts with my professional experience as a civil engineer to help with the construction of infrastructure projects in Artsakh and Armenia. The last and third activism phase started and still continues, with the unfortunate assassination of my friend Hrant Dink. He was obsessed with the Armenian orphans left behind in Anatolia after 1915. He would always say, sometimes privately, sometimes publicly: 'We keep talking about the dead and gone Armenians, it is time to start talking about the living and surviving Armenians, even though they are Islamicized, they are hidden, or afraid to come out'. When I asked him: 'How do you know they are

Armenian?', he would smile and say: 'I know them from their eyes, and I know they know that I know'.

Unfortunately, he was assassinated in January 2007, and did not witness the phenomenon of hidden Armenians coming out and starting to return to their roots. The turning point in the re-awakening of the hidden Armenians was the 2009 start of the reconstruction of the Surp Giragos Church in Diyarbakir/Dikranagerd, followed by my piano concerts in the Surp Giragos Church in 2012 and again on April 23, 2015 on the hundredth anniversary of the Armenian Genocide, followed by Armenian language classes organized for them in 2013 and 2014 in Diyarbakir and Dersim, followed by several trips to Armenia organized for them in 2014 and 2015 from Diyarbakir, Dersim, Antep, Sason, Urfa, Mush, Van, and Hamshen regions of Artvin and Hopa. Initiating and organizing these events became my third phase of activism as the founder of Project Rebirth. I was encouraged to write about them, sharing my thoughts and emotions in articles for several English Armenian media websites. They were well received and generated a lot of interest, many of them eventually being translated to French, Russian, Italian, Spanish, Greek, Romanian, Swedish and of course, Turkish and Armenian. Some of these articles generated a lot of heated discussion, the highest readership counts or the largest number of comments. I was encouraged by many, many readers to put them together in a book, and here we are.

This book is dedicated to four people I was privileged to call friends, who played a major role in the turning events surrounding the hidden Armenians, or influenced me to take an active role in initiating and writing about these events:

> **Hrant Dink**, the brave Armenian journalist and Agos newspaper editor, having the courage as the first Armenian in Turkey to call upon the state to face its own history, but at the same time to advocate direct dialogue between Turks and Armenians about the 1915 events. His fiery articles and speeches encouraged democratization, freedom of speech and dialogue based on historic facts. His assassination triggered hundreds of thousands of Turkish citizens to question the state version of denialist history.

> **Fethiye Çetin**, the prominent Turkish lawyer who acted as Hrant Dink's lawyer before and after his assassination, and

author of the book 'My Grandmother' in which she described her hidden Armenian roots and her Armenian grandmother. Her book triggered thousands of hidden Armenians to start sharing their own hidden stories.

Vartkes Ergün Ayık, the chairman of the Diyarbakir Surp Giragos Church Foundation of Diyarbakir, who initiated the church reconstruction project despite numerous bureaucratic obstacles and fundraising challenges. Once the church was successfully reconstructed, it became a magnet attracting the hidden Armenians to come together and re-discover their roots.

Cem Özdemir, the co-chairman of the German Greens Party and the driving force in organizing the resolution in the German Bundestag Parliament to recognize the Armenian Genocide and acknowledge German responsibility as allies of Ottoman Turkey. As the son of Turkish guest workers settled in Germany, he showed the courage to initiate the parliamentary resolution despite multiple death threats.

I would like to thank my family, my dear wife Joy, my two sons Daron and Alexander, for supporting me and standing by me throughout these events, writing of the articles and the preparation of this book. Finally, to all my hidden Armenian friends, still hidden or no longer hidden, I wish them courage, perseverance, determination, hope and prayers for a safe and happy life with their loved ones.

— Raffi Bedrosyan[*]
Toronto, Canada
7 Nov. 2018

---

* For the author's biography, see page 232.

TRAUMA AND RESILIENCE

ARMENIANS IN TURKEY

Hidden, not hidden and no longer hidden

PART I

BLACK SEA

GEORGIA
Tbilisi ◉

Trabzon

Kars • • Gumri   AZERBAIJAN
• Tokat   Ani + Yerevan
                Echmiadzin + ◉   Karabagh
• Sivas   • Erzeroum
        • Erzinjan

TURKEY
        • Tunceli
                Sp. Garabed
        • Kharpert   +
Malatya   Moush   L. Van + Varak
        Bitlis •   + Van   • Tabriz
Diyarbekir •   Aghtamar

        • Mardin
• Aintab • Urfa
Iskenderoun   IRAN

• Aleppo   • Mosul

SYRIA Der Zor •   IRAQ

BLACK SEA   GEORGIA
TURKEY   ARMENIA
SYRIA IRAQ IRAN
MEDITERRANEAN SEA

HISTORICAL ARMENIA, THE
ARMENIAN REPUBLIC AND
KARABAGH

My Roots – Ovsanna, Onnik, Araxie, Agassi

In my past articles, I have told genocide survival stories of many hidden Armenians. Now, I will tell the survival story of my own parents – one very sad, the other funny, sort of.

When I was growing up in Istanbul, Turkey, stories about my grandparents were never mentioned at home. I was not even aware of the Armenian Genocide, the so called "1915 events," or the impact of these events on my grandparents. We were never told about these events at school, nor could we find anything in our Turkish history books or the Turkish media. Then an incident happened while I was in my second year in high school at the American Robert College in Istanbul. There was a competition for a scholarship as an exchange student to an American high school for a semester and I was selected one of the three finalists. In the final interview to select the winner, the Turkish teacher asked me the following question: "When you go to the US and you hear lies about Armenians murdered by the Turkish state during World War One, what are you going to say?" And I responded: "I think I would tell whatever I learnt in our history books." But when I went home that night, I decided to ask my grandmother about our family story. And for the first time, she told me.

My maternal grandparents were from Bursa, 160 kms (100 miles) away from Istanbul. Sometime in the early 1910s, my grandfather, a successful and wealthy pharmacist named Onnik Saraylian, weds a very beautiful but uneducated girl named Ovsanna Ghugasian, my grandmother. They have a daughter named Mari, who would later become my aunt. Then the war starts in 1914 and my grandfather is called back into the army as a pharmacist and all contact is lost with him. My grandmother is already pregnant with a second child. The dreaded deportation orders for the Bursa Armenians come in mid-1915. My grandmother's pleas that she is pregnant, that her husband is an army pharmacist are all in vain, and she is forced to join the deportation convoy with her daughter Mari. It is summer, hot and humid, and the Armenians keep walking for days, for weeks, for months, thirsty and hungry, constantly harrassed by the escorting gendarmes. Near Konya in central Anatolia, my grandmother goes into labour one night and gives birth to a baby boy, who is supposed to be my uncle. Without much food nor water, there is no milk coming out of Ovsanna, and the baby boy lasts only ten days. Ovsanna is forced to

3

place the dead baby under a rock and prodded by the bayonets of the gendarmes, resumes her walk – all the way to Damascus. This is a distance of 1,400 kms (900 miles) on modern roads, but the deportation caravans are dragged on much longer routes to different locations in Anatolia before reaching Damascus. It is a miracle how Ovsanna and her daughter Mari survive the ordeal, followed by several other survival miracles within Damascus until the war ends in 1918 with the defeat of the Turks. Then Ovsanna makes the journey back home to Bursa in 1919. But she finds her house already occupied by a crowd of Muslim settlers, who violently assault her and don't even allow her entry to her own house. Ovsanna manages to find her way to Istanbul with her daughter Mari and finds shelter in the Samatya neighbourhood near the Armenian Patriarchate. The Armenian Patriarchate has set up registries and displays lists of newcomers to the city to aid families find lost relatives or children. Meanwhile, Ovsanna's husband Onnik has somehow survived the war in the army and goes to the Patriarchate every day to check the lists of newcomers. Another miracle, Ovsanna registers her name on the Patriarchate list and Onnik finds her. One would hope the reunion would have a happy ending but the story gets very unclear after this, as told by my grandmother. Shortly after the reunion, Ovsanna realizes she is pregnant again. But Onnik decides suddenly to leave his pregnant wife and daughter, and travels to Bulgaria, never to be heard of again. Ovsanna curses after her husband who abandoned her. She gives birth to a baby girl in 1920, who would become my mother. Without any husband or godfather, Ovsanna takes the baby to the Samatya Armenian church to be baptized. The priest directs the church janitor to be the godfather as the only male present in the church. He asks her what the name will be for the girl. Ovsanna is not even consulted, the janitor is a fan of Peruz, a popular Armenian oriental dancer at that time, and my mother is named Peruz. My mother never saw her father Onnik. My grandmother has never told us the reason why her husband Onnik suddenly abandoned her, but years later, my mother, as she neared her own death, speculated that most likely Onnik was not her real father and that Ovsanna had got pregnant after being assaulted and raped in Bursa. So, I will never know whether Onnik was my real maternal grandfather or not…

My paternal grandparents were both from Bardizag (Bahcecik) near Izmit, about 80 km (50 miles) from Istanbul. My grandfather Agassi was a

(Top) Bedrosyan family.
(Left) Ovsanna.

blacksmith and had opened his own shop near the port of Istanbul, after marrying my grandmother, Araxie. In his shop, he specialized in crafting metal springs and shocks for the horse carriages and the automobiles which had started to appear in the streets of Istanbul. But he also took orders for the manufacture of many custom iron works. One such order came from the American Robert College in 1914. For the annual Sports and Field Athletics Day, the school wanted Agassi to produce shot put balls, hammers and javelins. But a suspicious neighbor shopkeeper was convinced Agassi was producing bombs and arms for the Armenian revolutionaries, and informed the police, which would have led to certain arrest, jail and execution for my grandfather, no questions asked. Another but friendlier neighbor shopkeeper alerted Agassi, who immediately closed shop, ran down the street to the port and jumped into the first ship ready to depart, hiding in one of the lilfeboats on board. The ship happened to go to Romania. Meanwhile, Araxie is at home and pregnant. She gave birth to my father, Nubar, all alone, while her husband Agassi spent the war years in Romania, and returned home only in 1918 when the war ended.

So, both my grandmothers, Ovsanna and Araxie, gave birth to my parents, Peruz and Nubar, all alone by themselves, without having a husband beside them.

I will end this account with a funny anecdote. Years later, when Peruz and Nubar went on their first date in 1952 in an open air restaurant at an Armenian charity ball, both grandmothers, Ovsanna and Araxie, went to observe and inspect their children on their dates. A common friend witnessed the two women, standing next to each other but without knowing each other, peering into the restaurant through a chain link fence, checking out how the date was proceeding…

Needless to say, my decision to leave Turkey and come to Canada was made the night my grandmother Ovsanna told her story.

Esayan Primary School

I started my education at Esayan Primary School in Istanbul, one of 17 Armenian schools still functioning in Turkey. This school was founded in 1895 by two wealthy philanthropists, Mgrditch and Hovhannes Esayan brothers, to meet the growing demand of Armenian students in Istanbul.

One must remember that prior to the 1915 Armenian Genocide, there were over 1,000 Armenian schools in Ottoman Turkey, serving about 170,000 Armenian students. In the 1960s when I was in primary school at Esayan, there were zero Armenian schools and zero Armenian students existing in Turkey outside Istanbul, and less than 20 Armenian schools with about 3,000 students in Istanbul. The few Armenian families still living in Anatolia had no choice but to relocate to Istanbul, if they wished to have their children receive Armenian education.

I remember my Esayan days fondly and vividly, starting with the tiny kindergarden where I learned the numbers, and the Armenian and Turkish alphabets. The kids in grades two or three seemed to be so much older, bigger and faster than us when playing in the concrete playground sandwiched between the school and Surp Harutiun church. Our teachers varied from angelic to demonic, both Armenian and Turkish. Some practiced compassionate and passionate teaching techniques, while others believed in the law of the ruler, on your head, on your bum, or the most painful, on your curled fingers.

I had my first love affair in grade four, age nine. I was paired to walk with a sweet girl from another class during a school outing. By the time I was in grade five, we had become regular boyfriend-girlfriend. We exchanged photos, art work, paintings, messages and eventually love letters, but never directly, always via other students who acted as messengers and intermediaries... The exchanged material was of great interest to the intermediary girls in the class, who regularly passed judgment as to whether the affair was getting hotter or cooler. Her family was from Diyarbekir (Dikranagerd) in southeastern Turkey, and they had moved to Istanbul just before she was born. Anyway, we both graduated from Esayan Primary School, and then we never saw each other, as she continued her education at the Istanbul German High school, and I went to the English High School and American Robert College.

Years later, after I moved to Canada and started my studies in civil engineering at the University of Toronto, I received a phone call one night. The girl on the phone said: "Guess who I am." And I guessed right...

My girlfriend from grade five is my wife now. We went to university together, she became a pharmacist, and later in life, a fabulous ballroom dancer, while I became an engineer and pianist, and later in life, an activist and writer. In the meantime, we raised two boys, brought our parents from Turkey to Canada, lived through good times and tough times. The two Esayan graduates still love each other, as they grow better, not older...

Buyukada – Prinkipo Island - Medz Geghzi

When growing up in Istanbul, Turkey, my family had the privilege of spending summers in the largest of the Princes Islands, named historically as Prinkipo in Greek, Medz Geghzi in Armenian, and officially as Buyukada in Turkish. Although we were a lower middle income family unable to afford owning an apartment in Istanbul, my father chose to pay ever increasing rents for a residence in the winter all his life, in order to be able to provide his family a summer home on Buyukada.

The Princes Islands, an hour away from the mainland by boat, were historically used as a place of exile for Byzantine princes who had fallen out of favour with the Emperor. In Ottoman times, they were mostly inhabited by Greek fishermen, and starting from the 19th century, they became fashionable summer residences for the wealthy members of minorities, who commissioned Greek and Armenian architects to build ornate mansions for them, especially in Buyukada. During my growing years in the 1960s and 70s, these islands were the only freely multi-cultural, multi-ethnic locations in Istanbul, at least in the summers. In the journey from Istanbul mainland to these islands, the boat would first stop at Kinaliada or Proti, mainly inhabited by Armenians in the summer, then at Burgazada or Antigoni, taken over by Jews for the summer, then on to Heybeliada or Halki, inhabited by Turks and Greeks, and finally arrive at Buyukada, inhabited by all minorities, Armenians, Greeks and Jews. In the winters, the islands would be vacated by the minorities, and left to the Turkish locals who lived there all year around. There were no motorized vehicles allowed on the islands, except for emergency vehicles, and all transportation was by horse carriages, bicycles, boats or on foot.

The Turkish locals worked in the public sector of the local government, police and fire departments, operated all the banks, shops and restaurants, as well as the horse carriages. There was a tacit understanding that since their livelihood depended on serving the minorities in the summer, there should be friendly relations between them and the minorities. As a result, there was a great degree of tolerance and absence of discrimination in the

Buyukada-Prinkipo-Medz Geghzi.

islands, compared to elsewhere in Istanbul or the rest of Turkey. But still, interesting incidents happened and I remember some of them from my teenage years.

There were certain bullies or enforcers among the local Turks, who were ready to pick a fight with the minority youngsters at the slightest excuse. It could be a result of a refusal to the bully's demand to "borrow" a bicycle, refusal to give presents such as cigarettes, or refusal to give a boat ride. Since most kids smoked cigarettes at that time, these bullies would approach any Greek or Armenian kid and demand that they hand over their cigarette pack, or else. As a result, smart boys started carrying two cigarette packs on them, a cheap brand in their shirt pocket which could be given away as ransom to the bully, and a more expensive brand like Marlboro hidden in their pants...

Like most boys, soccer was a passion for me and I played a lot of soccer in Buyukada. Passionate matches would be played between teams of Armenians, Greeks, Jews and local Turks, often resulting in hot disputes which ended up in quarrels and fights. The fights were not only between the two teams, but sometimes even against the referee who gave or failed to give a favourable decision. There were times when a Greek referee ended up getting a beating from the Armenian team play against the local Turkish team or vice versa... In any case, there were also more serious

9

soccer matches arranged between the best teams of one island against another island. As I was a reasonably good player, I was selected to play on the Buyukada team to defend the "honour" of our island against Heybeliada. I was the only non-Turk on our team. The game attracted a lot of spectators, including the bullies of the island. I ended up scoring the winning goal. As a means of cheers and congratulations, the chief bully stated the following to me: "If you hadn't scored, if we didn't win, you would have got the first spit from me, followed by a good beating"…

Although all minorities and local Turks lived together and interacted on the island, minority kids usually chose their girlfriends or boyfriends from their own ethnic group, and "mixed" affairs were frowned upon, especially by the parents. One summer when I was sixteen, I ended up breaking this taboo by going out, for a few days only, with a Turkish girl, the daughter of the local bank director. The poor girl's family was so upset when they found out about this affair that she was forbidden to go to the beach for the rest of the summer and banned from going out of the house on her own…

This multicultural life in the Princes' Islands has mostly disappeared now, except in Kinaliada, where the Armenians still continue to flock in the summers. The three other islands are now taken over fully by Turkish residents, and invaded by mostly Arab tourists in the summer.

Life in the Turkish Army

I paid several thousand dollars for the privilege of serving in the Turkish army for two months… Before you condemn me as a traitor working against the Armenian cause, let me explain.

Several years after I came to Canada from Turkey, studied, graduated, settled, married and had a son, my parents still continued living in Istanbul. They kept saying they were too old and unwilling to relocate to Canada, and they had no one except me to take care of them in case of illness or other emergencies. As a Turkish citizen, I had to complete the compulsory military service in order to have the right to travel back to Turkey. And if I hadn't paid several thousand dollars, I would have had the privilege of serving in the army not for two but for eighteen months.

So, after having my head shaved, dressed up in the standard issue camouflage military wear and two size bigger boots, I started my military

Author in the Turkish Army.

service in Burdur, central Turkey, in the summer of 1989. The daily routine was mainly to learn how to march in unison for the "Big Parade" in front of the army chiefs of staff. I suspect these all-day long marching drills under the blazing sun, in an average temperature of 38 degrees Celsius (100 degrees Fahrenheit), also served to satisfy the secret sadistic desires of our sergeants, who loved barking orders at us. By the end of the day, our brown heavy wool military uniforms would transform into a yellowish beige due to the famous wind and dust of Burdur, caked with our own sweat.

But unfortunately, there would not be rest even at the end of the day, as we would have to attend "educational conferences" after dinner. History professors sent from Ankara would arrive to lecture us about "the enemies of Turkey." After explaining why and how each bordering neighbor state is hostile to Turkey, such as the Soviet Union, Iran, Iraq, Syria, Bulgaria and Greece, the professor would invariably point out that Turkey has an even worse enemy than all of these states combined – the Armenians. In these textbook indoctrination sessions, the professor would explain how the Armenians revolted and massacred the Turks in 1915, how the Armenians now lie and blame the Turks with genocide, and how the Armenians continue the killings by targeting the Turkish diplomats. But I was surprised that several fellow conscripts, mostly of Kurdish origin, would approach me after these sessions and confide in me that they know these lectures are lies, that their families live in former Armenian villages, that the houses they live in once belonged to Armenians, that they have an Armenian grandmother who was an orphan from 1915, and so on...

We were allowed to take a shower and wash our sweat and dust caked uniforms by hand once a week. But it was quite a production to go to the shower barracks, which was some distance up the hill. At the end of the first week, our platoon of 50 soldiers was organized in a line of 25 pairs of two, based on height, tall guys at the front, short ones at the back, and we had to march parade style to the showers. When we reached the showers, we observed that the shower system was basically a horizontal pipe high above, with several holes in it. We were told to find a hole in the pipe and stand under it. After every soldier stood under a hole, the commander would turn on the water. Unfortunately, there were not enough shower holes for all 50 of us, and the last two in the group, including me, were left out. The commander had a simple response: "No problem, you take a shower next week." After spending a second week in a uniform which had started to transform into a heavy duty cardboard, we again lined up to go up the hill to the showers. I ensured I was marching right at the front this time. When we reached the showers, the commander, who was a different guy, ordered the first two soldiers, including me, to stand aside. As the others lined up under the pipe, the two of us kept wondering what is going on, and the commander commanded: "You two will guard the uniforms, but no problem, you take a shower next week." The third week, with my uniform probably weighing heavier than me, and stinking probably from a mile away, I blended in and marched in the middle of the group, and successfully accomplished the mission of taking my first shower in the Turkish army, under the dreaded hole in the pipe.

But we had some fun times as well. Some evenings we were allowed to play soccer, and as I was a pretty good footballer at the time (some people say I still am...), I was selected to our battalion team to play against other army units. The games were quite brutal, all the hidden frustrations would come out, usually resulting in violent fights. Fights were quite common in the barracks, and even in the dining hall, fisticuffs would ensue for simple reasons such as not passing the bread or not serving the right portion of soup.

By the fifth week, the dusty air, the wool blankets and uniforms, but especially the daily marches under the hot sun caused dehydration and recurrence of asthma in me, an illness that I had as a child but which had gone away as I grew up. I simply couldn't breathe, and I fainted one day. The army doctor gave me a note to stay out of the sun and I was excused from the daily marches. So, I sat in the shade under a tree while my fellow conscripts still continued marching and singing for the glory of the heroic army. Of course, this started some jealous remarks against me, such as feigning asthma and cheating in order not to march. In the meantime, the soccer games continued in the evenings, preparing for a final game against another battalion. I had no problem running around in the cool evenings and our battalion commander ordered me to play on the soccer team. This resulted in even more intense jealous remarks against me, particularly by one soldier from a wealthy and influential Turkish family. And unfortunately, while I played in that final soccer game, the battalion commander arranged a beating of this soldier for "putting his nose in other people's business"…

So I survived my service in the Turkish army, despite the brainwashing lectures, insults, heat, dirt, sweat and sickness, and gained the right to visit my parents, who wished to live the rest of their lives in Turkey, whenever there would be a need to take care of them. However, the irony of all, was that a few short months after my army stint, my parents said: "Manches (my son), we decided to come to Canada after all"…

TAD – Turkish Armenian Dialogue

Almost thirty five years after graduating from the American high school in Istanbul, called Robert College, I re-connected with my high school buddies in 2005. Most of them had stayed in Turkey, and had established themselves successfully in various fields of business, finance, science, medicine and academia. This is not surprising as Robert College was one of the best schools, if not the top one, in Turkey. Of course, like most intellectuals, my buddies were also self declared experts in politics and history. Invariably, chats or discussions, whether online or around a drinking table, would lead to heated exchanges about past and present political issues. I was disappointed, but not surprised, that their understanding of the 1915 "Armenian events" was the latest Turkish state version of history. I say the latest version, because the Turkish state version of the "1915 Armenian events" has changed over the years. It has ranged from complete denial of the very existence of Armenians in Turkey, to Armenians revolting and mass murdering the Turks, to Armenians and Turks massacring each other, to Armenians being deported only from the eastern front war zones. The 2005 version was this last one, that the Armenians were safely and securely relocated from the eastern front war zones because of Armenian revolutionaries collaborating with the Russian enemies, and that some Armenians had died due to sickness and starvation resulting from the war conditions which affected even higher numbers of Muslims.

One day in mid 2005, I decided to open up to my buddies about the "1915 Armenian events," using the subject title "Benim Dert," meaning "My Trouble." I explained how my pregnant grandmother was taken from her home in Bursa (near Istanbul) in 1915, how she was forced to march in a deportation convoy all over Anatolia under severe heat and starvation conditions, how she gave birth to a baby boy (my uncle) near Konya who lasted only ten days without any milk coming from my grandmother, how she placed the dead baby under a rock and was forced to continue to march prodded by the bayonets of the Turkish soldiers, how she walked all the way to Damascus, how she miraculously survived and returned back to Bursa when the war ended in 1918, found her home occupied by new Muslim settlers who beat her up and threw her out of her home, and how she found her way to Istanbul. And I asked my highly educated Robert College buddies: "Was my pregnant grandma a revolutionary, was she a threat to the state, was she living in the eastern front war zone?" Unfortunately, the responses were mostly a repetition of the state version of history, as it is very difficult to suddenly abandon decades of brainwashing. Only one Turkish high school buddy, who was a doctor living in the US, acknowledged the 1915 events as "genocide" and personally apologized for what the Turkish state had done to the Armenians.

Encouraged by this friend's candid apology, I decided to start a dialogue with my highly intellectual high school buddies about the "1915 Armenian events," with the hopes of perhaps conveying to them some historical truths that they may not be aware of. I declared that all online discussions in this subject will be grouped under the heading TAD – Turkish Armenian Dialogue. There was a flurry of emails back and forth, between me and my buddies, but soon I realized that we were not having a dialogue. I was presenting to them what I knew as historic facts, from several international sources, American, German and even Turkish ones such as Taner Akçam, and they were counteracting with the Turkish state paid historians' denialist version. What we were having was a monologue, not a dialogue. So, I changed the heading of our chat group to TAM – Turkish Armenian Monologue. In the meantime, tragically, my close friend journalist Hrant Dink was assassinated in January 2007. After a few sympathetic condolence exchanges, the Turkish high school buddies stopped chatting about the 1915 Armenian events altogether, while I continued giving references from past history as well as current events, further showing facts concerning the Armenian genocide and the ongoing Turkish state denials. This phase of discussion was only one sided, and I defined it as AM – Armenian Monologue.

Then one day, while analyzing the three phases of discussion around the Armenian Genocide, a fellow pointed out that what we went through as TAD TAM AM when translated to Turkish would literally mean Taste Like Vagina...

I stopped discussing this subject with my high school buddies, as I reluctantly accepted the futility of dialogue with people brainwashed for several decades, especially after the main advocate of dialogue, Hrant Dink, was killed.

My attempts at dialogue failed but there is much hope in the younger generations of Turks, Kurds and Armenians for dialogue based on facts and truth, evidenced by thousands of Turkish university students studying and writing dissertations on the Armenian Genocide, thousands of young Kurds admitting and apologizing for their grandfathers' participation in the massacre and plunder of Armenians, and more importantly, thousands of hidden Armenians who are the grandchildren of forcibly Islamized, Turkified and Kurdified Armenian orphans, returning to their Armenian roots, language and culture.

Track One and a Half Diplomacy

For a few years in the early to mid 2010s, there were some encouraging signs that the Turkish state had started taking steps toward increased democratization and minority rights. For the first time since the founding of the republic in 1923, some of the properties belonging to minority foundations, which were seized by the state in earlier years, were returned to their rightful owners. For the first time, there was some freedom in the press, people could utter taboo words like "Armenian Genocide" without being charged with "Insulting Turkishness," arrested or jailed as per Article 301 of the Penal Code. For the first time, some churches and schools belonging to the minorities in Istanbul could be permitted to receive much needed renovations. For the first time, there was some acknowledgment of the 1937-1938 massacres perpetrated by the state on the Alevi population of Dersim. For the first time, the state allowed the Kurdish minority, making up about a quarter of the population in Turkey, to freely speak and write in their language, even giving them an official Kurdish TV channel on the state TV corporation.

Whether these small but encouraging steps taken by the state were genuine attempts of democratization, or merely tactical moves to impress the Europeans to finally admit Turkey into the European Union, they caused hope and optimism among the minorities. A few visionary Armenian individuals used this window of opportunity to initiate the reconstruction of the Diyarbekir Surp Giragos church. When a few years earlier, even getting a government permit to repaint a church or a school in Istanbul was unthinkable, suddenly it became possible to obtain all the necessary approvals from several ministries in Ankara for Surp Giragos church in far away Diyarbekir. Establishing warm relations with the Diyarbekir mayor and other local government officials resulted in further cooperation, and even funding for one third of the required budget for the reconstruction project.

During these few favourable years, I was also able to establish good relations with the Turkish state through the Turkish Ambassador in Ottawa and the Turkish Consul General in Toronto. I am certain they had received instructions from Ankara to make contact with "moderate" Armenians in the Diaspora. It was mutually beneficial to start a dialogue under those circumstances. I could initiate or follow up on certain approvals for the Surp Giragos church, start discussions with the state for the return or restoration of a few other churches in Eastern Turkey, impress upon the government officials the benefits of increased tourism and cultural exchanges by Armenians from Diaspora and Armenia travelling to Eastern Turkey (historic Armenia). When we visited Aghtamar in September 2012 with a large group of Diaspora Armenians

Surp Giragos church, Diyarbekir, before and after its renovation.

for the first Armenian mass to be held by the US Eastern Diocese Primate Archbishop Khajag Barsamian, I was pleasantly surprised to run into the attaché from the Ottawa Turkish Embassy at the ceremonies on the island. This was followed by several Turkish central and local government officials attending my first piano concert at the Surp Giragos church. Successful discussions with the Turkish officials contributed to the start of restoration projects at the medieval Armenian capital Ani near Kars, restoration of some churches in Malatya, Sivas and Van and more importantly, return of some properties belonging to the Surp Giragos church in Diyarbekir.

One specific project that I pursued with Turkish state officials was the restoration of the Varakavank Armenian monastery complex in Van near the shores of lake Van, now known as Yedi Kilise (Seven Churches) in the village of present day Yukari Bakracli. This historic monastery, dating back to the 11th century, comprised of six churches and a few other structures. It had served as a prominent religious and educational centre over several centuries. It rose to fame in mid 19th century when Mgrdich Khrimian, future head of the Armenian church, became the abbot of Varakavank in 1857. He established a printing house in the monastery and started publishing the first newspaper in historic Armenia, called *Ardziv Vasburagani* (The Eagle of Vasbouragan). He also started a modern school, teaching theology, music, Armenian grammar, geography and history. Famed novelist Raffi was one of the teachers. The monastery was sacked, mostly destroyed and all the monks murdered in 1915. During several discussions with the Ankara government and Van provincial officials, the state appeared to look favourably on the restoration of Varakavank and decided to allocate funds for it. The university in Van (Yirminci Yuzyil University) even started drawing up the architectural restoration plans. But then, we were informed, that the monastery is not in the ownership of the government and that the deeds were held privately. It was revealed that the family of a prominent Turkish newspaper editor owned the monastery. I initiated discussions with this editor through intermediary contacts. One may wonder how can a Turkish family own an Armenian monastery? The editor turned out to be quite a slippery character, publicly declaring that he is prepared to donate the monastery back to the Armenian Patriarchate, while informing us that

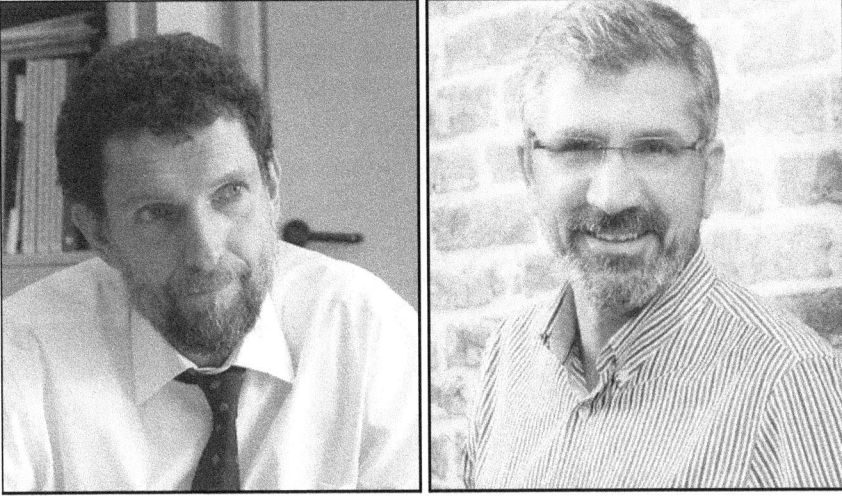

Osman Kavala (*l*) and Tahir Elçi (*r*).

he will sell it back to the state or the patriarchate for the right price. Eventually he stopped all communications stating that he is only one of the heirs and he cannot get the consent of the other six heirs.

During cordial and friendly discussions with Turkish government officials, sooner or later the elephant in the room, the subject of the Armenian Genocide, would invariably come up. Most of the officials would toe the official Turkish state policy of denial and argue about the benefits of establishing a historical commission for Armenian, Turkish and third party historians to deal with the matter. But to my surprise, some of the officials were much more open-minded, even privately acknowledging the historic facts and the truth of genocide, after reading Wolfgang Gust's book, *The Armenian Genocide: The Evidence from the German Foreign Office Archives*, which I presented to them as a gift. When Ahmet Davutoğlu, the former foreign minister who later became Prime Minister, visited Canada, the Turkish Consul General arranged for a private meeting for him to meet me. Davutoğlu advocated closer relations with the Armenian Diaspora and stated that "the Armenian Diaspora is also our Diaspora." I discussed with him the mutual benefits of advancing dialogue between Armenians and Turks, and between Armenia and Turkey, by opening the borders and suggested naming the border crossing "Hrant Dink Gate," honouring the most passionate advocate of dialogue who sacrificed his life trying to bridge the gap between the two peoples.

When there are no official relations between two states, the practice of non-governmental, informal and unofficial contacts and activities between private citizens or groups of individuals is called Track Two Diplomacy. In my case, as an Armenian individual dealing with Turkish government officials, we decided to name our communications Track One and A Half Diplomacy. These friendly communications with Turkish officials in Canada continued even after they were re-assigned to other posts such as the US, Egypt, Ukraine or back into Turkey.

Unfortunately, these small but encouraging steps toward increased democratization and dialogue came to an abrupt end in mid-2015. The increased demands of the Kurdish minority for more local autonomy, followed by increased activities of Kurdish militants, combined with too much Kurdish success in the June elections, triggered a complete reversal of the liberalization policies of the state. The full force of the Turkish army was unleashed against the Kurdish militants and general population of eastern and south eastern Turkey. The hidden Armenians were caught in the crossfires, suffering as much or even more than the Kurds. They lost their homes, their jobs, and in some cases, even their lives in the midst of the civil war. The Turkish army moved into many cities and towns of eastern and southeastern Turkey, including Diyarbekir, and the state passed legislation expropriating entire neighbourhoods for "security' purposes." The Armenian Surp Giragos church was also expropriated, becoming police and special forces headquarters to carry out operations against Kurdish militants. Along with the church, all the properties such as shops and houses belonging to the church were also expropriated. The Armenian Church Foundation immediately appealed the expropriation legislation and eventually succeeded in obtaining the return of the church, through the return of the other properties is still an ongoing process.

I would like to remember two precious friends in Turkey who tried so hard to start democratization.

In dealing with state officials about restoration of Ani and other churches, negotiating with the slippery newspaper editor about Varakavank, the biggest help came from an intellectual friend, Osman Kavala, founder of Anadolu Kultur, a non-governmental organization which had the objectives of acknowledging and promoting cultural diversity, promotion of dialogue and peace through the arts, culture and history of all peoples in Anatolia. Unfortunately, the state has responded to his relentless efforts toward democratization by arresting him on October 28, 2017. He is still being held in jail without any charges.

The organizer of the April 2015 Centenary Commemorations of the Armenian Genocide in Diyarbekir was a Kurdish lawyer named Tahir Elçi, chairman of the Diyarbekir Bar Association. He was also instrumental in organizing my piano concert in Surp Giragos church on April 23, 2015, attended by more than a thousand hidden Armenians. He was an advocate of peaceful negotiations between Turks and Kurds. Unfortunately, he was shot dead on November 28, 2015 while giving a speech, calling for an end to the violence in Diyarbekir, at a public square one block away from Surp Giragos church.

The increasingly authoritarian and repressive regime in Ankara has now wiped out all the small steps toward democratization, human rights, minority rights and freedom of speech. Along with the ultra-nationalistic approach of the Turkish state, any discussion of the Armenian Genocide or the return of Armenian properties is out of question, and therefore, our attempts at Track One and A Half Diplomacy are also dead. For now.

Ascent to Ararat

Ever since I was a child, every time I looked at a picture of Mount Ararat, I kept wondering how it would feel to be on top of it. After my first visit to Yerevan, where you are so close to the majestic mountain that you can almost touch it, climbing Mount Ararat became a real obsession, and one of the "Bucket List" items in my life.

I was fortunate enough to realize my dream of climbing Ararat in August 2013 when I was sixty years old, accompanied by my son, Daron, who had turned 27 that year. After getting all the required items on the climb list such as boots, gear, gloves, goggles and several layers of clothing, we flew from Istanbul to Van and then by mini-bus to Dogu Bayazit to meet our mountain guide and the other members of the "climbing expedition" team.

Dogu Bayazit is the easternmost district of Turkey, and part of the province of Agri. The name was changed from Ararat by the Turks. The former name of Dogu Bayazit was Daroynk, a continuously Armenian inhabited fortress town all the way back 2,700 years to the Urartu Kingdom. The Armenian Bagratid (Pakraduni) princes were the last rulers when the first Turks arrived in 1064, followed by the Mongols, and then the Ottomans. Even during Ottoman times, until the Armenian Genocide of 1915, the Armenian population of 12,000 formed 93 % of the population. Most of the Armenians were massacred during 1915, but some escaped to Eastern Armenia and Iran. At present, the entire 100,000 population of Dogu Bayazit is Kurdish, except for the Turkish administrative officials, police and security forces. Stones from demolished Armenian churches are re-used in many buildings. Gravestones mixed with skulls and bones from the destroyed Armenian cemetery are re-used as road building material and clearly visible on the shoulders of one of the main roads.

Our guide was an energetic young Kurd, who had climbed Ararat more than one hundred times. In the early 2000s and until the civil war between the Kurdish militants and the Turkish state shut down the mountain, climbing Ararat had become the main industry in Dogu Bayazit, catering to the needs of the mountain climbers, providing accommodation, guides, climbing gear, provisions, horses and other necessary supplies. Most climbers are mountaineer enthusiasts from Europe or the US with experience from previous expeditions. They have come to climb Ararat because its peak of 5,165 metres (17,000 feet) is even higher than Mont Blanc, the highest mountain in Europe at 4,808 m (15,770 ft). They have come to Ararat because of the legend of Noah's Ark. They have come to Ararat because they want to conquer yet another mountain, with lots of experience and months of training, while Daron and I have come to Ararat because we are Armenians, with zero experience and zero training, except for climbing stairs.

Our expedition team comprised of two Dutchmen, two Americans and us, the two Armenians. The Dutch and the Americans compared notes on their previous conquests, Mount Kilimanjaro in Africa, Mont Blanc and other European peaks, US peaks, etc. While they admired our guts for taking on this challenge without any previous experience and training, they also expressed their opinion that we would probably not be able to reach the peak. We could also tell that they were concerned we would hinder their climb, as we have to move up the mountain together as a team. In any case, one bright sunny morning, we started the climb, which would be over a three-day period. The first climb was to an altitude of 3,200 m (10,500 ft) where we would stay overnight in First Camp. It all

Majestic Mount Ararat towering over Yerevan.

went according to plan over a six-hour duration: we kept together as a team, the ascent was not too steep, with beautiful views of the plateau below, in hot weather temperatures of 30 degrees Celsius (86 Fahrenheit). Our main climbing gear, the tents, the sleeping bags, the food and other provisions were brought up to First Camp by a group of horses and the guide's helpers.

We all had dinner together with the guide, his helpers and the cook. Interesting stories were exchanged. The guide told us stories of accidents on the mountain, that if any climber is injured, there is no choice but being carried down by the other members in the team, that it is foolish to climb alone because once you get lost, you stay lost forever on the mountain, that the year before an Italian climber was lost and his frozen body was found after three months. The Kurdish cook told us about his father who had two wives, one Kurdish and one hidden Armenian who was Islamized. The father and his two wives had nineteen children, including the cook. The cook and his eighteen brothers and sisters had at least five children each. Therefore, in two generations, the family had expanded to almost one hundred people. No wonder the Turks are worried that the Kurds will soon become the majority of Turkey – hence Erdoğan's command to Turkish families to produce three children.

As we were dead tired, the sleeping bags set up on the rocky ground felt like the most comfortable bed in a five-star hotel, and we fell asleep immediately. The next morning after breakfast, we started a much more difficult and steeper climb toward Second Camp at an altitude of 4,200 m (13,700 ft). The entire terrain had become a steep volcanic staircase, zig zagging and finding the correct steps following the exact footsteps of the guide. If you don't step on the right rock, and mistakenly step on a loose rock, not only you may lose your footing and balance, but also endanger the climbers below you, hurling the loose rock onto their heads. The temperature started to go down along with the sun, and when we reached Second Camp, it was already down to 10 degrees Celsius (50 Fahrenheit). The view from the Second Camp is incredibly beautiful, as it is higher than the lower peak of Mount Ararat, and you can gaze down into the circular volcanic crater of the lower peak. There is almost no flat terrain at Second Camp, and the tents are set up on the edge of precipices. If you come out from your tent half asleep and take a few steps in the wrong direction, you can have a pretty fast climb down the mountain... After having a makeshift meal by the bonfire that we set up, we retired early to our tents, as the climb to the peak of Ararat would start around 2 am in the morning, in order to reach the peak at an estimated time of 8 am, and be able to return back to Second Camp in the afternoon that same day.

There were other climbing expeditions beside ours, with a few tents set up nearby. Suddenly, we heard a song from one of the tents – in Armenian: "Seghann e arat, timatsn Ararat...", this is a famous Armenian song meaning: "Our table is plentiful, Ararat is across from us, let's drink friends, our cups are full, let the Armenian wine taste sweet to us all." Life is full of surprises, so, we dressed up and went to the singing tent, where we found four Armenians from Yerevan, Armenia, a newly married couple with the husband a professional mountain guide, a girl and her uncle. After immediate embraces, kisses, several more songs and drinks, we decided to climb to the peak of Ararat not with the Dutch and the Americans, but with our new Armenian compatriots.

At 2 am, we started the ascent to the peak in pitch darkness but equipped with flashlights on our heads, under a drizzling rain and cold temperatures around 0 degrees Celsius (32 Fahrenheit). Thanks to the able leadership of our Armenian guide and new lifelong friend, we finally reached the summit of 5,165 m (17,000 ft) around 8 am, completely

On the summit of Mount Ararat with the Armenian flag.

covered in ice and very poor visibility. The temperature was down to minus 10 Celsius (14 Fahrenheit), with an even colder wind chill. My whole body was almost frozen, I could hardly stand or breathe, my knees were screaming with pain, I couldn't feel my fingers any more, but the emotional exhilaration that I experienced at the icy summit was indescribable. The six Armenians unfurled the Armenian flag, held hands, and sang the national anthem "Mer Hayrenik" and then the Armenian Lord's prayer "Hayr Mer." It was a moment that will stay with us until the end of our lives.

The descent from the peak would be easier and uneventful – or, that's what we thought. We reached down to Second Camp very quickly, met with our Kurdish guide, Dutchmen and American friends, and exchanged our experiences at the summit. Since it was still early in the day, we decided to continue climbing down to First Camp. The Dutch and Americans departed ahead of us. Our guide stated that he had to prepare the Second Camp for a new group and suggested that we follow the trail down to First Camp on our own. The weather had become sunny and warm again, Daron and I changed into shorts and t-shirts, and started our descent. Within half an hour, we were surrounded by clouds which seemed to rise from below us. Then disaster struck. We were in the middle of a snowstorm. In a few minutes, snow covered every single rock, boulder and all traces of a pathway disappeared under a blanket of complete whiteness everywhere. We didn't know where we were, where we came from or where we should go. I had flashbacks of the Italian climber found frozen after three months, as we started to panic. But then, we remembered we had packed a whistle for emergencies. After ten minutes of whistling, someone fortunately heard us and whistled back. An eternity of waiting and whistling followed, and finally another guide climbing up the mountain found us and showed the path down to the First Camp.

Anyway, we safely made our way down the mountain. During all this excitement, Daron had calmly collected rocks along the journey, filling up his sleeping bag, weighing at least 15 kilos (over 33 lbs). He carried the rocks down the mountain, on the plane from Agri to Istanbul, and then to Canada. The rocks are now placed in an antique hearth in our living room, so that we have Ararat in our home.

Now, every time I look at Mount Ararat in a picture or for real in Armenia, not only do I see our holy mountain, but I visualize how we climbed to the top and how we almost got lost on the way down. And I am happy, as Ararat has made us more Armenian.

Sense of Belonging, Integration or Acceptance

We Armenians, at least the ones in the Diaspora, are nomads. Survivors of the Armenian Genocide had to adapt very quickly to a new environment, a new country, a new language, a new culture, quite different from the homeland that they had lost forever. Imagine an orphan from Sepasdia or Kharpert ending up in Egypt or Greece or France, without speaking a word of Arabic, Greek or French, trying to learn a trade to earn a living. And yet, the Armenians not only survived but excelled, wherever they landed. And if the country or the city they landed was not good enough or safe enough, they were ready to relocate again to a better place. Most Diasporan Armenian families have moved not once but at least twice in their lives. The first move for the genocide survivors would be from their ancestral homeland in western Armenia or Cilicia to an Arab country such as Lebanon, Syria, or Egypt. Then, the family would move from these countries to Europe, United States or Canada. And most likely, move again in the new adopted country from a smaller city to a bigger and better city.

In the case of my family and my wife's family, the genocide survivor generations moved from homeland to Istanbul, then the next generation moved from Istanbul to Canada, and following the nomadic trend, it looks like our children are moving from Canada to the United States. It is our wish and expectation that, sooner or later, hopefully sooner, the last move will be back to Armenia as repatriates. Each move costs so much turmoil, stress, frustration and anxiety, a giant emotional soup with ingredients ranging from nostalgia to anger, sadness to thanksgiving. And no matter how much we try to adapt, no matter how successfully we try to integrate, no matter how much we accomplish, there is always a sense of yearning, a sense of not belonging, simply not enough acceptance, something not just right in these adopted living places.

In my case, growing up in Istanbul, I always felt we Armenians were not accepted and treated equally, even before I found out about the realities of the 1915 genocide at the age of seventeen. No matter how many close Turkish friends I had, no matter how well I interacted at school with my Turkish teachers and classmates, no matter how much I tried to be "one of the group," I always felt deeply, inexplicably, inevitably that Armenians were disliked by the Turks. I knew how individual Turks liked or loved me, but I also knew that Turks collectively would dislike, hate and discriminate Armenians collectively. After I found out about the genocide and what happened to my family, my efforts simply stopped to be "one of the group," to be accepted or to belong. My feelings toward individual Turkish friends did not change at all, but my feelings toward Turks collectively changed drastically. The feelings of non-acceptance and dislike became mutual. I stopped questioning why Turks dislike the Armenians and I accepted it as an unalterable reality, because I started disliking Turkish society as a whole. I still liked or loved individuals, say an Ahmet or an Ayse, but only because I disassociated them from the broader Turkish society.

When I came to Canada all by myself at age eighteen, I was fortunate enough to integrate very quickly, thanks to my English language skills and excellent education that I had received at the American Robert College in Istanbul. I excelled at university, established friendships with many Canadians and multi cultural immigrants, as well as within the Toronto

Armenian community. Of course, I had severe money problems but that was not a deterrent to make friends. I remember clearly I came to Canada with exactly $750 in my pocket, and deposited $690 to the University of Toronto the next day for tuition fees, leaving me the grand total of $60 for food and accommodation for the first month, until I found several part-time jobs after school hours. There were quite interesting experiences but let me tell only one. I was moving furniture for $2 per hour and one day a lady hired us to move furniture from another city to Toronto. We rented a truck, drove an hour away to the other city, filled up the truck with her furniture and drove back an hour to Toronto. But when she looked for the keys to open the door of her Toronto house, the lady realized that she had left them at her place in the other city. Unfortunate for her, but fortunate for me, as I ended up making an extra $4 retrieving the key, which means we had a feast and a party that night... My financial situation improved dramatically when I started giving piano lessons at $5 an hour. I could even start saving funds toward our wedding... Anyway, those penniless days were soon over after university. My wife and I were able to start successful careers, establishing ourselves in both Canadian and Armenian communities, providing for the best schools for our boys and living in the best neighborhoods. However, despite our material success, or perhaps because of it, the issue of acceptance or sense of belonging was always lingering for newcomers like us.

When I went to Armenia and Artsakh, I felt again some sense of not completely belonging there. I met and interacted with people from all walks of life, from the president and high government officials to construction labourers, from old professors to young students, from oligarchs to the poor unemployed or retired, from the most urbane to the rural villagers. Emotionally I felt like I was at home and welcomed by all, but logically I kept questioning whether I could fit in, whether I would be accepted as one of them, or I would always be labeled as a diasporan outsider despite all good intentions.

So at the end of the day, despite all efforts to belong or to be accepted, despite all success, accomplishments, love and respect from friends, colleagues and communities in Turkey, Canada or Armenia, I haven't found a sense of feeling completely at home in any of the three places... The lingering question of "What am I doing here, why am I here?" comes out inevitably.

There is no escape of the ever-present and continuing trauma of the Genocide. Some Armenians are pre-occupied with the past every day, thinking, feeling, talking about it every day. It brings them together, keeps them together, to the degree that it defines their existence, their sense of community, their sense of identity as Armenians, which often leads them to be ghettoized in their adopted countries with minimum interaction with non-Armenians. There are also Armenians who feel suffocated by the pain of the past or its constant reminders, and they search for a new identity in their adopted country by trying to completely integrate into the mainstream community and disengaging themselves from the Armenian community. In both extremes, the sense of belonging is incomplete. Then there are the hidden Armenians in Turkey, who suffer the most, with almost no sense of belonging. Surrounded by Muslim Turks or Kurds, they know they are different from them, hated and discriminated by them no matter how hard they try to appear to be like them. Once they reveal their Armenian identity, the rejection is even worse. If they try to move away from their Muslim environment and integrate into the Armenian community of Istanbul, they are shunned by the local Armenian community and especially the Istanbul Armenian Patriarchate, until and unless they fulfill the requirements of baptism to become Christian Armenians and learn to speak Armenian reasonably well.

In short, this search of identity and a sense of belonging is a damning legacy and continuing trauma of the Armenian Genocide, our "djagadakir" in Armenian, meaning "the writing on our forehead."

My Speech at Massachusetts State House

On April 20, 2018, I was invited to be the keynote speaker at Massachusetts State House in Boston on the occasion of the 103rd Commemoration of the Armenian Genocide. The audience included American senators, state representatives and other elected officials, ambassadors, clergy, community leaders and invited Armenian American citizens. Here is what I had to say:

Distinguished guests, clergy and elected representatives,

I am truly honored and humbled to be here with you this morning. I will tell you a story of one hundred years in fifteen minutes, a story about the living victims of genocide, a story of Armenian orphans left behind in Turkey after their parents perished in 1915. It is the story of these orphans, who were forcibly Islamized, Turkified and Kurdified, and yet, secretly kept their Armenian roots, and passed this secret on to the next generations, despite all attempts of assimilation.

There were thousands of Armenian orphans taken to Turkish state orphanages, were given Turkish names, forcibly converted to Islam and Turkified, and beaten up if they were ever heard speaking any Armenian. There were thousands of physically fit Armenian boys sent to military schools to become soldiers in the Turkish army. There were thousands of Armenian girls sold as slaves. Slave markets, abolished in Turkey in 1908, were re-opened in 1915 and these Armenian girls were sold for the price of a lamb. But girls from wealthy families fetched higher prices because whoever took them would also end up owning the properties and assets of the girls' perished family. And there were thousands of Armenian children snatched from their parents along the deportation routes as they passed through numerous villages and towns toward the Syrian Desert. All these orphans became slaves, servants, maids, sons and daughters, wives or mistresses in Muslim Turkish and Kurdish homes. But it turns out they secretly kept their Armenian identity, and they passed it on to the next generation, often at their deathbed.

Almost hundred years after the genocide, the grandchildren of these orphans have shown the courage to reveal their Armenian identities openly, and expressed their wish to return to their Armenian roots, language and culture. There is widespread hatred and discrimination against Armenians in Turkey, and the hidden Armenians' decision to reveal their original identities is quite dangerous, with the risk of losing their homes, jobs, friends, or even their lives as they face a hostile state, neighbors, employers, and even hostile members of their own family who wish to remain Muslim Turks and Kurds.

The main trigger for the hidden Armenians' critical decision to return to their roots was the 2011 reconstruction of an Armenian church in Diyarbekir province in southeastern Turkey. Surp Giragos is the largest Armenian church in the Middle East, which was taken over by the Turkish state and used as military headquarters in 1915 while the Armenian population of the city was driven out and massacred. Its belltower was bombarded by cannon-fire for being higher than the

Author at Massachusetts State House, 2018.

minarets of Turkish mosques in the region. Beside the Armenian orphans that were left behind after the genocide, there were also 4,000 Armenian churches and school buildings left behind in Turkey. If not burnt and demolished outright, these churches and schools were converted to Turkish mosques, government buildings, community centres, banks, banquet halls, even a whorehouse. After the war ended, the Diyarbekir church was used as a state warehouse for a while and eventually abandoned, left in ruins with a collapsed roof. In 2010, a few Armenian individuals took the initiative to reconstruct this church, getting approvals from the local and central government in Turkey and organizing fundraisers from Armenian communities worldwide. This was the first and only reconstruction of an Armenian church in Turkey. At the opening of the church, along with local and foreign dignitaries including the US Ambassador to Turkey, the vast majority of the attendees were people appearing as Turks and Kurds, but in reality, hidden Armenians. Like a magnet, the church attracted hidden Armenians not only from Diyarbekir, but also from other regions of Turkey, who came together, supporting one another, exchanging stories, organizing monthly breakfast meetings. I initiated cultural events in the church by giving a piano concert, which was followed by other concerts, exhibitions and conferences. Armenian language classes were organized for the hidden Armenians, and as a reward to the graduates of the language course, I planned a trip for them to Armenia. In cooperation with the Armenian Ministry of Diaspora, the hidden Armenians toured cultural and historic sites in Armenia, helping them return to their roots. This trip was followed by other trips for hidden Armenians from other regions of Turkey. Each trip encouraged more and more hidden Armenians to come out and return to their original roots. For the 100th anniversary of the Armenian Genocide, I gave another concert at Surp Giragos church, attended by a thousand hidden Armenians, and the commemoration of genocide became rather a celebration of rebirth for the survivors, and we decided to officially name these initiatives as Project Rebirth, providing a wide network of connections and support.

Unfortunately, all these initiatives came to an end in late 2015, when the Turkish state decided to respond harshly by military means to the Kurdish minority demands for local autonomy. The war between the Turkish army and Kurdish militants resulted in thousands of people killed, thousands of buildings burnt down and half a million people left homeless. The hidden Armenians and Surp Giragos church in Diyarbekir were caught in the crossfires. The church was expropriated by the Turkish government and it again became military headquarters for the Turkish army, just like one hundred years ago, history repeating itself. Our church foundation immediately appealed the expropriation legislation and was successful in reversing the legislation. However, the church and the surrounding region are declared a military zone and the church is still closed to the public. The unsuccessful coup d'etat in 2016 brought further repressions and gross human rights violations against civilians, resulting in hundreds of thousands losing their jobs, their homes, or arrested without any charges. Our hidden Armenians are now back into survival mode and Project Rebirth, instead of organizing Armenian language classes or trips to Armenia, is helping them with legal, social and relocation assistance.

The hidden Armenians have survived for a hundred years and this last crisis shall also pass. But I ask you to consider the following:

If a man is murdered, and the perpetrator takes over the murdered man's orphaned children by force, takes over the murdered man's property and possessions, this would be recognized as a crime in any society, developed or not. If the perpetrator covers up and denies the crime, or threatens anyone who dares speak up about the crime, this would also be recognized as a further crime. You wouldn't think: "Well, I am doing business with this man even though he is a murderer, so I better keep quiet." Instead, you would take steps to bring the perpetrator to justice. But if an entire people, an entire nation is murdered, if the orphaned children of an entire people are taken by force and assimilated, if the properties and assets of an entire people are taken over by the perpetrator, isn't this a crime? If the perpetrator denies the crime or threatens anyone who dares speak up against the crime, is this acceptable? Genocide denied is genocide continued. Armenians worldwide, hidden Armenians in Turkey still suffer the consequences of the genocide. Genocide denied is also genocide repeated. If the Armenian Genocide was recognized and the perpetrators brought to justice, the Jewish Holocaust could have been prevented. Hitler wouldn't have stated: "After all, who remembers the Armenians," before ordering the destruction of Jews in Poland. Some of his generals got their training in genocidal policies in Turkey, as Germany was an ally of Ottoman Turkey during the First

World War. But Germany did recognize the Armenian Genocide, and even acknowledged its own responsibility two years ago. Many states in Europe, Latin and South America have also recognized the Armenian Genocide. I know I am preaching to the converted here. The State of Massachusetts was one of the earliest states in America recognizing the Armenian Genocide. 47 other states have also done so. I ask you, whether Democrat or Republican, to call upon your federal colleagues in the House and Senate, to call upon your President, to recognize the Armenian Genocide. I ask you to urge them to be on the side of truth and justice, instead of being on the side of genocide perpetrators and deniers. This is not an issue contrary to national interests or strategic partnerships. This is an issue of human rights, human conscience and human decency. It is the right thing to do. Thank you and God bless you all.

What If…

Sometimes I start thinking, or rather, fantasizing, about future political scenarios. I use the word fantasizing, because these scenarios that come to my mind have nothing to do with the past or present realities. But still, once the question "what if" enters my mind, the future scenarios start taking shape.

What if Turks stop the denials and acknowledge the Armenian Genocide? What if Turks are ready to compensate for the Armenian losses suffered during and after the Genocide?

What if Azeris accept the reality of Artsakh/Karabagh independence? What if Artsakh joins Armenia forming a single state?

What if Kurds gain local autonomy or independence from Turkey?

What if Turkey breaks up? What if Armenians regain eastern Turkish territories as per Sevres Treaty and the Kurds establish a state on southeastern Turkish territories? What if Turkey accepts these scenarios peacefully?

What if Georgia goes along and cooperates with all these new developments on its borders?

In the short term, or even the long term, or forever, none of these scenarios would ever become reality. But what if, miraculously, they become reality?

Continuing the fantasy, what if all these states, existing, expanded or newly created, develop friendly relations, cooperating and collaborating economically, politically and culturally? What if all the states are convinced of mutual benefits of cooperation, harmony and trust to serve their best national interests?

Further continuing and concluding the fantasy, I start visualizing an economic federation or union of five states, gathering together under the banner of Anatolia Caucasus, consisting of Turkey, Kurdistan, Georgia, Azerbaijan and Armenia. While each state maintains its existing capital, Kurdistan gets Diyarbekir as capital. Istanbul would become the economic centre of the federation, with economic leadership rotated among the five states and all decisions discussed in simultaneous translation into five official languages. The economic power, natural resources, human capital and the geographic advantages of this federation would rival the European Union. Russia, United States and the EU would compete to establish good relations with this new entity.

Then again, I would come upon a news item about another incident of hatred or discrimination by Turks against the Armenians, or yet another attack by Azeris against the Armenians, and poof!... the fantasy would disappear.

PART II

PART II

Surp Giragos church had more than 200 deeds showing that a significant portion of the Diyarbekir city center belonged to the church prior to 1915. At present, several apartment buildings, state schools, offices, and shops are on these lands. So, the long and difficult process has begun, to reclaim these lands and properties by their rightful owner, the Surp Giragos church.

Evolving Armenian Realities and the Surp Giragos Dikranagerd Church[*]

I would like to share my thoughts about Armenian realities—evolving ones, forgotten ones, and new ones.

Until 20 years ago, the Armenian reality was mainly Soviet Armenia and the diaspora. Then, a double miracle happened and we had a free and independent Armenia and Karabagh, creating a new reality, which became the triangle of Armenia, Karabagh, and the diaspora. And yet, throughout the past century, there's been an often forgotten or dismissed reality—the Armenians remaining in Turkey. This is a tiny community of about 60,000, generally called Bolsahays as they live mostly in Istanbul, which was the intellectual, cultural, political, industrial, and social center for Armenians before 1915. Although they are called Bolsahays, they come mostly from the historic homeland, where they lived continuously for

* *Armenian Weekly*, 1 July 2011.

more than 3,000 years. These people are not exactly diasporan or Hayasdantsi. So, how do you define them? Where do we place them in the Hayasdan-Artsakh-Spiurk triangle? I suggest placing them in the middle, in the heart of the triangle. Let me explain.

For almost a century now, despite the hardships, pain, and grief caused by the Turkish state, despite the discrimination, harassment, and insults hurled at them by the general Turkish population, these Armenians have continued to preserve their identity and carry the heavy burden of protecting the legacy and heritage left behind by their ancestors, at least in Istanbul, keeping an open and active the Armenian Patriarchate, more than 30 churches, nearly 20 schools, and two hospitals. Until recently their efforts were all managed defensively, in a survival mode, until one Armenian, originally from Malatya, stood up in Istanbul and called upon the Turks and Turkish state to face their past, stop falsifying historical facts, and talk about the remaining Armenians. He stood up as an advocate of dialogue and a bridge between Turks and Armenians. Unfortunately, the enormous impact of Hrant Dink's critical message and the new reality was only understood after his murder.

Around the same time, another Armenian in Istanbul, this time from Dikranagerd/Diyarbekir, stood up and declared that the historic Surp Giragos church had to be reconstructed. This church, with its seven altars and capacity of 3,000 people—the biggest Armenian church in the Middle East—was partially destroyed by cannon fire in 1915 and left in ruins, on its last legs after its roof collapsed. Until recently, the Turkish state had not allowed even minor repairs to the Armenian schools and churches in Istanbul, let alone the full reconstruction of a historic church in Anatolia. And yet, Vartkes Ergun Ayik persevered; he hired expert architects, historians, and builders, obtained all the required permits and approvals, and even more incredibly, convinced the Diyarbekir municipal government to pay for one third of the church's reconstruction. The construction is now underway, with two thirds completed, and more than half of the financing also secured.

This church had more than 200 deeds showing that a significant portion of the Diyarbekir city center belonged to the church prior to 1915. At present, several apartment buildings, state schools, offices, and shops are on these lands. So, the long and difficult process has begun, to

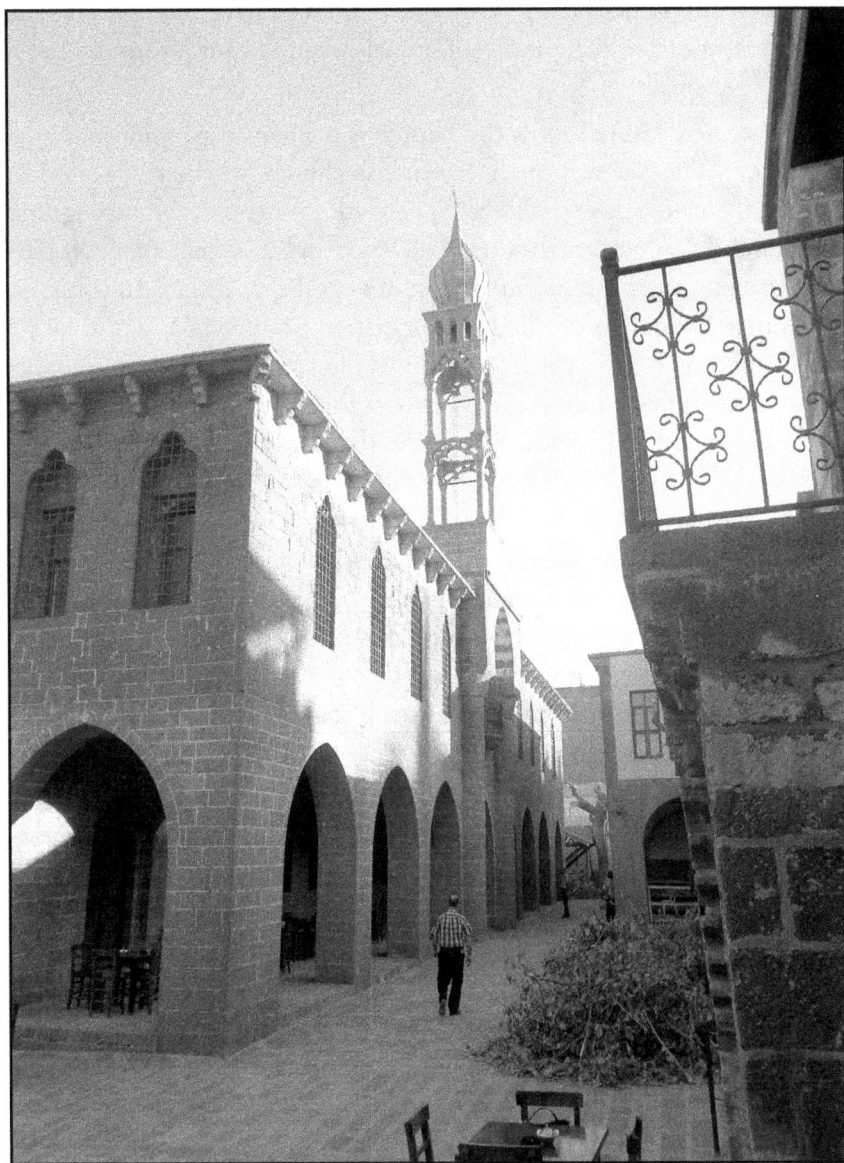

St. Giragos Church, Diyarbekir, 2014.

reclaim these lands and properties by their rightful owner, the Surp Giragos church.

This is the first time Armenians have begun to reconstruct a building in their ancestral homeland. It is the first time they have claimed the land and properties from their ancestral homeland, after losing them in 1915. This is a new reality.

Another new reality is how this church is helping shape public opinion in Turkey. Whoever sees the Surp Giragos church, whether in person or through the media, keeps asking, "Where are the people who belonged to this church?" "Where are they now?" "Where did they go, and why?" The ever-changing and most recent version of the official Turkish state history claims that Armenians revolted on the eastern front during World War I to join the Russians and that, as a result, the Ottoman state temporarily deported them from only the "eastern war zones" to the south toward the Syrian desert. But Diyarbekir was not in the eastern front, nor in the war zone; nor was there any Armenian revolt. As these facts become evident, Turkish citizens—both Turks and Kurds—have started to question the falsified history. Still a tiny percentage, there is nevertheless an ever-increasing number of Turkish citizens, especially of the younger generations, who have started "seeking the truth" and demanding that the state face its past and stop its denialist policies. There are also Turkish citizens who are fully aware of the truth and have developed a guilty conscience about their ancestor's past evil deeds. This year [2011], the April 24, 1915 events were commemorated in five Turkish cities, including Diyarbekir. This is another new reality.

The church, when reconstruction is completed, will become a historic destination of pilgrimage for all Armenians—a memorial and reminder of the past Armenian presence in Anatolia, and a hope for the future.

Armenians are few in number, and Bolsahays are even fewer, but by engaging in a dialogue with liberal-minded Turks and Kurds eager for the democratization of Turkey, and through cooperation with their colleagues in the media, academia, law, construction, finance, and political fields, these few Armenians remaining in Turkey are learning how to undo past wrongs much more effectively than the diaspora. No matter how often Diaspora Armenians gather together to hear their leaders give speeches demanding the return of their lands or to stop the denial, the deeds and results achieved inside Turkey are much louder than the words outside.

The diaspora's efforts surely serve a useful purpose in helping younger Armenian generations keep their identity, or even in reminding foreign politicians of the past injustices, but in terms of reversing these injustices, the Armenians remaining in Turkey are starting to play a vital role through dialogue and cooperation with their fellow Turkish citizens.

The Armenians in Turkey, therefore, deserve the maximum support of their fellow Armenians in the diaspora and Armenia. And this is the most important new Armenian reality.

Searching for Lost Armenian Churches and Schools in Turkey*

On July 21, [2011] the U.S. House Foreign Affairs Committee overwhelmingly adopted the Berman-Cicilline Amendment based upon the Return of Churches resolution spearheaded by Representatives Ed Royce and Howard Berman, with a vote of 43 to 1, calling on Turkey to return stolen Armenian and other Christian churches, and to end the repression of its Christian minorities.

Where are these lost or stolen Armenian churches in Turkey? How many were there before 1915, the turning point in the Armenians' world, when they were uprooted and wiped out from their homeland of more than 3,000 years? How many churches are there now? Considering that every Armenian community invariably strove to build a school beside its church, how many Armenian schools were there in Turkey before 1915, and how many are there now? How many Armenian churches and schools are left standing now in Turkey is the easier part of the issue: There are only 34 churches and 18 schools left in Turkey today, mostly in Istanbul, with less than 3,000 students in these schools. The challenging and frustrating issue is how many were there in the past.

Recent research pegs the number of Armenian churches in Turkey before 1915 at around 2,300. The number of schools before 1915 is estimated at nearly 700, with 82,000 students. These numbers are only for churches and schools under the jurisdiction of the Istanbul Armenian Patriarchate and the Apostolic Church, and therefore do not include the numerous churches and schools belonging to the Protestant and Catholic

* *Armenian Weekly*, 1 Aug. 2011.

Armenian parishes. The American colleges and missionary schools, mostly attended by Armenian youth, are also excluded from these numbers. The number of Armenian students attending Turkish schools or small schools at homes in the villages are unknown and not included. Finally, these numbers do not include the churches and schools in Kars and Ardahan provinces, which were not part of Turkey until 1920, and were part of Russia since 1878.

The two maps show the wide distribution of Armenian churches and schools in Turkey before 1915. The two lists for the Armenian churches and schools are by no means complete, but should be regarded as a preliminary study that can serve as a foundation for further research. The place names are based on the old Ottoman administrative system, instead of that of modern Turkey. They are ably assembled by Zakarya Mildanoglu, from various sources such as the Ottoman Armenian National Council Annual reports, Echmiadzin Journal, Vienna Mkhitarists, and studies by Teotig, Kevorkian, and Nishanyan.

Lost Churches
Adana: Center and villages, Yureghir, Ceyhan, Tarsus, Silifke, Yumurtalik, Dortyol, Iskenderun, 25 churches
Amasya: Vezirkopru, Mecitozu, Merzifon, Havza, Gumushacikoy, Ladik, 15 churches
Ankara: Center, Haymana, Sincan, 5 churches
Antakya: Center, Samandagh, 7 churches
Antep: Center, Nizip, Halfeti, 4 churches
Arapkir (Malatya): Arapkir and Kemaliye villages, 19 churches
Arganimadeni (Elazig): Erganis, Siverek, Bulanik, Kahta, 10 churches
Armash (Akmeshe): 2 churches
Artvin: Center and villages, 11 churches
Balikesir: Balikesir, Mustafakemalpasha, Biga, Bandirma, 6 churches
Bayburt: Bayburt center and villages, 34 churches
Beshiri (Diyarbekir): Beshiri and villages, 14 churches
Bilecik (Bursa): Golpazar, 4 churches
Bingol (Genc): Center and villages, 11 churches
Bitlis: Center and villages, 30 churches
Bitlis: Tatvan, Ahlat, Mutki, Hizan, 66 churches
Bolu: Duzce, Akyazi, 5 churches

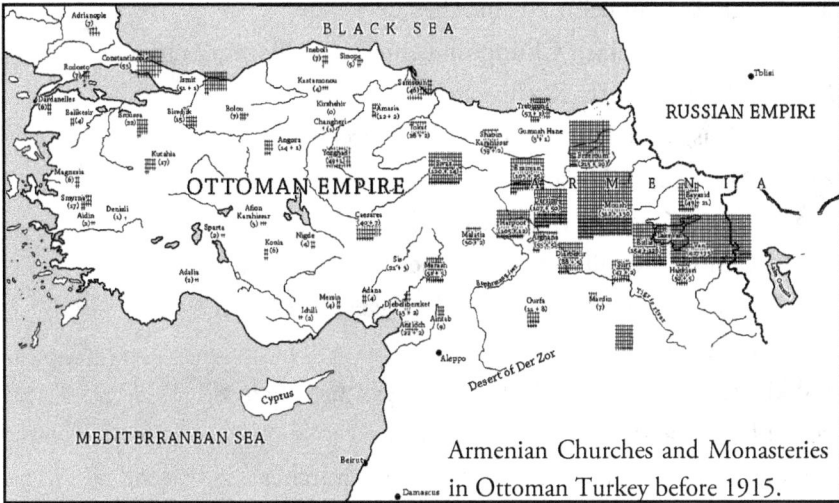

Armenian Churches and Monasteries in Ottoman Turkey before 1915.

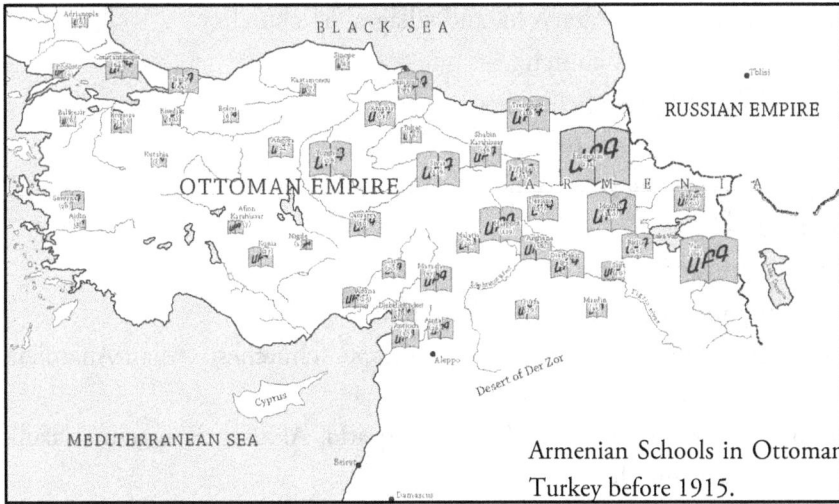

Armenian Schools in Ottoman Turkey before 1915.

* Both maps based on originals published in the *Armenian Reporter International*. The data is derived from the 1913 population survey conducted by the Armenian Patriarchate of Constantinople.

Bursa: Center, Orhangazi, 11 churches

Charsancak (Tunceli): Mazgirt, pertek, Pulumur, Hozat, and villages, 93 churches

Chemishgezek (Tunceli): 20 churches

Chungush (Diyarbekir): Chungush center and villages, 2 churches

Dersim: Hozat, Pertek, 28 churches

Divrigi (Sivas) Center and villages, 25 churches

Diyadin (Erzurum): Diyadin and villages, 4 churches

Diyarbekir: Center and villages, 11 churches

Edirne: Center and villages, 4 churches

Egin (Erzincan): Kemaliye, Ilic, and villages, 17 churches

Egin: 3 churches

Eleshkirt (Erzurum): Eleshkirt and villages, 6 churches

Ergani: Ergani and villages, 11 churches

Erzincan: Erzincan center and villages, 52 churches

Erzurum: Center, Aziziye, Yakutiye, Ashkale, Narman, Ispir, Oltu, Shenkaya, Horasan, Pazaryolu, and villages, 65 churches

Giresun: Tirebolu, 1 church

Gumushane: Center, 4 churches

Gurun (Sivas): Center and villages, 5 churches

Harput (Elazig): Harput center and villages, Karakochan, Palu, Keban, 67 churches

Hinis (Erzurum): Hinis and villages, 19 churches

Hoshap: Hoshap and villages, 14 churches

Istanbul: European/Trachean region, 36 churches; Asian/Anatolian region, 8 churches; total 44 churches

Izmir: Center and villages, Manisa, Turgutlu, Akhisar, Bergama, Nazilli, Odemish, 23 churches

Izmit: Gebze, Kocaeli, Sakarya, Kandira, Geyve, Karamursel, 50 churches

Kastamonu: Tashkopru, Boyabat, Inebolu, 7 churches

Kayseri: Center and villages, Nigde, Aksaray, Bor, Nevshehir, Tomarza, Develi, Bunyan, Talas, 57 churches

Kemah (Erzincan): Kemah and villages, 14 churches

Kighi (Bingol): Kighi and villages, 58 churches

Konya: Center, Bor, Burdur, Nevshehir, 7 churches

Kutahya: Center, Tavshanli, 7 churches

Lice: Lice and villages, 19 churches

Mardin: Center and villages, 3 churches

Mush: Center and villages, Batman, Malazgirt, Bulanik, Varto, Hizan, 148 churches

Ordu: Karaduz, Ulubey, 3 churches

Palu (Elazig): Palu center, Kovancilar, Karakochan, and villages, 44 churches

Pasinler (Erzurum): Pasinler and villages, 4 churches

Pulumur (Tunceli): Pulumur and villages, 6 churches

Rize: Yolusti, 1 church

Samsun (Canik): Center and villages, 43 churches

Samsun: Ordu, 1 church

Shebin karahisar: Shebinkaya center, Giresun, and part of Sivas, 32 churches

Silvan (Diyarbekir): Silvan and villages, 34 churches

Sivas: Center and villages, Hafik, Zara, Ulash, Yildizeli, Sariz, Bunyan/ Ekrek, Gemerek, 110 churches

Tercan (Erzincan): Erzincan and Tercan villages, 33 churches

Tokat: Center and villages, 32 churches

Trabzon: Center and villages, Of, Machka, Surmene, Akchaabat, Fatsa, Yorma, Arakli, 89 churches

Urfa: Center and villages, Birecik, Siverek, Suruch, Hikvan, Harran, Bozova, Halfeti, 17 churches

Van: Center and villages, Edremit, Gurpinar, Edremit, Ozalp, Ercish, Timar, muradiye, Tatvan, Bashkale, Gevash, Bahchesaray, Chatak 322 churches

Yozgat: Center and villages, Bogazliyan, Sarikaya, Cayiralan, Sorgun, Shefaatli, and villages, 51 churches

Yusufeli (Artvin): Center and villages 4 churches

Zeytun (Marash): Center and villages 14 churches

Lost Schools

Adana: 25 schools, 1,947 boys, 808 girls, 2755 students, 40 male, 29 female, 69 teachers

Aghtamar: 32 schools, 1,106 boys, 132 girls, 1238 students, 36 male teachers

Amasya-Merzifon: 9 schools, 1,524 boys, 814 girls, 2,338 students, 54 teachers

Ankara: 7 schools, 895 boys, 395 girls, 1,290 students, 20 male, 9 female, 29 teachers

Antakya; 10 schools, 440 boys, 47 girls, 487 students, 10 male teachers

Antep: 9 schools, 898 boys, 798 girls, 1606 students, 31 male, 27 female, 58 teachers

Arapkir: 18 schools, 713 boys, 223 girls, 936 students, 23 male, 2 female, 25 teachers

Armash: 2 schools, 190 boys, 110 girls, 300 students, 5 male, 1 female, 6 teachers

Bandirma: 8 schools, 700 boys, 644 girls, 1,344 students, 22 male, 13 female, 35 teachers

Bayburt: 9 schools, 645 boys, 199 girls, 844 students, 27 male, 5 female, 32 teachers

Beyazit: 6 schools, 338 boys, 54 girls, 392 students, 11 male, 2 female, 13 teachers

Bilecik: 10 schools, 1,120 boys, 143 girls, 1,263 students, 18 male, 3 female, 21 teachers

Bitlis; 12 schools, 571 boys, 63 girls, 634 students, 20 male teachers

Bursa: 16 schools, 1345 boys, 733 girls, 2078 students, 34 male, 20 female, 54 teachers

Charsancak: 12 schools, 617 boys, 189 girls, 806 students, 16 male, 2 female, 18 teachers

Chemishgezek: 12 schools, 456 boys, 272 girls, 728 students, 14 male, 1 female, 15 teachers

Cyprus: 3 schools, 63 boys, 37 girls, 100 students, 8 male, 1 female, 9 teachers

Darende: 2 schools, 260 boys, 70 girls, 330 students, 4 male, 1 female, 5 teachers

Divrigi: 10 schools, 757 boys, 100 girls, 857 students, 18 male, 2 female, 20 teachers

Diyarbekir: 4 schools, 660 boys, 324 girls, 1014 students, 18 male, 9 female, 27 teachers

Egin: 4 schools, 541 boys, 215 girls, 756 students, 13 male, 9 female, 22 teachers

Erzincan: 22 schools, 1389 boys, 475 girls, 1864 students, 54 male, 9 female, 63 teachers

Erzurum: 12 schools, 485 boys, 10 girls, 495 students, 12 male teachers

Erzurum: 27 schools, 1,956 boys, 1,178 girls, 3134 students, 44 male, 41 female, 85 teachers

Gurun: 12 schools, 736 boys, 78 girls, 814 students, 18 male, 2 female, 20 teachers

Harput: 27 schools, 2,058 boys, 496 girls, 2,554 students, 49 male, 9 female, 58 teachers

Hinis: 8 schools, 352 boys, 15 girls, 367 students, 11 male, 1 female, 12 teachers

Ispir (artvin): 3 schools, 80 boys, 3 male teachers

Istanbul: 40 schools, 3,316 boys, 2,327 girls, 5,643 students.

Izmir: 27 schools, 1,640 boys, 1,295 girls, 2,935 students, 55 male, 54 female, 109 teachers

Izmit: 38 schools, 5,900 boys, 3,385 girls, 9,285 students, 142 male, 82 female, 224 teachers

Kastamonu; 3 schools, 110 boys, 50 girls, 160 students, 2 male teachers

Kayseri: 42 schools, 3,795 boys, 1140 girls, 4,935 students, 107 male, 18 female, 125 teachers

Kemah: 13 schools, 646 boys, 28 girls, 674 students, 16 male teachers

Kighi: 9 schools, 645 boys, 199 girls, 844 students, 27 male, 5 female, 32 teachers

Konya; 3 schools, 213 boys, 137 girls, 350 students, 6 male, 6 female, 12 teachers

Kutahya: 5 schools, 825 boys, 349 girls, 1174 students, 16 male, 7 female, 23 teaches

Lim and Gduts Islands, Van: 3 schools, 203 boys, 56 girls, 259 students, 5 male, 1 female 6 teachers

Malatya; 9 schools, 872 boys, 230 girls, 1,137 students, 16 male, 3 female, 19 teachers

Marash: 23 schools, 1,261 boys, 378 girls, 1,669 students, 34 male, 10 female, 44 teachers

Mush: 23 schools, 1,034 boys, 284 girls, 1318 students, 31 male, 4 female, 35 teachers

Palu: 8 schools, 505 boys, 50 girls, 555 students, 14 male, 1 female, 15 teachers

Pasen: 7 schools, 315 boys, 7 male teachers

Samsun (Canik): 27 schools, 1,361 boys, 344 girls, 1,705 students, 44 male, 15 female, 59 teachers

Shebinkarahisar: 27 schools, 2,040 boys, 105 girls, 2,145 students, 38 male, 4 female, 42 teachers

Siirt: 3 schools, 163 boys, 84 girls, 247 students, 9 male, 2 female, 11 teachers

Sis/Cilicia: 7 schools, 476 boys, 165 girls, 641 students, 15 male, 4 female, 19 teachers

Sivas: 46 schools, 4,072 boys, 459 girls, 4,531 students, 62 male, 11 female, 73 teachers

Tokat: 11 schools, 1,408 boys, 558 girls, 1,966 students, 37 male, 13 female, 50 teachers

Trabzon: 47 schools, 2,184 boys, 718 girls, 2,902 students, 72 male, 13 female, 85 teachers

Urfa: 8 schools, 1,091 boys, 571 girls, 1,662 students, 19 male, 7 female, 26 teachers

Van: 21 schools, 1,323 boys, 554 girls, 1,877 students, 47 male, 12 female, 59 teachers

Yozgat: 12 schools, 1,179 boys, 557 girls, 1,736 students, 30 male, 13 female, 43 teachers

Zeytun: 10 schools, 605 boys, 85 girls, 690 students, 14 male, 1 female, 15 teachers

These churches and schools were the lifeblood of the Armenians in Turkey. These buildings witnessed countless Armenians' baptisms, weddings, and funerals; they served as learning centers where eager teachers transferred knowledge to the children; and these buildings became community gathering centers for happy times and sanctuaries during troubled ones, until the bitter end in 1915. As the Armenian population got wiped out of Anatolia in 1915, so did these churches and schools. Along with the hundreds of thousands of homes, shops, farms, orchards, factories, warehouses, and mines belonging to the Armenians, the church and school buildings also disappeared or were converted to other uses. If not burnt and destroyed outright in 1915 or left to deteriorate by neglect, they became converted buildings for banks, radio stations, mosques, state schools, or state monopoly warehouses for tobacco, tea, sugar, etc., or simply private houses and stables for the Turks and Kurds.

At present, out of the 34 active Armenian churches in Turkey, only 6 are left standing in Anatolia. The biggest of these buildings is Surp Giragos church in Dikranagerd/Diyarbekir, the largest Armenian church in the Middle East, which is now being reconstructed as an Armenian church, under the jurisdiction of the Istanbul Armenian Patriarchate. The process of re-claiming more than 200 deeds of lost lands and property belonging to this church has also been initiated. The project funding and construction is already two-thirds complete, with an expected church opening and first Holy Mass to be performed on Oct. 23, 2011. At present, pilgrimage tours are being organized for this historic occasion, along with visits to other historic sites in Eastern Turkey such as Aghtamar/Van and Ani/Kars, continuing to Armenia and Javakhk. There will be more announcements about these tours in the near future.

Sources
* Zakarya Mildanoglu, *Agos* newspaper April 22, 2011, Istanbul, Turkey.
* Ottoman Armenian National Council, annual reports 1910-1914, Istanbul, Turkey.
* *Echmiadzin Journal*, Yerevan, Armenia 1965-1966 all journals.
* Dr. H. Hamazasp, *Armenian Monasteries in Anatolia*, 9 volumes, Vienna Mkhitarist Union, 1940, Vienna, Austria.
* Raymond Kevorkian and Paul Paboudjian, *Les Arméniens dans l'Empire ottoman à la veille du génocide*(Armenians in the Ottoman Empire before the Genocide), Paris, 1992.
* Teotig Lapjinjian, *Hayots Koghkota* (Armenian Golgotha), 1923, Istanbul, Turkey.
* Vijagatsuyts, *Kavaragan Azkayin Varjaranats Turkiyo*, Dedr A-B, Vicag 1901 Darvo (Report on Armenian Schools in Anatolia, Turkey, Booklets 1 and 2, 1901 Status) Armenian National Education Commission Central Directorate, Istanbul, Turkey.
* Sevan Nishanyan, *Adini Unutan Ulke* (The Country That Forgot Its Name), Everest Press, 2010, Istanbul, Turkey.

Setting the Record Straight: List of Churches in Turkey[*]

The recently appointed ambassador to Turkey, Francis Ricciardone, responding to questions submitted by Senator Robert Menendez (D-N.J.), made incorrect claims about churches in Turkey. We would like to provide some facts for the ambassador's attention.

As *Armenian Weekly* readers know from a recent article published in the paper, the approximate number of Armenian churches in Ottoman Turkey prior to 1915 stands at 2,300, while the number of active Armenian churches in Turkey today is 34—28 in Istanbul, and six in Anatolia. The article had further qualified that these numbers only represented Armenian Apostolic Churches under the jurisdiction of the Istanbul Armenian Patriarchate. When the pre-1915 number of numerous Armenian Catholic, Protestant, and Evangelical churches are to be added to the 2,300 Armenian Apostolic Churches, plus the Greek churches, plus the Catholic, Protestant, and Orthodox churches belonging to the various European communities in Ottoman Turkey, the number of Christian churches easily doubles up. It would take some research to define the exact number of Christian churches prior to 1915; however, it is relatively easier to determine the number of active Christian churches in Turkey today.

The following list gives the Armenian churches still standing in Turkey, both in Istanbul and in Anatolia:

Armenian Apostolic Churches in Turkey

In Istanbul:

Christ the King Armenian Church (Kadıköy, Istanbul)

Church of the Apparition of the Holy Cross (Kuruçeşme, Istanbul)

Holy Archangels Armenian Church (Balat, Istanbul)

Holy Cross Armenian Church (Kartal, Istanbul)

Holy Cross Armenian Church (Selamsız, Üsküdar, Istanbul)

Holy Hripsimiants Virgins Armenian Church (Büyükdere, Istanbul)

Holy Mother-of-God Armenian Apostolic Church (Bakırköy, Istanbul)

Holy Mother-of-God Armenian Church (Beşiktaş, Istanbul)

Holy Mother-of-God Armenian Church (Eyüp, Istanbul)

Holy Mother-of-God Armenian Church (Ortaköy, Istanbul)

---

[*] *Armenian Weekly*, 23 Aug. 2011.

Holy Mother-of-God Armenian Church (Yeniköy, Istanbul)

Holy Nativity of the Mother-of-God Armenian Church (Bakırköy, Istanbul)

Holy Resurrection Armenian Church (Kumkapı, Istanbul)

Holy Resurrection Armenian Chapel (Taksim, Istanbul)

Holy Three Youths Armenian Church (Boyacıköy, Istanbul)

Holy Trinity Armenian Church (Galatasaray, Istanbul)

Narlikapi Armenian Apostolic Church (Narlıkapı, Istanbul)

St. Elijah The Prophet Armenian Church (Eyüp, Istanbul)

St. John the Baptist Armenian Church (Üsküdar)

St. John the Evangelist Armenian Church (Gedikpaşa, Istanbul)

St. John the Evangelist Armenian Church (Narlıkapı, Istanbul)

St. John the Forerunner Armenian Church (Bağlarbaşı, Uskudar, Istanbul)

St. George (Sourp Kevork) Armenian Church (Samatya, Istanbul)

St. Gregory the Enlightener (Sourp Krikor Lousavoritch) (Ghalatya, Istanbul)

St. Gregory the Enlightener (Sourp Krikor Lousavoritch) Armenian Church (Kuzguncuk, Istanbul)

St. Gregory the Enlightener (Sourp Krikor Lousavoritch) Armenian Church (Karaköy, Istanbul)

St. Gregory the Enlightener (Sourp Krikor Lousavoritch) (Kınalıada, Istanbul)

St. James Armenian Church (Altımermer, Istanbul)

St. Nicholas Armenian Church (Beykoz, Istanbul)

St. Nicholas Armenian Church (Topkapı, Istanbul)

St. Santoukht Armenian Church (Hisar, Istanbul)

St. Saviour (Sourp Pergitch) Armenian Chapel (Yedikule, Istanbul)

St. Sergius Armenian Chapel (Balikli, Istanbul)

St. Stephen Armenian Church (Karaköy, Istanbul)

St. Stephen Armenian Church (Yeşilköy, Istanbul)

St. Takavor Armenian Apostolic Church (Kadıköy, Istanbul)

Saints Thaddeus and Barholomew Armenian Church (Yenikapı, Istanbul)

St. Trinity (Sourp Yerrortutyoun) Church (Pera, Istanbul)

St. Vartanants Armenian Church (Feriköy, Istanbul)

The Twelve Holy Apostles Armenian Church (Kandilli, Istanbul)

Of the Armenian Apostolic Churches still standing in Istanbul, only 28 are active at present; the rest are closed due to lack of clergy and/or lack of congregation.

In Anatolia

Holy Forty Martyrs of Sepasdia Armenian Church (Iskenderun, Hatay)
Holy Mother-of-God Armenian Church (Vakıflıköy, Samandağ, Hatay)
St. George (Sourp Kevork) Armenian Church (Derik, Mardin)
St. Gregory the Enlightener Armenian Church (Kayseri)
St. Gregory the Enlightener Armenian Church (Kırıkhan)
St. Giragos Armenian Church (Diyarbakır) (Under Reconstruction)

Armenian Catholic Churches in Turkey

St. Mary Armenian Catholic Church (Beyoğlu, Istanbul)
St. Jean Chrisostomus Armenian Catholic Church (Taksim, Istanbul)
St. Leon Armenian Catholic Church (Kadıkoy, Istanbul)
Assumption Armenian Catholic Church (Büyükada, Istanbul)
Armenian Catholic Church of Immaculate Conception (Koca Mustafa Paşa, Istanbul)
St. Saviour Armenian Catholic Church (Karaköy, Istanbul)
St. Gregory the Illuminator Armenian Catholic Church (Ortaköy, Istanbul)
St. Paul Armenian Catholic Church (Büyükdere, Istanbul)
St. John the Baptist Armenian Catholic Church (Yeniköy, Istanbul)
Of the Armenian Catholic Churches in Istanbul, only the first four are active.

Armenian Evangelical/Protestant Churches in Turkey

Armenian Evangelical Church (Pera, Istanbul)
Armenian Evangelical Church (Gedik Paşa, Istanbul)

Until recently, the Armenian Church Foundations and the Istanbul Armenian Patriarchate had great difficulty in preserving or protecting the church buildings and schools under their jurisdiction; there would be no permission from the government to carry out minor repairs or even paint the deteriorating church and school buildings. But there has been an improvement with the present government, which has restored the Holy Cross Church on Aghtamar Island on Van Lake, albeit as a state museum, and has given permission to the repair and reconstruction of a few historic churches, most notably the Surp Giragos church in Diyarbekir.

To provide a complete picture of churches in Turkey today, we present below a lists of non-Armenian churches.

Greek Orthodox Churches
Fener Greek Orthodox Ecumenical Patriarchate, Fener
Panagia Mugliotissa, H. Georgios Poteras, Fener
Aya Irini, Topkapı
Aya Yorgi, Büyükada
Hagios Poliektus, Topkapı
Havariyyun, Fatih
Kanli, Fatih
Nikolaos, Ayakapı
Kyriaaki, Kumkapı
Panagia Elpida, Kumkapı
Theodoros, Yenikapı
Panagiea, Altımermer
Menas,
Georgios,
Khristos Analepsisi,
Nikolaos,
Konstantinos,
Helene, Samatya
Panagia, Belgradkapı
Nikolaos, Topkapı
Demetrios, Sarmaşık
Georgios, Edirnekapı
Panagia, Salmatomruk
Panagia Hançeriotissa, Tekfursarayı
Panagia Suda, Eğrikapı
Panagia Blakherna, Demetios Kananou, Ayvansaray
Panagia Balinu, Taksiartes, Balat
Hpasaskave, Hasköy
Konstantinos ve Helene, Beyoğlu

Panagia, Galatasaray

Trias, Taksim

Panagia Evangelistria, Dolapdere

Demetrios, Athanisios, Kurtuluş

Dodeka Apostoloi, Feriköy

Hristos Metamorphosisi, Şişli

Panagia, Beşiktaş

Phokos, Ortaköy

Demetrios, İoannes Prodromos, Kuruçeşme

Taksiarkhes, Propethes Elias, Arnavutköy

Khralamsok, Bebek

Panagia Evangelistira, Boyacıköy

Taksiarkhes, İstinye

Nikolaos, Panagia, Yeniköy

Panagia Pege, Silivrikapı

Nikolaos, Georgios, Khristos, Büyükada

Trias, Hsypridon, Khristos, Heybeliada

Georgios, Khristos, Burgazada

Khrasitos, Kınalıada

Heuphemia, Trias (Aya Triada), Kadıköy

Hioannes Khrysostomos, Kalamış

Georgios, Yeldeğirmeni

Prophetes Elias, Üsküdar

Pantelemion, Georgios, Kuzguncuk

Georgios, Çengelköy

Hristos Metamorphosis, Kandilli

Konstantinos ve Helene, Paşabahçe

Paraskeve, Beykoz

Paraskeve, Konstantinos, Tarabya

Paraskeve, Büyükdere

İoannes Prodromos, Yenimahalle

Georgios, Khristos Analepsis, Bakırköy

Stephanos, Yeşilköy

Demetrios, Panagia, Prophetes Elias, Büyükada

Nikolaos, Prophetes Elias, Heybeliada

İoannes Prodromos, Burgazada

Panagia, Kınalıada

Georgios Metokhi, Fener

Georgios Metokhi, Yeniköy

Georgios Metokhi, Heybeliada

İoannes Prodromos Methokhi, Balat

Panagia Kaphatiane, Hnikolaos, İoannes Prodromos, Galata

Balıklı Hagia Kharalampos, Silivrikapı

Haigoi Anargiroi, Silivrikapı

Hristos Genesis, Arnavutköy

Although these Greek churches are still standing, very few are active as there are virtually no Greeks left in Turkey. The last census numbers indicate a population of less than 2,000, which means there are about 20 Greeks left for each Greek church in Turkey.

European Catholic Churches
Saint Benoit (French), Galata

Saint Esprit (French), Beyoglu

Saint Antoine(French), Beyoglu

Santa Maria (İtalian), Tünel

Sankt Georg (Austria), Karaköy

Saint Pierre et Saint Paul (French), Galata

Notre Dame de l'Assumption (French), Moda

St Augustine (French), Fenerbahçe

Czestochova Meryem Ana (Polish), Polonezköy

Anglican Churches
English Consulate Anglican Chapel, Galatasaray

Kirim Anglican Church, Beyoğlu

Pera Resurrection Church- Aynalıçeşme Beyoğlu

All Saints Anglican-Presbyterien, Moda

Protestant Churches
German Protestant Church, Tarlabaşı, Beyoğlu

Netherlands Consulate Dutch Chapel, Beyoğlu

Swedish Lutheran, Tünel

Istanbul Nehir Pentecostal, Harbiye
İstanbul Altıntepe Protestant, Altıntepe

Other Orthodox Churches
Russian Orthodox, Galata
Sveti Stefan Bulgarian Orthodox, Balat

In recent years, a few Christian churches have been created in resort areas such as Antalya and Bodrum, frequented by European retirees, but these are not recorded.

When responding to Sen. Menendez's questions, perhaps the ambassador only relied on information provided by Turkish government sources, which could sometimes be unreliable on issues related to "past history" or to present concerns such as Christian missionary activities. One remarkable example of this is a January 2007 dated Turkish Security General Directorate circular, which indicated that while there were 77,777 mosques in Turkey at the end of 2006, the number of non-Muslim religious institutions had climbed to 373. The circular expressed concern that this number had increased greatly from 273 in 2005, mostly due to illegal missionary activities of Protestant Christians. Of the 373 recorded religious institutions, 321 were Christian churches, including 90 Greek Orthodox (75 in Istanbul), 55 Armenian (48 in Istanbul), 60 Assyrian, 3 Chaldean, 4 Bulgarian, 1 Arabic Orthodox, 53 Christian churches for foreigners, and 52 illegal Protestant Missionary churches. In addition, 36 Jewish Synagogues and 9 Jehovahs Witness temples were recorded. Interestingly, there were more than 900 "gathering centres" (*cemevi*) recorded for Alewites as cultural centers, since they are not recognized as belonging to an official religion.

What is Turkey Returning to Armenians?[*]

The Turkish government recently announced that real estate assets confiscated by the State, which once belonged to Armenian, Greek, and Jewish charitable foundations, would be returned to the rightful owners, and that the government would pay compensation for any confiscated property that has since been sold to third parties. This is definitely a long

---

[*] *Armenian Weekly*, 31 Aug. 2011.

overdue positive step in the right direction by the Turkish government, when compared with decades long injustice and discrimination of the past Turkish governments against its non-Muslim citizens. While this decree was hailed by the EU, Turkish media as well as the minority charitable foundations in Turkey, it was met by the Armenian Diaspora as an insufficient gesture at best, a cynical political trick at worst. Perhaps the following facts can help put the issue in context.

In 1936, the Turkish government required the non-Muslim minority charitable foundations to submit a list of all their real estate assets to the state, which they did. In 1974, during the height of the Cyprus crisis and with inflamed hatred toward the Greeks, the Turkish government installed by the 1971 coup d'etat decreed that any assets not shown on the 1936 lists, that is, properties deeded to the charitable foundations after 1936, are illegally obtained and therefore, must be seized by the Turkish state. Some 1,410 properties willed or gifted to non-Muslim charitable organizations from 1936 to 1974 were confiscated by the State, thus suddenly depriving the foundations from their beneficial uses and revenues. These assets included apartment, school and office buildings, houses, shops and vacant land, mostly in or near Istanbul, where most of the remaining non-Muslim minority citizens in Turkey lived. The present government decree pledges to return 162 of the 1,410 assets confiscated in 1974. Over the past several years, the charitable foundations had tried through Turkish legal channels to get back these assets but to no avail. They had recently applied to the European Court of Human Rights, which had already ruled against the Turkish state on a number of cases.

Below is a partial list of the Armenian charitable foundation assets to be returned by the government:

1. Gedikpasha Armenian Protestant primary school – the building is already demolished, at present used as a park.

2. Gedikpasha Armenian Protestant Church – one apartment building in Kumkapi, a restaurant, a playground.

3. Surp Harutyun Armenian Church – several flats in Beyoglu.

4. Ferikoy Surp Vartanants Church – an apartment building and a vacant lot in Sisli.

5. Kurucheshme Surp Khatch Yerevman Church – one building in Arnavutkoy.

6. Kumkapi Surp Harutiun School – a store in Kumkapi and a store in Kadikoy.

7. Kumkapi Mayr Asdvadzadzin Church – a flat in Eminonu.

8. Yenikoy Surp Asdvadzadzin Church – a vacant lot in Istinye.

9. Bomonti Mkhitaryan Armenian Catholic School – school buildings, two shops and a flat in Sisli.

10. Yedikule Surp Prgich (Holy Saviour) Armenian Hospital – a total of 19 properties, including one building lot, a house and four shared lots in Sariyer, a residential building in Moda, 2 residential buildings in Sisli, one flat in Beyoglu, one store in Kapalicarsi Covered Bazaar, a house in Uskudar, one apartment building, one flat and a warehouse in Kurtulus, a four storey hotel in Taksim, a retail and office commercial building in Beyoglu, a flat in Chamlica, a 47,500 sq. m. vacant lot in Beykoz, and a 44,000 sq. m. land adjacent to the Hospital, formerly the gardens of the Hospital, presently used as Zeytinburnu Soccer Stadium, a sports building, a parking lot and a tea garden, and last but not least, the valuable office building called Selamet Han in Eminonu, Istanbul.

It is noteworthy to emphasize the significance of the Selamet Han office building, which was donated in 1953 by well known businessman and oil magnate Calouste Gulbenkian. The impressive six storey art nouveau style building was built in early 20th century by Armenian architect Hovsep Aznavour, builder of many of Istanbul landmarks in the Pera/Beyoglu district. The Selamet Han building, confiscated by the state in 1974, fell into disrepair and is now in a dilapidated condition. The Surp Prgich Foundation has announced that as soon as the building is given back, it intends to restore it and put into use as a boutique hotel, to generate much needed revenues for the hospital operations.

The recent government decree at last and at least partially addresses the injustices of the 1974 confiscations, by pledging to return about ten percent of the 1,410 properties, mostly in Istanbul. However, there is a massive list of properties and assets belonging to the thousands of Armenian churches, monasteries and schools in Anatolia, lost after 1915. One example to illustrate the enormity of this issue is the case of the Surp Giragos Armenian church in Diyarbekir, which by itself had owned more than 200 properties in central Diyarbekir prior to 1915. Another interesting example is the Sanasaryan High School in Erzurum. This school, which provided education of such a high caliber that it even surpassed the Istanbul Armenian schools in the late 19th century, was closed down in 1915. It is still a little known fact in Turkey that Mustafa Kemal Atatürk, when drumming up support and organizing the resistance to the Allied occupation of Anatolia, convened the famous Erzurum Congress in this Armenian school in July-August 1919. The Sanasaryan School Foundation had built and owned one of the largest office buildings in Istanbul in the late 19th century in order to support the Sanasaryan School in Erzurum. It is also a little known fact that the famous Sanasaryan Han Office Building in Istanbul was seized first by the Ottoman and then the Turkish Republic governments and converted into the General Security and Police Headquarters of Istanbul. This building became notorious for the imprisonment, torture and murder of hundreds of intelligentsia during the military government regimes in the 1970s and 1980s.

One last glaring example involves the lands belonging to the Surp Agop Armenian Cemetery, which were confiscated in the 1930s by the Istanbul municipal government. These lands were deeded in the 16th Century by the Ottoman Emperor Sultan Suleiman the Magnificent to the Armenian people for cemetery uses, as a reward to his personal cook Manuk Karaseferyan of Van, who saved the Sultan from a poisoning plot against him by the Germans and Hungarians after the campaign to take Budapest. The Armenian cemetery was in use for nearly four centuries from 1560s to 1930s. As these vast lands lie adjacent to the most popular road in the centre of the city, they were deemed most valuable by the Istanbul government and expropriated from the Armenian Surp Agop Foundation without any compensation, despite years of legal struggles. At present, these lands are occupied by the State Radio and Television Headquarters, the Turkish Armed Forces Istanbul Headquarters, the Military Museum, many fashionable hotels such as Hilton, Regency Hyatt, Divan, several apartment and office buildings, as well as the expansive Taksim Park, which has walkways made from the marble of Armenian tombstones.

The decree by the present government may seem insufficient or insignificant, but everything is relative, and this is an enormous first step of a long journey in the right direction when compared with past Turkish government policies. This journey requires mutual empathy, cooperation, encouragement and, above all, the uncovering of all hidden historic facts on the path to the creation of a common body of knowledge.

A Series of Firsts in Armenian-Turkish Relations[*]

During the third week of October [2011] several firsts were accomplished in Turkey with respect to the future of Turkish-Armenian relations, the significance of which will be more apparent in the coming months and years. Naturally, every precedent-setting event is the result of many years of hard work and determination in overcoming equally hard circumstances and mindsets.

The largest Armenian church in the Middle East, Surp Giragos of Dikranagerd/Diyarbekir, became the first Armenian church in Anatolia to go through a complete reconstruction after willful destruction and neglect since 1915. This was the first "first."

The consecration of the restored church took place on Sat., Oct. 22, and the first Mass was conducted on Sun., Oct. 23, in the presence of nearly 3,000 Armenian worshippers from Europe, North America, Armenia, and from within Turkey. The moving ceremonies were attended not only by Armenians but also Turkish citizens of Kurdish origin, who are the majority population in southeastern Turkey, as well as several prominent Turkish intellectuals who traveled from Istanbul. Together, they prayed for dialogue, peace, and empathy—spiritual values usually absent among the three peoples. This was another first.

Due to this absence of such precious spiritual values, an untold numbers of Armenian individuals and families have stayed hidden among Turks and Kurds since 1915. Recently, however, many have started "coming out" and declaring themselves Armenian. Some decide to be identified as Muslim Armenians, some go one step further and become Christian Armenians. A few of them were even baptized in the newly consecrated Surp Giragos, which has already become a beacon for all Armenians within Turkey. This was also a first.

More than 200 deeds were recently discovered, showing church ownership of many properties around Diyarbekir prior to 1915, and legal

---

[*] *Armenian Weekly*, 7 Nov. 2011.

processes and negotiations have started to recover these properties, which is another first.

A group of around 25 Armenians traveled from North America to Turkey to witness these historic events, led by two prominent religious leaders, Archbishop Khajag Barsamian, Primate of the Eastern Diocese of the Armenian Apostolic Church of America, and Archbisop Vigen Aykazian, President of the National Council of Churches of Christ in the U.S. The group—which included doctors, lawyers, engineers, businessmen, and retirees—shared the recognition that the reconstruction of Surp Giragos was significant for all Armenians worldwide, serving as a reminder of Armenians' historic presence in Anatolia, as well as a future pilgrimage site.

These individuals had also recognized that financing its reconstruction would be much more meaningful than any church reconstruction in the United States, and even in Armenia. And so they donated generously for a far-away church in southeastern Turkey, traveled there to see it come to fruition, and also promised to act as fundraisers toward shortfalls in the project budget. This was also a first for Diaspora Armenians.

In the spirit of cooperation, the local Diyarbekir municipal leaders decided to participate in the church reconstruction project and financed one third of the project costs. They acknowledged the role their forefathers played in the Armenian Genocide, and assisted the reconstruction effort to "make up for the past events." They greeted the visitors with signs in Armenian welcoming them "to their home"—another first.

Back in Istanbul, in a similar spirit of cooperation, the mayor of Istanbul welcomed the American Armenian group and the two Archbishops, and provided a snapshot of the accomplishments and challenges of running one of the biggest cities of the world. He was asked what steps he is taking to promote the Armenian-built and -owned buildings sprinkled all over Istanbul, and he responded very positively, saying they're correcting all guidebooks, inserting plaques and audio messages at prominent Armenian buildings, and describing the significant contribution and legacy of Armenians in Istanbul architecture, arts, and theatre. This was another first.

In another meeting in Istanbul, the group met with one of the most influential corporate leaders of Turkey, with interests in media, energy, transport, mining, construction, and banking. Members of his corporate team and a member of the Turkish Parliament representing Istanbul accompanied him. The group discussed opening the Turkey-Armenia border and increasing trade, jobs, and investments on both sides of the border. "We are ready to cooperate with the Armenians, once the politicians resolve their differences," said the corporate leader, and the group suggested that since "people vote in the politicians, especially influential people like him can sway politicians." The member of parliament present also responded favorably to the questions from the group regarding issues facing the Istanbul Armenian community and the impact of the current task of rewriting the Constitution on the minorities. This dialogue was another first.

And yet, despite all these positive firsts and precedent-setting events, we also experienced multiple negative—more usual—events in October. The undeclared civil war between the Turks and Kurds intensified. Kurdish militants murdered 24 Turkish soldiers, and the Turkish army responded by killing several Kurdish militants. Turkish jets flying from the Diyarbekir military base bombed several Kurdish targets within Turkey and in northern Iraq.

Then the earthquake struck Van and prevented our group from traveling to Van and Aghtamar. The predominantly Kurdish-populated region complained about the Turkish state not helping them, while ultra-nationalist factions of the Turkish media rejoiced that the earthquake was a "divine punishment" meted by God upon the Kurds. These were not firsts, unfortunately; simply a continuation of decades-old practices.

On the other hand, in some Armenian circles, any communication with the Turks is still frowned upon as treachery. It is thought that any dialogue with Turks about culture, academic cooperation, economy, or trade is merely following Ankara's narrative, which requires that Armenians set aside their quest for truth, justice, and security.

The time has come to realize that it is essential to engage in direct dialogue with the Turks. My late friend Hrant Dink's statement is a timely reminder. He said: "Both Armenians and Turks are clinical cases. Armenians are suffering from trauma (of the 1915 events); Turks are suffering from paranoia (of the consequences of accepting the 1915 events). Who will cure them? What is the prescription? The Armenian will be the Turk's doctor, the Turk will be the Armenian's doctor. The prescription will be dialogue."

Although still few in numbers, there is an increasing number of Armenians and Turks engaged in dialogue, in academia, the media, arts, sciences, law, business, and other professions, which has started to produce real results in improving Turkish-Armenian relations.

Without dialogue, the Surp Giragos church could not have been achieved.

Without dialogue, none of the firsts described above could have been achieved.

Dersim: A First Step in Facing the Past in Turkey[*]

Turkish Prime Minister Recep Tayyip Erdoğan last week apologized on behalf of the Turkish Republic for the 1937-38 Dersim massacres. In his speech, Erdoğan showed documents dated August 1939 that stated the Turkish government had organized military operations resulting in the deaths of more than 13,000 civilians in the province of Dersim. Erdoğan further defined these events "as the most tragic events of our recent past," adding, "this disaster should now be questioned with courage."

Dersim is an eastern province of Turkey, bordered by the Erzincan, Elazig, and Bingol provinces. During Ottoman times, the Dersim region formed part of Harput province, adjacent to Erzurum province. Its population is comprised of mainly Kurds of the Alawi sect, Shiite Muslims often persecuted by the majority Sunni Muslim Turks.

In the Ottoman period and, later, the Turkish Republic, the central government had difficulty establishing authority in this region, controlled mostly by Kurdish feudal lords and tribal chieftains. The killings took place when the Kurdish population of the region resisted the efforts of the newly formed Turkish Republic to exert its authority there. After disarming the local population and arresting its leaders, the Turkish Army attacked the entire region, killing indiscriminately. Women and children trying to hide in caves were either smoked out or burned alive by sealing the cave entrances. Army planes dropped bombs and poison gas on the fleeing civilians. One of the bomber pilots was Sabiha Gökçen, Mustafa

---

[*] *Armenian Weekly*, 1 Dec. 2011.

Kemal Atatürk's adopted daughter and a war hero in Turkey, whose name was later given to one of the two Istanbul airports. All arrested Kurdish leaders were hanged. The number of dead ranged from 13,000 according to Turkish sources—40,000 to U.S. and 80,000 to Kurdish sources. One fact remains clear: Dersim was de-populated, with most of the remaining population forcefully deported to western Turkey "in order to accelerate the Turkification of this rebellious group." Decades later, these people were allowed to return to Dersim, which was renamed Tunceli province. For the past two decades, it has become one of the hotbeds of the Kurdish resistance movement.

Many interesting twists of events led Erdoğan to issue the official apology about the Dersim massacres. Two years ago, when Erdoğan first attempted to end the Kurdish resistance peacefully, one of the leaders of the strongly nationalistic main opposition party, the CHP, roared that the correct way to deal with the Kurdish Question was not through peaceful means, but through tried and true methods used in Dersim in the 1930s. Ironically, the main opposition party is now headed by Kemal Kilicdaroglu, an Alawite from Dersim. (One of his party members recently demanded that Turkey face its past and apologize for the Dersim massacres; for this outburst, he now faces party discipline hearings.) The main motive behind Erdoğan's apology seems to be to put the blame of the Dersim massacres squarely on the CHP opposition party, which was in full control of the government in the 1930s—in the era of Atatürk, Ismet Inonu, and Celal Bayar—as well as to attempt to lure the votes of the ethnic Kurdish population. Another opposition official from Diyarbekir praised Erdoğan and criticized his own party for not issuing the apology, and was immediately expelled from the CHP. A member of of Erdoğan's governing party proposed to delete Sabiha Gökçen's name from the Isanbul Airport, and was promptly silenced by Erdoğan. In the meantime, Kilicdaroglu accused Erdoğan of treason and said he wouldn't be surprised if Erdoğan apologizes to the Armenians next. Erdoğan responded: "How dare you compare me to the Armenian Diaspora!"

There are several Armenian connections to the Dersim story, both ironic and tragic. During the height of the 1915 deportation and massacres, several Armenian groups from neighboring provinces sought refuge in Dersim. An estimated 25,000 Armenians from Erzurum and Erzincan survived under the protection of the Dersim Kurds, and most of

Survivors of the Dersim Massacre on display, 1938

these Armenians converted to the Alawite religion. It is said that one of the reasons for the fury of the violent attacks by the Turkish army in the 1930s was vengeance toward these Kurds who saved the Armenians in 1915. It is also said that a significant portion of the Dersim massacre victims were converted Armenian women and children.

In stark contrast, the war hero and pilot Sabiha Gökçen, who bombed the people of Dersim, was in fact an Armenian girl from Bursa, adopted by Atatürk after being orphaned during the genocide. We cannot help but wonder ironically: What did Sabiha Gökçen think when bombing the people below? That she was a Turk bombing the Kurds? Or did she know that she was an Armenian bombing Armenians? The revelation of Sabiha Gökçen being Armenian was exposed with documentation by Armenian journalist Hrant Dink in 2004, which started the ball rolling toward his targeted assassination by the "Deep State" in 2007.

The hidden Armenians of Dersim have recently "come out" and officially formed the Dersim Armenians Union, some even changing their names and religion from Islam to Christianity. Their leader has recently stated that nearly three quarters of Dersim villages are inhabited by hidden Armenians, but many are scared to reveal their real identities.

All these interrelated facts lead toward Turkey's inevitable need to face its past—and not only the selective good heroic deeds of its forefathers. Prime Minister Erdoğan has taken a first step by acknowledging and apologizing for the Dersim massacres. Other events that Turkey must face include the so-called 1942 Wealth Tax imposed on minorities, which resulted in the total transfer of their wealth to Turks, and the violent Sept. 6-7, 1955 events, which resulted in the minority Greek population fleeing Turkey. But the biggest elephant in the room remains: facing the truth about the 1915 genocide.

Justice as Joke: The Trial of Hrant Dink's Murderers[*]

When Hrant Dink was assassinated in front of the *Agos* newspaper offices in Istanbul, Turkey, five years ago on Jan. 19, 2007, the significance of this heinous act was not immediately understood. Neither the Turkish people nor the Turkish state, "deep" or otherwise, realized that this was not another murder of a journalist, so tragically common in Turkey. No one in Turkey could predict that this murder would become a turning point for Turkey on such far-reaching issues as democratization, freedom of speech, the "deep state," and Turkish-Armenian relations from the present all the way back to 1915. Although the assassin was caught almost immediately by police, perhaps even leading one to wonder about their prior knowledge, the question of "Who ordered the assassination?" could not be answered five years ago—and cannot be answered now, after five long years of a trial completed just two days before the fifth anniversary of the shooting. It seems, however, that the end of the trial is not the end of this case. The spontaneous support shown by several hundred thousand ordinary people who took to the streets during Hrant's funeral is now being repeated after five years with outrage at the trial verdict and demands for truth.

Why was this trial deemed unfair by the people, by civil society? First, we need to provide context for the general situation in Turkey. For five years, government leaders said the Dink murder was one of many acts by Ergenekon, the "deep state" organization, which organized attacks on minorities, and both Muslim and Christian religious institutions, to create an atmosphere of anarchy and terror, ripe for a coup d'etat by the military. The murder of Catholic priest Santoro in Trabzon, the murder of three Christian missionaries in Malatya, uncovered plans of mosque and

[*] *Armenian Weekly*, 13 Feb. 2012.

Hrant Dink.

museum bombings, hidden cache of arms, and thousands of communications toward the planning of a coup d'etat have all been presented as incriminating evidence to arrest and imprison several hundred retired and active military leaders, bureaucrats, professors, lawyers, journalists, and businessmen deemed Ergenekon members. After the assassination, Prime Minister Recep Tayyip Erdoğan himself said to the Dink family, "They are after me as well."

The police arrested three and charged 16 other suspects in connection with the murder. The trial proceeded at a crawling pace, with the Dink family lawyers stonewalled at every session, and a determined group of supporters called "Hrant's Friends" attending every session demanding justice. Discouraged by the pace of the trial, the Dink family took the case to the European Human Rights Court (EHRC), which promptly assessed and passed its judgment in December 2010: The state had neglected to provide protection for Hrant Dink despite known threats so that state officials must share responsibility in the assassination for ignoring the known threats. The EHRC also targeted the Istanbul and Trabzon Security Departments for being negligent, as they failed to prevent the assassination despite being aware of an imminent plan for the murder. Following the EHRC verdict, the lawyers for the Dink family demanded that 30 bureaucrats from the Istanbul and Trabzon government offices, as well as the National Intelligence Organization, also be questioned and charged. The court turned down the request.

The lawyers for the family also produced massive amounts of indisputable evidence that demonstrated the presence of a plan for the murder; of several persons communicating before, during, and after the murder; and, more critically, several government officials being informed of the plan, and either ignoring, praising, or consenting to it, and then deliberately covering up their involvement. Destroyed evidence included several tapped telephone conversations between police officials and informers, and sworn evidence of several police officers against their superiors who knew about the planned murder. Evidence refused by the court included footage of the actual murderer and accomplices captured by a store security camera; cellular phone conversations immediately before, during, and after the murder between the murderer and at least four others; and communications between the Dink murder suspects and military leaders already imprisoned for belonging to the Ergenekon "deep state" terrorist organization. Another example of scandalous treatment of evidence included the deliberate tampering, forging, and concealing of past communications by police officials, which turned notification of the impending murder into information about the murder after the fact. And while the evidence showed that Trabzon police had tapped the phone lines of some suspects and had even physically trailed them, when asked for the records by the court, the police said they had done no such thing. When it was revealed that the Trabzon Police indeed had the records, the court was told they were deleted. The evidence presented by the family lawyers also showed that Istanbul police had obtained the video footage of the crime scene on the day of the murder and had destroyed part of it. The Telecommunications Directorate, the regulator of cellular telephone operators, resisted providing the court with records of the suspects' phone conversations, either among themselves or with police officials, until two weeks before the verdict. Ironically, all of these facts were widely covered by the media, including the transcript of several wiretapped conversations between the suspects and police officials. One of these conversations is disgustingly clear: immediately after the murder, a Trabzon informer asks, "Is he [the shooter] one of our boys?" and the Trabzon police officer responds, "Yes, but he wasn't supposed to run away after the shooting."

Why did the verdict cause an uproar?

As stated previously, in addition to the person who pulled the trigger—who was sentenced earlier—a total of 19 people were charged in Hrant's murder for belonging to a terrorist organization planning the murder, for providing logistics and training, and for arranging the murder weapon. Eighteen of the suspects were acquitted from the charge of belonging to a terrorist organization planning the murder. Only one person was charged with planning the murder and helping the assassin.

None of the 30 state bureaucrats or police officials were even brought to trial for questioning. All of these "untouchables" kept their jobs and some were even rewarded with promotions. The then-governor of Istanbul ran for parliament and got elected as a member of Erdoğan's party. The then-Istanbul Police chief got appointed as governor of the Osmaniye province. The then Trabzon police chief got promoted to head of the General Security Directorate. In short, the government managed to achieve something unbelievable, going from being a target of the "deep state" to becoming an accomplice of the "deep state" in the murder of Hrant Dink.

In another twist of irony, the government went a step further and jailed a journalist for publishing a book exposing the role of bureaucrats in the Dink murder, on charges of abetting the Ergenekon terrorist organization. The presiding judge said that although he acquitted the suspects from belonging to a terrorist organization, it does not mean that they did not belong to a terrorist organization, and that there simply was no evidence. The government officials said that they did everything the judiciary demanded of them. Prime Minister Erdoğan and President Abdullah Gul tried to convince the protesting masses that there is always the appeal process and not to worry.

During the initial trials, Hrant's son said, "the court was making fun of us." Upon hearing the verdict, Hrant's lawyer said, "they saved the best joke for last." As Hrant's friends, it is very difficult not to be discouraged. However, one has to realize why the state had to align with the "deep state" when its judiciary system came to this verdict in the assassination case of Hrant Dink, the first Armenian in Turkey who had dared the Turkish state to face its past and stop denying the truth about 1915: Any admission of guilt by the Turkish state in this murder would go all the way back to admission of guilt in 1915—a very long chain of dominoes that has already started to move, judging by the reaction of a growing number of people in Turkey demanding the truth.

Lies, Damned Lies, and Billboards[*]

Posters that warned "Don't be deceived by Armenian lies!" were placed throughout Istanbul during the week leading up to the Feb. 26 protest in Taksim Square, held to commemorate the 20th anniversary of Khojali.

Who organized the event? Who financed it? Why was it being held now, all of a sudden, after 20 years of silence about Khojali in Turkey?

Apparently, for answers, one must go back quite some time, all the way to 1915. Yes, 1915, a date dreaded by Turks, a date Armenians spread lies about non-stop—lies that most of the world outside of Turkey believe, and that, even worse, many Turks within have also started to believe. These lies have got to be stopped before it is too late, before more Turks are deceived by the Armenians, before the upcoming 100th commemoration—in 2015—of the 1915 events.

Until recently, if you spread these lies in Turkey, you were labeled a "traitor," convicted for "insulting Turkishness," jailed and beaten. If you happened to be named Hrant Dink, you were silenced with a bullet to the back of your head. But many Turks have now started to believe these lies, and have started to empathize with the Armenians, with Hrant, even carrying signs declaring, "We are all Armenians, We are all Hrant."

Just a month ago, when the trial of Hrant's murderers ended with a cover-up, when the presiding judge declared that there was "no evidence of organized murder, even though I sense there is a deep organization behind the murder," some treacherous Turks poured into the streets carrying the dreaded signs that declared they were "all Armenian, all Hrant," and demanding justice, demanding the state face its past.

In the meantime, the French, who have believed the Armenian lies for a long time, went one step further a month ago when they passed a law that would punish anyone who denied these lies. In fact, a Turkish minister, ironically the one responsible for European Union accession talks, decided to challenge this law by declaring that there was never an Armenian

---

[*] *Armenian Weekly*, 8 Mar. 2012.

Genocide. He got into some trouble with the Swiss authorities, who continue to believe the lies.

The time had come, therefore, for the "real" Turks to act, to show the "traitorous" Turks—and the rest of the world—that they would not be deceived, that only they knew the truth, and that they would make sure the Armenians stopped lying and learned the truth, or else...

And the posters came out on Feb. 26 in Taksim Square, in central Istanbul, with the following humane messages addressed to the Armenians and traitorous Turks:

"You are all Armenians, you are all Bastards"

"Today Taksim, tomorrow Yerevan, we may suddenly come there one night"

"Grey Wolves are here, where are the Hrants?" (The grey wolf is a symbol of the ultra-nationalist Turks)

"Grey wolf Ogun" (referring to Hrant's killer)

"Grey wolf Catli" (referring to the mobster ordered by the Turkish state to go after ASALA)

"Hrant's bastards cannot scare us"

"Agri Mountain [Mount Ararat] will be your graves"

"Let Armenia be wiped out"

The French were also remembered, as rolls of toilet paper marked "Sarkozy toilet paper" were distributed to the protesting crowds. And yes, there were also some messages about the Azeri Khojali victims. But it was apparent that the crowds were more pre-occupied with the Armenians and traitorous Turks, their 1915 stand, and their grief over and demands for justice for Hrant. The Khojali incident was just the occasion to vent their hatred and anger.

The event could have been regarded as routine, as just another spontaneous anti-Armenian hate show so common among the Turkish people, brainwashed with the racist Ittihadist ideology for several generations. Usually, however, the elite "brainwashers" stay hidden behind the curtain during these events. On Feb. 26, they did not see the need to hide. The governor of Istanbul attended the event, and it became clear that the expensive posters placed throughout Istanbul—on prominent city-owned billboards and subway stations—were subsidized by the government, using taxpayer money, including that of the Armenian community of Istanbul.

But even more remarkable was the presence of the Turkish minister of interior, who was at the front of the rally, instigating hatred and discrimination through his statements. After defining Armenians as "blood suckers" and "heartless, pitiless murderers," he continued, "The spilled Azeri blood is Turkish blood, and as long as the Turkish nation lives, we will seek revenge for this spilled blood." Remembering the true objective of the event, he announced that "the Turkish nation has absolutely nothing to be ashamed of in its history, not in Turkey, not in the Balkans, Azerbaijan, or Kazakhstan!" Apparently, while Prime Minister Erdoğan insists on an historical commission to investigate 1915, and the U.S. State Department parrots the same position, the minister of interior already knows the truth and has announced the conclusion of the investigation.

It seems that the ever-changing state policy on how to deal with the 1915 events is changing once again. The official position over the past 90 years has moved from complete silence, to theses that "Armenians never lived in Turkey" (or "Armenians massacred Turks," or "Armenians and Turks killed each other during the war," or "Armenians were only deported on the eastern war front," or "Armenians died of hunger and disease"), to the latest thesis: "Armenians committed genocide." Of course, the other new thesis is that "the French also committed genocide." But there is also an official policy that does not seem to be changing, no matter who controls the government—the state or deep state, military or civilian, left or right, Ittihadist or nationalist, secular or moderate Islam—and that is: "We killed in the past. If necessary, we will kill again." If Erdoğan is serious about showing that his regime is different from his predecessors', he will have to start by asking for the resignation of his interior minister.

Revisiting the Turkification of Confiscated Armenian Assets[*]

If one person murders another, then takes over that murdered person's property and possessions, he would be living off the proceeds of his crime.

[*] *Armenian Weekly*, 17 April 2012.

Once authorities discover his crime, he would be found guilty—by any court, anywhere—and then sentenced, punished, and forced to return the unlawfully obtained property and possessions. But if a people murders another people, and takes over the property and possessions of the murdered people, it seems that different rules apply, and the guilty—and their children—can continue living off the proceeds of the crime. It also seems that their successors can continue to threaten the successors of the murdered people with new murders, if, that is, they dared to mention the murder, or dared to demand the return of their property and possessions. This is the evolving saga of the Turkish and Armenian peoples from 1915 to today.

The 1915 murder of a people—or perhaps, more correctly, the attempted murder of a people—not only resulted in wiping out the Armenians from their 4,000-year-old homeland within a matter of 1-2 years, but also initiated an ongoing process of wealth, property, and asset transfer from Armenians to Turks. This process, started in 1915 by the Ittihadist leadership of Ottoman Turkey, continued uninterrupted with the successor Turkish Republic for many decades using various legislative decrees. It was completed with the total and legal Turkification of all Armenian assets and properties—of the Armenians' economic presence— in what is now the Turkish republic.

This essay will attempt to explain the legal Turkification process, provide examples illustrating the enormity of the assets involved, and discuss recent initiatives to reverse this process (including steps taken by Armenians, and steps announced by the present Turkish government).

***

Kilifina uydurmak, in Turkish, means to "fit the sword to the sheath." One would normally expect that the sword is made first, and the sheath to fit it. But if there is an unacceptable action first, followed by other actions needed to give it the appearance of a proper action—that is, to "make right" the original action—then this phrase is used to define the situation. "Fit the sword to the sheath" is a perfect description of the legislative process of the Turkification of Armenian assets.

On May 27, 1915, just weeks after the deportation of Armenians had begun in April 1915, the Ottoman Parliament passed the Deportation Legislation. This was followed by the Liquidation Legislation, which tried to give some semblance of legality to the plunder of Armenian assets that took place after the deportations. This legislation, dated June 10, 1915, and further reinforced on Sept. 26, 1915, directed the formation of Liquidation Commissions in the provinces where the deportations occurred. The legislation defined the Armenians as "transported persons" and their assets as "abandoned assets," as if the Armenians had willingly abandoned them. It provided the first steps to liquidate the assets, and gave the state power to decide to whom the assets should be given, or sold, and for how much, without the approval of the owners (but on their behalf). By January 1916, there were 33 Liquidation Commissions formed, covering all of the interior provinces, recording, listing, appraising, and holding on deposit some of the assets for future return to Armenians, but also selling or distributing other assets to Muslim refugees. The legislation also stipulated that assets belonging to Armenian charitable foundations, such as churches or schools, be transferred to the State Directorate of Charitable Foundations or the State Treasury. Cash and movable assets of the transported persons were to be collected and kept in a Special Trust account on behalf of the owners. Naturally, having the pick of any asset left behind, thousands of government officials and members of the Liquidation Commission enriched themselves, as did thousands of local Turks and Kurds who seized the houses, farms, orchards, warehouses, factories, mines, hotels, shops, stores, tools, and livestock once owned by Armenians.

The whereabouts of the dossiers belonging to these 33 Liquidation Commissions is a mystery. The Turkish state, which boasts that all their archives are open (and persistently calls for Armenian archives to be opened even though they are, in fact, open), continues to keep these crucial records of Armenian assets a secret. Interestingly, in 2005 when the present Turkish government attempted to comply with European Union (EU) modernization initiatives by translating, digitizing, and opening up the old Ottoman land registry and deed records to the public, it was prevented from doing so by a stern warning—dated Aug. 26, 2005—from the National Security Committee of the Turkish Armed Forces. "The Ottoman records kept at the Land Register and Cadaster Surveys General Directorate offices must be sealed and not available to the public, as they have the potential to be exploited by alleged genocide claims and property claims against the State Charitable Foundation assets," read the warning. "Opening them to general public use is against state interests."

When the Ottomans were defeated and the Ittihadist leaders fled Istanbul in a German submarine, the newly elected Ottoman government on Jan. 8, 1920, rescinded the Liquidation Legislation and directed the return of all Armenian assets, or equivalent compensation, to their rightful owners. Unfortunately, the Istanbul government itself got liquidated before the legislation was implemented, and the nationalist government gaining strength in Ankara immediately took steps to abolish it. It seems that the Ankara parliamentarians, who were mostly Ittihadists, were more pre-occupied with the Armenian assets than the "Liberation War" raging against the Greeks raging at the time. These Ittihadists, gathered around Mustafa Kemal Atatürk, had two strong motives to join the Ankara government: First, to ensure that they held on to the assets that they had plundered, and to ensure that they prevented these assets from being returned to any surviving Armenians; and second, to escape any prosecution and punishment for "crimes against humanity" by the Ottoman Istanbul government and the Allied forces occupying Istanbul, who were actively searching for them.

The Ankara parliament later annulled the legislation of the Istanbul Parliament, reinstated the Ittihadist Liquidation Legislation on Sept. 14, 1922, and appointed new members for the Liquidation Commissions, thereby enriching local notables. The term "transported persons" was changed to "persons lost or fled from the country." The legislation stated that if these persons ever returned, they would receive their assets and deposits; otherwise, all assets would be sold with the proceeds going to the state treasury, after verification by the courts regarding lost or fled persons. As the requirement of court verification for lost or fled persons proved difficult, the legislation was revised on April 29, 1923, giving lost or fled persons, or previous owners, four months (if within the country) or six months (if abroad) to claim their assets. In September 1923, the parliament passed legislation banning the return of Armenians to Cilicia and the east. With further amendments in a new legislation dated March 13, 1926, the state sold the assets to local Turkish investors with a low 1915 wartime assessment on the assets instead of current values. (It is estimated that the assets' value would have increased by more than 12 times from 1915-26.) It was also specified that any returning Armenians would not receive the actual assets, but cash, based on the legislated 1915 valuation. This legislation was in effect until 1988; if, until then, any

Armenian came to claim compensation, it would have been assessed based on 1915 valuation. In August 1926, legislation was brought in for the state to nationalize any assets left behind and not claimed by the Armenians prior to the 1924 Lausanne Treaty.

Another legislation, dated May 31, 1926, enabled families and heirs of "martyrs"—officials executed by the Istanbul government for their role in the Armenian deportations—or Ittihadists assassinated by Armenians, to receive pensions deemed "blood money" from the revenues of the Armenian assets. This legislation was also in effect until 1988.

In addition to the Armenian assets held by the Turkish state, the issue of assets held by individual Turks was the subject of fierce debates in parliament. Since most of these assets were held without any documentation, there were problems in their transfer and sale. On May 24, 1928, new deeds were prepared for the Armenian assets, and on June 2, 1929, new legislation gave the right to title and deed to possessors of real estate for a specified period. Accordingly, any vacant land such as fields, orchards, and farmland held for 15 years since 1914, and any buildings or other real estate held for 10 years since 1919, became the legal property of the individuals who had bought, stolen, occupied, or seized them.

The legal Turkification of the assets was now complete. Yet, not all of the individuals who had bought the assets from the state treasury were able to make the required payments. New amendments were approved in 1931 that reduced and then canceled debts and mortgages to the treasury, thereby encouraging the growth of the "Turkified" economy.

The deposits held by the state treasury on behalf of the deported people was handled by legislation dated May 24, 1928, which legalized the straight transfer of the funds to the state budget, starting with 300,000 Turkish liras in 1928. Based on a proportional increase of the Turkish state budget 920 times from 1928 to 2008, this would be equivalent to 276 billion Turkish liras today, or US$150 billion. Another 3.9 million Turkish liras from the Armenian deposits was transferred to the state budget by 1931, marked as revenue from the assets or taxes on the assets.

It is difficult to assess the value of the Armenian assets seized by the Ottoman and Turkish Republic governments and by individuals, but existing pieces of the puzzle can provide a glimpse into the enormity of the theft. In 1916, the sum of five million Ottoman Turkish liras, equivalent to 30,000 kilograms of gold, was transferred by the Ottoman government to the Reichsbank in Berlin. This large sum of money, deposited during wartime, would be the aggregate of Armenian deposits and sums gained from the Liquidation Commissions. There are further unknown gold deposits at the Deutche Bank. During U.S. Senate discussions related to the Armenian assets, the figure of $40 million was mentioned. In terms of real assets, Ittihadist leader Talat Pasha's own records indicate that in 1915, 20,545 buildings, 267,536 acres of land, 76,942 acres of vineyards, 703,941 acres of olive groves, and 4,573 acres of mulberry gardens were allocated to Muslim settlers out of the assets seized from Armenians.

Based on a population loss of 1.5 million, and 10 persons to a family, the loss of houses alone would number at least 150,000. There were 2,900 Armenian settlements emptied of their population; in these settlements, there were 2,300 churches and 700 schools under the jurisdiction of the Istanbul Armenian Patriarchate and the Apostolic Church. Once the Armenian Catholic and Protestant churches and schools are added to this sum, the number easily exceeds 4,000. Most of these churches and schools had their own charitable foundations to generate revenue for their upkeep and maintenance. For example, the Surp Giragos Armenian church in Diyarbekir/Dikranagerd, one of the largest churches in the Middle East with a large parish and community, owned more than 200 properties in Diyarbekir as part of its charitable foundation. The foundation of the Sanasaryan College in Erzurum/Garin owned several shops and houses in Erzurum, as well as the Sanasaryan Office building in Istanbul, to pay for the school's expenses. The two Armenian hospitals, Surp Prgich (Holy Savior) and Surp Hagop, had vast holdings in Istanbul to pay for the hospital building and staff expenses, as well as to provide subsidized medical care to poor Armenians.

All of these assets, except the two hospitals and some of the Istanbul Armenian churches and schools, disappeared after 1915. If not destroyed outright or left to deteriorate, the church and school buildings were converted into banks, mosques, state schools, community centers, stables, or warehouses. Armenian houses were taken over by local Turks and Kurds, or by Muslim refugee settlers from the Balkans. The Armenian economic assets such as farms, orchards, olive groves, stores, factories, mines became the foundation stones of the Turkish economy and the starting capital of most of the wealthy Turkish industrialists of today. The Turkish government continued the seizure of Armenian assets and the legalization of it up until the 2000s. With legislation brought in 1974, more than 1,400 legally obtained assets of the Istanbul Armenian charitable foundations since 1936, were declared illegal and seized by the state.

In the last three years, the Turkish state has taken some steps to reverse the process of nationalizing Armenian assets. After losing several cases— taken by Istanbul-Armenian charitable foundations to the European Human Rights Court—related to the seizure of assets, the state recently announced that 162, or about 10 percent, of the assets seized after 1974 would be returned to the Armenian charitable foundations. Although this is an encouraging first step, there is no mention of any return of the assets seized in 1915. And the figure of 162 pales in comparison with the hundreds of thousands of seized assets.

When the Turkish state decided to restore the Aghtamar Holy Cross church in Van, it did so only by converting it to a state museum. When Armenian communities raised funds worldwide to restore the Surp Giragos church in Diyarbekir as a working church, the Turkish state refused to provide any funding. The process of reclaiming the 200 properties belonging to Surp Giragos church is ongoing through the courts and negotiations with the Diyarbekir city government. The Istanbul Armenian Patriarchate has now decided to go to court to reclaim the Sanasaryan Office building in Istanbul as the first test-case related to the return of an Armenian asset seized in 1915. Indications are that the government will vigorously challenge this case, as it may set a precedent for multiple claims to follow.

The murdered people cannot be reclaimed nor returned. But their assets can and must be reclaimed by their successors. The assets seized by the murderers can and must be returned by their successors. This would be a start in the process, based on dialogue and non-violence, of facing the past.

Sources

* Ayşe Hür, "Ermeni Mallarini Kimler Aldi" (Who Got the Armenian Assets?), *Taraf*, Istanbul, March 2, 2008.
* Taner Akçam, *Ermeni Meselesi Hallolmustur*, Iletisim Yayinlari, Istanbul, 2008.
* Uğur Üngör, "Confiscation and Colonization: The Young Turk Seizure of Armenian Property," *Armenian Weekly Magazine*, April 2011.
* Nevzat Onaran, *Emvali Metruke Olayi: Osmanlida ve Cumhuriyette Ermeni*

ve Rum Mallarinin Turklestirilmesi (The Abandoned Assets Event: The Seizure/Turkification of Armenian and Greek Assets), Belge Yayinlari, Istanbul 2010.

* Raffi Bedrosyan, "Searching for Lost Armenian Churches and Schools in Turkey," *Armenian Weekly*, Aug. 1, 2011.

* Raffi Bedrosyan, "What is Turkey Returning to Armenians?" *Armenian Weekly*, Aug. 31, 2011.

A Flower or an Oak Tree?[*]

For the past few weeks, we have been reading the unbelievably emotional and informative revelations of Nanore Barsoumian, *Weekly* assistant editor, and Khatchig Mouradian, Weekly editor, in their travels in eastern Turkey, where they searched for traces of a three-thousand-year-old Armenian presence in the region that suddenly disappeared in 1915.

In one of the articles, Mouradian describes his travels to Chunkus, a district of Diyarbekir, where all 10,000 of the Armenian inhabitants were massacred and thrown into a deep abyss called Dudan during the summer of 1915. Although still denied by the Turkish state, it is indisputably documented by multiple countries' diplomatic representatives and historians, as well as by survivor and perpetrator accounts, that what happened in Chunkus also happened in all of Ottoman Turkey—in the east, west, north, south, and central regions. Only the applied mode of the Armenians' destruction differed from region to region. While Armenians in the north were thrown into the Black Sea, or driven to the desert in death marches from the west, east, central, and south regions under the guise of deportations "to keep them away from the war zone," officials in the Diyarbekir region achieved the unique distinction of the highest percentage of Armenian massacres (97% of the deportees), without the need to deport any distance, immediately outside the city walls.

In another article, Barsoumian describes her emotions travelling as a "tourist" in Diyarbekir, where these sad events took place, and yet, where there is now a newly reconstructed church, Surp Giragos—the largest Armenian church in the Middle East, and the first church reconstructed in Turkey since 1915. And she asks difficult questions: Who am I, why

* *Armenian Weekly*, 12 July 2012.

am I here, how am I connected to these lands, what is next, what is a church without its congregation, where do we go from here?

While these questions may be rhetorical or impossible to answer, I will still attempt to find some answers, as I myself ask these same questions on a daily basis.

Using Hrant Dink's famous quote, 1915 is a trauma for the Armenians, who cannot rest until their pain and losses are acknowledged and addressed, and are a paranoia for the Turks, who fear any acknowledgment will result in massive financial and territorial compensation. Dink's prescription for both afflictions was always dialogue. Unfortunately, his message was not well understood by either Armenians or Turks while he was alive, and after a brief period of empathy following his murder—seen with the spontaneous outpouring of sympathy by several hundred thousand Turkish citizens during his funeral—his message continues to fall on deaf ears, of both the Turkish and Armenian governments, as well as a majority of the Turkish people and the Armenian Diaspora.

But one must not generalize. Dialogue between Turks and Armenians for the sake of dialogue will not serve any purpose if both sides just parrot their positions; this can only be defined as monologues, as ineffective as two people shouting at each other from the top of two faraway mountain peaks. Therefore, real dialogue can only start between people who have a desire for a common body of knowledge about the 1915 events. And such people exist in Turkey today, perhaps small in number, but increasing every day, and increasingly in influential positions. Most Turkish citizens are brainwashed with the official state version of history about 1915 because of the educational system and constant hate-mongering against the Armenians in the media; however, people in Turkey can no longer be defined as a homogeneous, uniform group. There are serious clashes between the Turkish state and the sizable Kurdish minority—up to a quarter of the Turkish population—which wants greater autonomy and language rights.

For the first time in the history of the Turkish republic, the force of the "deep state," consisting of key military, judicial, media, academia, and business personalities that governed by a secular Kemalist agenda, has been broken and replaced by a moderately religious group of politicians who have started questioning the past deeds of the previous Kemalist governments. There are numerous bright personalities in politics, academia, media, publishing, NGOs, arts, and literature that can be defined as "opinion makers" and who have started pulling Turkey toward democratization, freedom of speech, and freedom of thought—and who have acknowledged the truth and organized apology campaigns about 1915. In a way, any new perspective on dealing with the 1915 events has become a barometer to gauge the level of democratization in Turkey. There are countless Turkish and Kurdish families that have Armenian roots going back to 1915, most commonly through Armenian girls or boys rescued/hidden/abducted. There are also countless other Turkish and Kurdish families with Armenian roots that have converted to Islam or have hidden their identity since 1915. These various groups have one thing in common: They have started to openly question the official state version of history regarding 1915.

To answer Barsoumian's question—What is next?—dialogue and contact with these various groups of non-uniform Turkish citizens is the way. We can cite very few examples of Armenian attempts for dialogue with the "opinion makers." To date, the only serious and successful Armenian initiative of dialogue in the academic field has been through the Zoryan Institute. This resulted in many young Turkish historians and academias cooperating not only with Armenians but also international colleagues, in producing the most serious research on 1915. Within Turkey, the only other successful dialogue has been in the media, by the dedicated team at *Agos* newspaper, following in the footsteps of Hrant Dink. The third example are the pilgrimage tours to Anatolia, organized by the Armenian Church in recent years, bringing Diaspora Armenians to their roots and face to face with the Turkish/Kurdish people now living there, often leading to the conclusion that both sides have more in common than they realized.

Dialogue about the truth of 1915 with opinion makers in Turkey and ordinary Turkish/Kurdish citizens would have one far-reaching result—it would create voters in Turkey knowledgeable about the genocide. Voters would vote in parliament members and governments that, in turn, would need to set policies and decisions according to the voters' preferences, sooner or later. Perhaps this is a very long winding road, but at the end, decisions respecting the truth of 1915 taken in the Turkish Parliament would be far more effective than any decisions taken by the parliaments of, say, France or Uruguay.

Barsoumian's questions regarding Surp Giragos are noteworthy. By reconstructing this church as an Armenian church again, we have created rock solid evidence and a reminder to the Turks and Kurds that there was a sizable Armenian population in this region before 1915. The church has already become a pilgrimage destination for all Armenians worldwide, with almost 4,000 people attending the opening ceremonies in October 2011, and 400 worshippers during Easter 2012. More significantly, this church has quickly become a liberating beacon to all people in Turkey, showing that they can now stop hiding the truth about the past, with many increasingly revealing stories about their region, province, village, or family. Where no Armenians officially existed in Turkey, there are now Armenian associations formed in places like Dersim, Sason, Bitlis, Malatya, or Sivas. An Armenian-language course organized in Diyarbekir had 41 students enrolled and already graduated. There will be a concert by an Armenian pianist at Surp Giragos in September 2012, the first concert of Armenian and classical composers since 1915. Perhaps Surp Giragos will not be a church without a congregation, after all. While Barsoumian likens Surp Giragos to a beautiful flower in a dying forest, perhaps a more apt description would be a revived oak tree, giving birth to many new budding plants after a forest fire.

Hidden Truths or Lies[*]

In a matter of years beginning in 1915, an entire people was wiped out from its homeland of several thousand years. But how can you wipe out the remnants—its creations, assets, traces, its very existence—from the collective memory of those who remained in that country, or, for that matter, from the collective memory of the rest of the world? This has been an immense challenge for successive Turkish governments, a mission that was mostly successful for almost four generations. And yet, here and there the lies or the hidden truths kept coming out with increasing frequency, especially in recent years.

[*] *Armenian Weekly*, 23 Nov. 2012.

Hiding the truth and historic facts about 1915 from its own people has been the policy since the founding of the Turkish Republic in 1923, through indoctrination of the education system, control of the media and academia, destruction of Armenian buildings and monuments, and so on. But the facts, perhaps still secret within Turkey but widely known in the outside world, are now being revealed to the masses in Turkey, because of increased liberalization, the internet and pioneering academicians and media opinion-makers who dare to speak the truth in Turkey. As a result, the citizens of Turkey, who for four generations were hidden from the facts, are now amazed to learn that a people called Armenians lived in Anatolia for several millennia, but somehow all suddenly disappeared in 1915. In this article, I will try to give a few paradoxical examples of the attempts in hiding the truth, versus the ones uncovering it.

The second largest and most modern airport in Turkey is called the Istanbul Sabiha Gökçen International Airport, named after the adopted daughter of Mustafa Kemal Atatürk, the first female pilot in Turkey, a hero who helped put down the Alevi/Kurdish rebellion in Dersim in 1936-38 by bombing the rebels from her plane. Her photos and accomplishments are prominently displayed on billboards at the airport, and are seen by millions of passengers. And yet, there is another side to her story: Her real name is Hatun Sebilciyan, an Armenian girl from Bursa, who was orphaned in 1915, adopted by Mustafa Kemal Atatürk, and given the Gökçen (azure, color of the sky in Turkish) surname by him after completing pilot training. Former *Agos* editor Hrant Dink became a marked man by the "deep state" in Turkey when he first uncovered this truth after interviewing Sebilciyan's surviving relatives in Lebanon in 2001. This fact was deemed an "insult to Turkishness" by the military, the media, and the government. Another recently uncovered fact: The people being bombed in Dersim were not rebels, but mostly women and children; the leaders were already hanged the previous year, a fact acknowledged and apologized for by Prime Minister Recep Tayyip Erdoğan, mostly to score political points against the governing party at the time (the current opposition party). To add more to the sad irony, these women and children were mostly remnants of the 25,000 Armenians who had sought refuge and found shelter with the Dersim Alevi Kurds in 1915. It is not certain whether Sebilciyan/Gökçen knew that she was

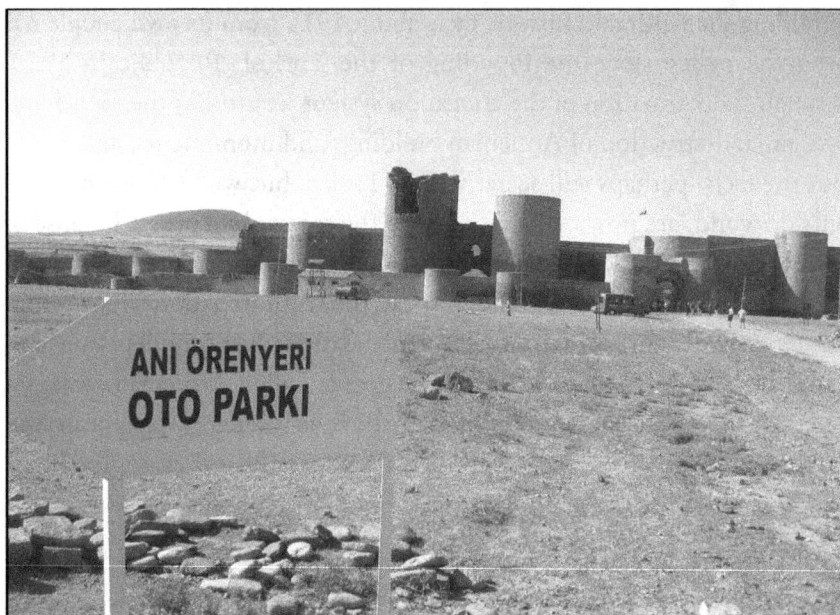

Ani, the Medievan Armenian capital.

Armenian, or if she knew that the women and children she bombed were Armenian.

The ancient city of Ani near Kars, situated on the Armenian border separated by the Akhurian river, is known as the "city with 1,001 churches." It is a former capital of the Armenian Bagratid Kingdom, and had a continuous Armenian presence from the 5th-17th century. It reached its glory days in the 10th and 11th centuries, when it became a central gateway on the Silk Route; its growing population of 100,000 even exceeded Constantinople at the time. Most of the buildings and churches are now destroyed, but the main Ani cathedral, Dikran Honents church, the Sourp Prgich church, and the city walls are still standing, with clearly visible Armenian writings carved in the stone walls. After years of neglect (or target practice) by the Turkish military on the remaining buildings, the current Turkish government has opened up Ani to tourists and has started some preliminary restoration efforts. However, there is not a single word about Armenians in the Turkish guidebooks or historic descriptions on Ani. The standing churches and buildings are referred to as belonging to the Georgians or the Seljuks. Even the name Ani is now spelled with an i without the dot, or "Anı"—which means "memory" in Turkish—so that the Armenian Ani connection to this city will disappear. The denial policy and the paranoia linked to 1915 has stretched so far that even the Armenian presence in Ani is being denied.

The museum in Kars exhibits historical artifacts collected from the region—wood-carved church doors, stone tombstones, carpets, and dowry chests. Descriptions explain that the ancient ones are from the Urartians, the more recent ones from the Russians or Georgians. And yet, all these artifacts have clearly visible Armenian writings carved in the wood or stone or woven into the fabric. Again, here, the denialist paranoia has gone to extreme limits, but it can only fool a few Turks who cannot recognize the Armenian alphabet.

The Holy Cross church on Aghtamar Island near Van dates back to 921 AD. It was built by the Armenian King Gagik, together with a palace and other buildings on the island. Armenian priests lived there continuously until 1915. All the buildings on the island were willfully destroyed by the Turkish army from the 1920s to 1950s, and only through the intervention of renowned Kurdish author Yashar Kemal was the Holy Cross church building spared. The current Turkish government decided to restore the church as a state museum in 2007. While there are beautiful Armenian writings carved on the church walls, both inside and outside the building, there is not a single word in the descriptive plaques or guidebooks indicating that this is an Armenian church. Even the name of the island was changed to "Akdamar," meaning "white vein" in Turkish, so that the Armenian Aghtamar connection would disappear. Why this fear, this paranoia? How can these moves convince anybody in Turkey or the outside world that this is not an Armenian church?

In Istanbul, almost all of the prominent historic buildings built from the 17th-20th century—such as the Ottoman imperial palaces, mosques, military barracks, universities, schools, or fountains—were built by Armenians. Led by the renowned Balyan family, royal architects for several generations, teams of Armenian tradesmen and craftsmen were involved in all aspects of the royal construction projects, including stone masonry, tile and mosaic manufacturing and setting, plumbing, foundations, glassworks, and metal works. And yet, until 10 years ago, official guides would tell tourists that Italian contractors named Balianis were involved in the construction of these buildings. Similarly, at least a quarter of the buildings in the historic Pera district, along the main thoroughfare called Istiklal

Caddesi, were either built by Armenian architects or owned by Armenians. Millions of Istanbul citizens and tourists live, work, and play in these buildings, without realizing their historic Armenian connection. Two years ago, when the Hrant Dink Foundation published a book on Armenian architects of Istanbul, and hosted an exhibition displaying photos of the buildings, it was like a revelation, causing uproar and amazement among the media and general public.

The government policy of forced amnesia over an Armenian presence prior to 1915 extends beyond architects and builders. Armenians served as ministers in the Ottoman government from the early 1800s until 1915 and were in charge of key ministries such as the treasury, armaments, mint, public works, customs, and post office departments. Tens of thousands of Armenians worked in the bureaucracy, army, and state hospitals. And the Turkish government has not only hidden their contributions but their very existence, as well. As a result, the general Turkish population has only recently started to realize the important role played by the Armenians in the Ottoman public sector. The contributions of Armenians in the private sector, of course, are completely and forcefully hidden, because all Armenian assets and properties—such as farms, factories, mines, warehouses, businesses, orchards, and buildings—were plundered and taken over by the Turkish/Kurdish leaders and the general public in 1915. In fact, the very foundation of the Turkish private and public sector economy and industry, the start-up of wealthy individuals and corporations, is based entirely on the seized Armenian assets; therefore, this is an understandable component of the denial policy.

The positive contributions by Armenians during the Turkish Republican era are also kept hidden. The introduction of the Latin alphabet and conversion from Ottoman Turkish to modern Turkish was implemented by an Armenian linguistics expert, Prof. Agop Martayan. In gratitude, Kemal Atatürk gave him the surname of Dilacar, meaning "the one who unlocks the language." In Turkish textbooks, he is referred to as A. Dilacar, with his first name Agop never spelled out. When he passed away in 1978, the Turkish media printed his obituary as Adil Acar, further Turkifying his given name. Another example of a hidden truth is the case of Armenian musician Edgar Manas, the composer of the Turkish national anthem, a fact only known by a few Armenians and completely covered up by the Turks.

Surp Khach church on Aghtamar island.

Holy Mother of God cathedral in Aintab was built by Sarkis Balyan. It was later used as a prison and then turned into Kurtulus mosque (Liberation mosque).

Why this fear, this paranoia, resulting in total denial? It goes beyond the denial of the historical facts of 1915. It is the denial of the existence of an entire people on these lands. Is it fear over the Armenian assets and properties left behind? Is it the simplistic argument: If Armenians never lived here, there could not have been a genocide? But then, if Armenians never lived here, how could they have massacred the Turks, as is claimed by the Turkish version of official history? Rather than speculate about the answers, I'll refer instead to the remarks made by prominent Kurdish professor Ismail Besikci, the recent recipient of the Hrant Dink Foundation Peace Award:

"The Ittihadists [Committee of Union and Progress] had devised a plan to reorganize the Ottoman Empire on the basis of Turkish ethnic identity. The nationalization of the Ottoman economy was a further significant target. But Greeks, Armenians, and other Christian people, as well as Islamic but non-Turkish people such as Kurds, non-Muslim Turkish and Kurdish people such as Alevis, presented significant obstacles to the execution of this Turkification project. They would get rid of the Greeks by forcing them into exile to Greece. The Armenian population would be eliminated under the guise of forced deportation into the desert. Then, the Kurds would be assimilated into Turkishness, and the Alevis into Islam. The wealth and immovable properties of the Greeks, forced into exile, and the Armenians, perished through genocide, would be confiscated by Muslim Turkish notables. A huge, widespread looting operation took place of the assets left behind by the Armenians and Greeks, helping the Ottoman economy, and then the Turkish economy, to be nationalized. Today, the source of the wealth of the haute bourgeoisie is the Armenian and Greek assets. In Kurdish areas of Turkey, the source of wealth of the Kurdish tribe leaders is again the Armenian and Syriac assets."

As Besikci has said, it has become apparent that the experiment of trying to convert a multi-ethnic, multi-religious, multi-cultural Anatolian society into a monolithic, mono-ethnic, single-religion Turkish nation, and then denying this fact, has failed. The hidden truths about the fate of the Armenian and Greek people, and their assets, can no longer be denied within and outside Turkey, despite state efforts. The assimilation of the Kurds did not succeed, despite state efforts.

As another Kurdish intellectual has very appropriately remarked, for many years the Turks denied that Armenians were ever killed on these lands, and also denied that Kurds ever lived on these lands. An increasingly larger number of opinion-makers in the Turkish media and academia have started to reveal the hidden truths, and sooner or later, the people of Turkey will realize that the historic facts are different than what they have been told by the state. As it becomes apparent that the hidden truths cannot be hidden any longer, the challenge for the Turkish government will be how to revise its stance from denial to acceptance of the truth, and how to deal with the truth vis a vis its own citizens as well as the outside world. It is hoped that this process will be carried out within the norms of dialogue, the establishment of a common body of knowledge.

"2012 Declaration": A History of Seized Armenian Properties in Istanbul[*]

After two years of painfully detailed research through thousands of documents, the Hrant Dink Foundation in Istanbul has produced a monumental work on the history and present status of the properties that once belonged to the Armenian charitable foundations in Istanbul— properties that were all seized by the Turkish government during the last few decades. The comprehensive study, some 400 pages long, for the first time compiles a list of the seized properties, illustrating the overall picture and enormity of the plunder suffered by the Armenian schools, orphanages, churches and hospitals in Istanbul that were dependent on the property income for survival.

The book's title, *2012 Declaration*, is a reference to the Turkish state's 1936 Declaration ordering all minority charitable foundations to list their assets and properties. During the height of the Cyprus crisis in 1975, the state arbitrarily legislated that any properties that were obtained by minority charitable foundations after 1936 through donations, inheritance, wills, and gifts, were deemed illegal, since they had not been listed in the 1936 Declaration. *2012 Declaration* makes reference to this illogical legislation and exposes the legalized but unlawful seizure, or state robbery, that took place years ago, and the recent small steps taken to undo the gross injustice.

The book is not a mere historical document providing an inventory of physical properties, or statistical records and legal statements. Rather, it is

---

* *Armenian Weekly*, 6 Dec. 2012.

a story of enormous human suffering, ranging from children being thrown out of their schools, to orphans no longer being able to find a home; the most tragic story involves the seizure of a summer camp complex of buildings literally constructed by orphan children (including Hrant Dink himself) by the Turkish state, to be sold to Turkish individuals.

The four members of the Hrant Dink Foundation—Mehmet Polatel, Nora Mildanoglu, Ozgur Leman Eren, and Mehmet Atilgan—sifted through the patriarchate, church, and school archives, government deeds and title records, foundation lawyers' personal archives, old maps and surveys, purchase and sale agreements, and Hrant Dink's own research files, to produce this concise history of each charitable foundation, including the location and type of properties gifted to each foundation and then seized by the state, and more than 200 photographs. The most heart-breaking aspect of this historic document are surely the photographs, some of which are reprinted here. The research team's attempts to obtain documents from government offices, however, were mostly unsuccessful, even though they were equipped with the force of legislation called the Freedom of Information Act; they were told that the 1915-25 era deed and title records of the Armenians are still not open to the public, due to the official paranoia that exists, defined as "threats to state security."

This article will attempt to summarize the 400-page document and give some striking examples of Istanbul-Armenian history.

***

First, some excerpts from the book's Introduction Section: "This book is not the story of seized buildings made of stone or cement, but the story of flesh-and-bone human beings. These seized institutions and buildings were the cherished belongings of human beings rich and poor, young and old, men and women, who had worked hard to create or acquire them. These unjustly seized buildings gave life to the schools, churches, orphanages, and retirement homes of the whole community. The social and cultural fabric of Turkish-Armenians depended on this economic foundation. It is our wish that similar injustices will not be carried into the future, as people read in this book the documented "why" and "how" of the attempts to wipe out the life and culture of our community. The issue is not only the seizure or return of the properties, but understanding this dimension of history and passing it on to future generations. As long as the ancestral people of these lands are marginalized or defined as "others," as long as minorities are not seen as equal citizens, the democratization efforts in Turkey will be stunted. It is our wish that this study will contribute to facing history."

The book then lists the Armenian charitable foundations and their assets. There were 53 Armenian charitable foundations in Istanbul, administering 18 schools and orphanages, 48 churches, 2 hospitals, and 20 cemeteries of the Istanbul-Armenian community, supported by the rental revenue and assets that they owned or received through wills and gifts. These foundations owned 1,328 properties, of which 661 were seized by the state for several reasons. The study could not determine the fate of 87 properties. After exhausting all legal means available to get back the seized properties from the state through the Turkish courts, over the last 10 years some of the foundations have taken their cases to the European Human Rights Court. As they began to win all of their cases, and since the European court decisions were binding on Turkey through European Union accession expectations, the Turkish state recently decided to amend the 1975 legislation related to the foundations (which had enabled their legal but unlawful seizure). With an improved piece of legislation, 143 properties, or about 10.77 percent of the 1,328 properties, have now been returned to the Armenian foundations.

The types of seized properties were residential apartment buildings, residential apartment units, house dwellings, vacant lots, orchards, fountains, stores/shops, warehouses, factories, commercial buildings, office buildings, office units, hospitals, workplaces, summer camps, churches, schools, and cemeteries.

The "owner status" of the seized properties are listed as unknown, municipal government, state treasury, public building, vacant, lost deed/ title, individually owned, owned by other foundation, or owned by the State General Directorate of Foundations.

The process by which the foundation obtained properties is listed as follows: donation, will, purchase, by Ottoman Sultan decree. The process by which the foundation lost properties is listed as follows: seizure by state, made public by state, sale to individuals or corporations.

The book explains some of the stories of seizure in great detail. Some examples are provided below.

Mkhitaryan Bomonti School

This is the tragic story of a 200-year-old Armenian school that ended up being a tenant in the building it used to own. Nevertheless, it is a story with a happy ending.

The Armenian Catholic Mkhitarists in Venice founded a boys' school in 1830 in the Pera neighborhood. In order to serve the increased student population with better educational facilities, the school foundation decided to move the school to a larger building, and in 1958, purchased the present site at Sisli-Bomonti neighborhood for 710,000 Turkish liras from a woman named Emine Tevfika Ayasli. The school name was changed to the Private Bomonti Armenian Catholic Primary School. In 1979, the State Charitable Foundations Directorate started a court case against the Armenian school; since this school was not listed in the 1936 Declaration, they argued, the purchase of the new school building was illegal. The directorate demanded that the purchase be cancelled and the building returned to the seller, or the heirs of the seller. The court accepted the argument, and in 1988 the Appeal Court turned down the Armenians' appeal. The school building deed was turned over to the former owner, who was deceased; as per the directions of her will, it was deeded to her brothers and to the Ankara Ayas Municipality. (It is interesting to note that Ayasli's will was prepared years after the school building was legally sold to the Armenian school foundation.) The brothers sold their share of the building to a construction company specializing in apartment buildings, named Miltas. In 1998, the Ankara Ayas Municipality entered into a tenancy agreement with the school and started charging rent. But the other owner, Miltas, objected to the tenancy agreement and started court proceedings to have the school vacate the building. In February 1999, Miltas won the case, and the same day the school's contents (including students' desks, library shelves and books, kindergarden toys and the school piano) were moved outside into the school yard. Faced with an incredible situation of suddenly having no school in the middle of the winter, the Armenian parents, in an exceptional fashion, resorted to civil disobedience, and start camping out in the school yard. The public outcry forced the mayor of Istanbul Sisli Municipality to intervene, and he arranged to buy the shares of Miltas, the construction company. He also struck an agreement with Ayas Municipality to have the school continue to function by paying rent to

Ayas Municipality. Naturally, the school lost most of its students after these disturbances and the student population dropped to 35. Meanwhile, the school foundation went to court to re-claim the building. In November 2012, two days before the publication of this book, the court case ended with victory for the Armenian school and now, the deeds have finally been returned to the Armenian foundation and the school has stopped paying rent.

Tuzla Armenian Children's Camp

In the 1950s, the Armenian Protestant Church in the Gedikpasa neighborhood of Istanbul served as the arrival point for many poor and homeless Armenian orphans, especially from the interior of Turkey. These children, numbering in the 60s, received their education at the Gedikpasa Armenian Protestant School in the winter under tolerable conditions, but had nowhere to go during the summers. The church foundation decided to purchase a vacant treed lot near the Marmara Sea in the Tuzla municipality for a summer camp for these children. In October 1962, the purchase was completed from an individual named Sait Durmaz, and registered to the church foundation, according to all applicable legal procedures. From then on, every summer, the children, aged 8-12, were given the task of building camp buildings, supervised by a builder named Tuzlali Hasan Kalfa. The children first erected the poles and the canvas tents they would live in during construction. Then they dug a water well, taking turns pumping the water needed for construction. Then the foundations were prepared. Since the sea was only 500 meters away, they carried all the sand and gravel from the beach by wheelbarrows. Slowly but surely, over three summers, the vacant land was transformed into a summer camp complex with buildings, dormitories, dining halls, play areas, a soccer field, pond, and gym. The children stocked the pond with frogs and ducks. Armenian boys and girls learned how to talk, sing, play, cook, and clean together in Armenian. Hrant Dink was one of those boys; his wife Rakel was one of those girls.

Happy days came to an end when the State Charitable Foundations Directorate applied to the courts in February 1979 to reverse the purchase agreement and have the property returned to its previous owner, arguing that the Gedikpasa Church Foundation had no right to purchase the property. After four years of trials, the court cancelled the summer camp deed and returned the property to its former owner, Sait Durmaz, including the extraordinary facilities that the children had constructed. The camp, imprinted in the memory of 1,500 Armenian children, became abandoned, with rusting bed frames, broken windows, and overgrown weeds. In 1987, the Appeal Court approved the previous court decision. The owner sold the camp to new purchasers, who in turn sold it again. Several court applications by the Armenian foundation in the 2000s, and most recently in August 2011, were all turned down. One of Hrant's last articles titled "Humanity, I take you to court!..." was a solemn cry in the face of this gross injustice.

Kalfayan Orphanage

In 1865, a cholera epidemic in Istanbul left many children behind as poor orphans. An Armenian nun named Srpuhi Nshan Kalfayan decided to care for 17 orphan girls, aged 2-10, at her home. She also started teaching them handcrafts and sewing. These personal efforts led to the founding of one of the most important Armenian educational institutions in Istanbul, the Kalfayan Orphanage School. The orphanage survived until the late 1960s, when the school building was expropriated without compensation and demolished in order to build the expressways leading to the Bosphorus Bridge crossing between Europe and Asia. The foundation owned a large parcel of land where it planned to transfer the orphanage school. The State Charitable Foundations Directorate argued that since this land was not registered in the 1936 Declaration, building a new orphanage there could not be allowed, and that the orphans and their teachers should be redistributed to other orphanages. Repeated applications did not yield any results and 150 people, the combined total of orphans and staff, spent the next 30 years in various dilapidated buildings, until a new arrangement was made in 1999 to share the school building of the Semerciyan School in Uskudar.

***

In a previous article titled, "Special Report: What is Turkey Returning to the Armenians?" I referred to another significant state seizure of Armenian properties. The Surp Agop Cemetery lands, which was decreed by Ottoman Sultan Suleiman to the Armenian community in 1550 as a reward to his Armenian cook, Manuk Karaseferyan of Van, who had uncovered a plot to poison the emperor by German spies during the siege of Budapest. The cemetery was used for 400 years until the 1930s, when the Istanbul municipality expropriated the lands after years of legal wrangling. At present, these lands, which are now in one of the most valuable and fashionable districts of Istanbul, are occupied by the State Radio and Television Headquarters, the Turkish Armed Forces Istanbul Headquarters, the Military Museum, many expensive hotels such as Hilton, Regency Hyatt, Divan, and several apartment and office buildings, as well as the expansive Taksim Park, which has some walkways made from the marble of Armenian tombstones.

The *2012 Declaration* book documents the Armenian properties lost in Istanbul, mainly during the 1970s, with the illogical but legal argument that if the charitable foundations had obtained properties after 1936, they would be deemed illegal because they had not been included in the 1936 Declaration. But the extent of this gross injustice would pale in comparison when we consider the amount of Armenian properties seized or lost after 1915, not only in Istanbul, but all over Anatolia, especially in historic Armenia. To illustrate the sheer enormity of the loss, consider these numbers: There were more than 4,000 Armenian churches and schools in Anatolia, each with its own land, each with its own income generating additional lands, properties, and assets. The recently reconstructed Surp Giragos church in Diyarbekir had over 200 separate deeds and titles to different properties such as shops, houses, farms, and orchards, which were taken over by the government and private individuals, erecting apartment buildings, office buildings, state schools, shops and houses, even a highway. Thankfully, the process to take these properties back has already started in Diyarbekir. The above-mentioned figures are only for Armenian churches and schools, that is, community owned buildings. Add to those numbers the properties owned by private Armenian individuals, such as houses, shops, farms, orchards, factories, warehouses, mines, and so on, and it becomes quite difficult to grasp the enormity of this wealth transfer.

Hrant's Message and the Way Forward[*]

On the sixth anniversary of his assassination and more significantly, on the sixth anniversary of the Turkish state's inability or unwillingness to find his real killers, Hrant Dink was remembered by tens of thousands of

[*] *Armenian Weekly*, 24 Jan. 2013.

people in many countries as well as in Turkey, including Istanbul, Ankara, Izmir, Diyarbekir, Malatya, and Bodrum. Throughout the world, Turkish and Armenian speakers repeated his vision and message of direct dialogue between Turks and Armenians. Year by year, instead of gradually diminishing in numbers toward oblivion, as is the case for other assassinated journalists in Turkey, there is a snowballing increase in the number and intensity of people attending the Hrant Dink commemorations, protesting and demanding justice, as well as adopting Hrant's message with more determination. It is not the tiny Armenian community in Turkey, but Turks (and Kurds) from all walks of life who have embraced Hrant as a tragic hero. The momentum is building to declare Hrant a martyr—the first shared martyr by the historically opposing nations of Armenians and Turks.

But what exactly was Hrant's message? He would define Armenians and Turks as two sick people, clinical cases—Armenians suffering from trauma (obsessed with 1915) and Turks suffering from paranoia (fear of consequences of acknowledging 1915). He would advocate Armenians and Turks to be each other's doctors, with dialogue as the only prescription. And he would clap his large hands vigorously, exclaiming, "There is no other medicine, no other doctor, no, no, no." He knew dialogue would be useless if one couldn't discuss the painful year of 1915, but only pleasant subjects such as Turks' and Armenians' shared values, shared culture, shared foods like dolma and kebab. He knew that dialogue would also be useless if one was unable to really "listen and hear," in addition to talk. And most importantly, he knew that dialogue would be useless if one didn't know the real historical facts of 1915. After being systematically brainwashed by the state with ever-changing official versions of history, people in Turkey have now finally started to learn the true historic facts, reasons, and consequences of 1915, not just the Turkish version versus Armenian version. So, if and when there is willingness to talk and listen, both sides can and should engage in direct dialogue, without the need to convince third parties to pressure the other side.

Hrant had studied zoology, and he would explain that if you remove any living organism from its natural environment, you would cause its extinction. He would then say, "If you remove an entire people from its land where it has lived continuously for 3,000 years, even if you transport them with great care in "golden airplanes," this would still be similar to taking an axe to the roots of an ancient tree." He didn't need to explain 1915 with long words; in a corner of the *Agos* newspaper, every week, he would place some facts about a village or town in Anatolia—could be in west, east, north, south, or central Anatolia—giving the Armenian and total population numbers, the names and numbers of churches and schools there, before 1915. He would have photos of these active Armenian churches and schools in that village or town before 1915, and photos of these non-existent churches or schools today, totaling more than 4,000 buildings. That would be enough for anyone to understand the reality of 1915.

But he wouldn't only talk about the Armenians gone or dead in 1915. He was much more interested in talking about the Armenians who remained, who stayed in Anatolia, who stayed and survived, but no longer as Armenians. These were the Armenians who survived by converting to Islam, by assuming Turkish, Kurdish, or Alawi identities. These were the Armenian girls and boys captured or sold, kept hidden, protected or married to Turks and Kurds. And entire Armenian villages that converted to Islam, or stayed protected by friendly Kurdish and Alawi leaders. Hrant was obsessed with this subject. What happened to these people? Did they secretly keep their Armenian identity? Did they pass it on to the next generations? Where are they now? How many are there? If there are "hidden Armenians," what would be the trigger for them to "come out of hiding"?

Genocide is not a single event but a continuous process. It is not only denial of a genocide that continues it, but also assimilation and conversion that continue it. Scholars have recently started defining genocide not only as the destruction of an oppressed nation, but also the construction of the oppressor nation—using assimilation and conversion processes. For Armenians, these processes continued on all fronts.

Hrant didn't or couldn't write much about this sensitive subject, but he was preoccupied by it, gathering stories, anecdotal evidence, always encouraging others to find out more. Clearly, this was not a subject that could be researched openly and scientifically, but whenever a new revelation came out about hidden Armenians in Anatolia, he would be greatly excited. His lawyer Fethiye Çetin's book *My Grandmother* was only an example of the fate of the hidden Armenians. In an interview with London filmmaker Nouritsa Matossian for the documentary "Hrant Dink: A Heart of Two Nations," Matossian asked him, "Do you see

Armenian faces in Anatolia?" Hrant: "Yes, often." Nouritsa: "Apparitions [meaning, ghosts]?" Hrant: "Apparitions *and* real ones." One could tell that Hrant, the emotional Hrant with the biggest heart, was like a child who had a secret he could hardly keep.

The answer to the question that kept him wondering—What would be the trigger for the hidden Armenians to come out?—came four years too late for Hrant to witness, unfortunately. The trigger was the reconstruction of the Diyarbekir Surp Giragos church in 2011. Thousands of Anatolians, young and old, Turkish and Kurdish, in appearance and identity, returned to their Armenian roots with the reopening of this church. Some got baptized in the church, some changed their Turkish names to the Armenian original, some changed their identity to Armenian but remained Muslim (a new phenomenon of Muslim-Armenians), some started learning the Armenian language. Hrant would have danced with joy to see an 11-year-old Kurdish girl not only learning Armenian but also singing Armenian songs at the first Armenian concert in the Diyarbekir Surp Giragos church in 2012. Hrant would have danced on the table after seeing a thousand people from Adiyaman, Amasya, Arapkir, Dersim, Diyarbekir, Elazig, Harput, Hemshin, Istanbul, Kastamonu, Kayseri, Malatya, Musadagh, Sason, Sinop, Sivas, Tokat, Van, and Yozgat organize activities together and celebrate Surp Hagop Day in December 2012, singing Armenian songs, even though no one knew how to speak Armenian.

Hrant was an Anatolian Armenian and wished to have the same democratic rights as all other citizens of the state, without being excluded, without being discriminated against, without being pressured to lose his identity. Armenians wished to have exactly the same things 100 years ago—no more, no less. The state felt threatened, and when fear got combined with opportunity it wiped out the Armenian identity in Anatolia to build a Turkish identity that excluded all others, including Greeks, Assyrians, and Kurds. The enormous transfer of wealth and assets from Armenians to Turks has added to the fear and paranoia of the state in facing its past. A new Turkish identity, which does not fear diversity or minority identities, needs to be created in Turkey in order to face both the past and the future. The state has finally started this process with the Kurds, but not the Armenians. The Kurds have started this process with the Armenians, openly acknowledging their role in 1915, and starting to make amends. It is hoped that Turks will see the light and follow them.

The Real Turkish Heroes of 1915[*]

Germany has decided to name several neighborhoods, streets, buildings, and public schools in Berlin and other German cities after Adolf Hitler and other Nazi "heroes."

If the above statement were to be true, how would you react? How do you think Germans would react? How do you think Jews still living in Germany would react? My guess is that you, the Germans, and the Jews would all find it inconceivable, offensive, and unacceptable.

And yet, it is true in Turkey, where it is acceptable to name several neighborhoods, streets, and schools after Talat Pasha and other *Ittihad ve Terakki* (Committee of Union and Progress) "heroes" who not only planned and carried out the Armenian Genocide, but were responsible for the loss of the Ottoman Empire itself.

At last count, there were officially eight "Talat Pasha" neighborhoods or districts, 38 "Talat Pasha" streets or boulevards, seven "Talat Pasha" public schools, six "Talat Pasha" buildings, and two "Talat Pasha" mosques scattered around Istanbul, Ankara, and other cities. After his assassination in 1922, Talat was originally interred in Berlin, Germany, but his remains were transferred to Istanbul in 1943 by the Nazis in an attempt to appease the Turks. He was re-buried with full military honors at the Eternal Freedom Hill Cemetery in Istanbul. The remains of the other notorious *Ittihat ve Terakki* leader, Enver Pasha, were also transferred in 1996 from Tajikistan and re-buried beside Talat, with full military honors; the ceremony was attended by Turkish President Suleyman Demirel and other dignitaries.

Is this hero worship misguided or deliberate? Is the denial of 1915 only state policy, or is it wholeheartedly accepted by the Turkish public, brainwashed by the state version of history?

Undoubtedly, there was mass participation in the genocide committed by the *Ittihat ve Terakki* leaders, resulting in the removal of Armenians from their homeland of 3,000 years, as well as the immediate transfer of their wealth, property, and possessions to the Turkish and Kurdish public,

---

[*] *Armenian Weekly*, 29 July 2013.

and to thousands of government officials. Yet, despite this mass participation and the hero worship, there were also a significant number of ordinary Turks and Kurds, as well as government officials, who refused to participate in the massacres and plunders. There is complete silence and ignorance in Turkey about these righteous officials who refused to follow government orders and instead tried to save and protect Armenians. They paid dearly for their actions, often with the loss of their positions or even their lives as a consequence. This article will cite some examples of these real and unsung heroes.

Celal Bey was the governor of Konya, a vast central Anatolian province and a hub for the Armenian deportation routes from north and west Anatolia to the Syrian desert. He knew exactly what the Armenians' fate would be along these routes, or if they survived the deportations and reached Der Zor; he was previously the governor of Aleppo and had witnessed the atrocities there. Celal Bey had attempted to reason with the *Ittihat ve Terakki* leaders, saying that there was absolutely no Armenian revolt in Anatolia, nor in Aleppo, and that there was no justification for the mass deportations. However, one of his subordinates in Marash inflamed the situation by arresting and executing several Marash Armenians, triggering a resistance by Armenians. As a result, Celal Bey was removed from his governor's post in Aleppo and transferred to Konya. Once there, he refused to arrange for the deportation of Armenians in Konya, despite repeated orders from Istanbul. He even managed to protect some of the Armenians who were deported from other districts and arrived in Konya. By the time he was removed from his post, in October 1915, he had saved thousands of Armenian lives. In his memoirs about his Konya governorship, he likened himself to "a person sitting beside a river, with absolutely no means of rescuing anyone from it. Blood was flowing down the river, with thousands of innocent children, irreproachable old men, and helpless women streaming down the river towards oblivion. Anyone I could save with my bare hands, I saved, and the rest went down the river, never to return."

Hasan Mazhar Bey was the governor of Ankara. He protected the Ankara-Armenian community by refusing to follow the deportation orders, stating, "I am a *vali* [governor], not a bandit. I cannot do this. Let someone else come and sit in my chair to carry out these orders." He was removed from his post in August 1915.

Faik Ali (Ozansoy) Bey was the governor of Kutahya, another central Anatolian province. When the deportation order was issued from Istanbul, he refused to implement it; on the contrary, he gave orders to keep the deported Armenians arriving in Kutahya from elsewhere, and treat them well. He was soon summoned to Istanbul to explain his insubordination, and the police chief of Kutahya, Kemal Bey, took the opportunity to threaten the local Armenians—either convert to Islam or face deportation, he said. The Armenians decided to convert. When Faik Ali Bey returned, he was enraged. He removed the police chief from his post and asked the Armenians if they still wished to convert to Islam. They all decided to remain Christian, except one. Faik Ali's brother, Suleyman Nazif Bey, was an influential and well-known poet who urged his brother not to participate in this barbarism and stain the family name. Faik Ali Bey was not removed from his post despite his offers of resignation. He ended up protecting the entire Armenian population of Kutahya, except for the one who converted to Islam and was deported.

Mustafa Bey (Azizoglu) was the district governor of Malatya, a transit point on the deportation route. Although he was unable to prevent the deportations, he managed to hide several Armenians in his own home. He was murdered by his own son, a zealous member of the *Ittihat ve Terakki* party, for "looking after infidels [*gavours*, in Turkish]."

Other government officials who defied the deportation orders included Reshid Pasha, the governor of Kastamonu; Tahsin Bey, the governor of Erzurum; Ferit Bey, the governor of Basra; Mehmet Cemal Bey, the district governor of Yozgat; and Sabit Bey, the district governor of Batman. These officials were eventually removed from their posts and replaced by more obedient civil servants, who carried out the task of wiping out the Armenians from these locations.

One of the most tragic stories of unsung heroes involves Huseyin Nesimi Bey, the mayor of Lice, a town near Diyarbekir. While the governor of Diyarbekir, Reshid Bey, organized the most ruthless removal of the Armenians in the Diyarbekir region—with a quick massacre, rather than lengthy deportation, immediately outside of the city limits— Huseyin Nesimi dared to keep and protect the Lice Armenians, a total of 5,980 souls. Reshid summoned Huseyin Nesimi to Diyarbekir for a meeting, but arranged to have his Circassian militant guard Haroun intercept him en route. On June 15, 1915, Haroun murdered Huseyin

Nesimi and threw him into a ditch beside the road. Since then, the murder location, halfway between Lice and Diyarbekir, has become known as *Turbe-i Kaymakam*, or the Mayor's Grave. The Turkish records document this murder as "Mayor killed by Armenian militants." In an ironic twist of history repeating itself, in October 1993 the Turkish state army attacked Lice, supposedly to go after the Kurdish rebel militants there; instead, they ended up burning down the entire town and killing the civilian population. This became the first case the Kurds took to the European Human Rights Court, resulting in a 2.5 million pound compensation against the Turkish state. At the same time, several wealthy Kurdish businessmen were targeted for assassination and murdered by then-Turkish Prime Minister Tansu Çiller. One of the victims was a man named Behçet Cantürk, whose mother was an Armenian orphan who had managed to survive the Lice massacres of 1915.

Governor Reshid was also responsible for firing and murdering several other government officials in the Diyarbekir region who had defied the deportation orders: Chermik Mayor Mehmet Hamdi Bey, Savur Mayor Mehmet Ali Bey, Silvan Mayor Ibrahim Hakki Bey, Mardin Mayor Hilmi Bey, followed by Shefik Bey, were all fired in mid- to late-1915. Another official, Nuri Bey, the mayor of first Midyat and then Derik, an all-Armenian town near Mardin, was also fired by Reshid Bey, and subsequently murdered by his henchmen. His murder was blamed on Armenian rebels. As a result, all of the Armenian males in Derik were rounded up and executed, and the women and children deported.

The names of these brave men are not in history books. If mentioned at all, they are labeled as "traitors" from the perspective of the official Turkish version of history. While the state and the masses committed a huge crime, and while that crime became a part of their daily life, these men rejected the genocidal campaign, based on individual conscience, and despite the temptation of enriching themselves. These few virtuous men, as well as a significant number of ordinary Turks and Kurds, defied the orders and protected Armenians. They are the real heroes and represent the Turkish version of similar characters in "Schindler's List" or "Hotel Rwanda." Citizens of Turkey today have two choices when remembering their forefathers as heroes: to either go with the mass murderers and plunderers who committed "crimes against humanity," or the virtuous human beings with a clear conscience who tried to *prevent* the "crimes against humanity." Getting to know these real heroes will help Turks break loose from the chains of denialist history over four generations and start to confront the realities of 1915.

Sources

* Tuncay Opçin, "Ermenilere Kol Kanat Gerdiler (They protected the Armenians)," *Yeni Aktuel*, 2007, issue 142.
* Ayşe Hür, "1915 Ermeni soykiriminda kotuler ve iyiler (The good and the bad in the 1915 Armenian Genocide)," *Radikal* newspaper, April 29, 2013.
* Seyhmus Diken, "Kaymakam Ermeniydi, Oldurduler... (The mayor was Armenian, they killed him...)," *Bianet*, April 23, 2011.
* Orhan Cengiz, "1915: Heroes and Murderers," *Cihan News Agency*, Nov. 2, 2012.
* Tuncay Opçin, "Ermenilere Kol Kanat Gerdiler (They protected the Armenians)," *Yeni Aktuel*, 2007, issue 142.
* Ayşe Hür, "1915 Ermeni soykiriminda kotuler ve iyiler (The good and the bad in the 1915 Armenian Genocide)," *Radikal* newspaper, April 29, 2013.
* Şeyhmus Diken, "Kaymakam Ermeniydi, Oldurduler... (The mayor was Armenian, they killed him...)," *Bianet*, April 23, 2011.
* Orhan Cengiz, "1915: Heroes and Murderers," *Cihan News Agency*, Nov. 2, 2012.

Where to Invest Our Resources?[*]

When visiting Armenia for the first time, one's itinerary invariably includes a multitude of churches and monasteries. Modern Armenia is the land of churches. Historic Armenia in Turkey was also a land of churches, with nearly 4,000 churches and monasteries. The Lake Van region alone had over 300 churches. The ancient city of Ani, dubbed the "city of 1,001 churches," contained 40 churches. We are proud of our churches, marveled at their architectural beauty and intricate construction techniques, and amazed at their settings, perched as they are on inaccessible mountain tops.

Yet, this obsession with churches, when combined with our tragic history, makes me think, "I wish we had fewer churches to visit, and instead many more victory monuments like Sardarabad. I wish our Armenian kings, princes, political leaders, and wealthy notables in the past

---

[*] *Armenian Weekly*, 17 Oct. 2013.

had spent less time, talent, resources, and money on these churches, and instead more on fortifications and defense of our lands and territories."

Delving into the reasons why these churches were built, it becomes apparent that it was not merely to meet the religious needs of the population; rather, it was to bring glory to the benefactor and perhaps help him "ease into heaven." Throughout history, our religious leaders have told benefactors that there is no better way to serve God, Jesus Christ, and Armenians than to build another church. Therefore, regardless of political, economic, or social realities and upheavals, Armenians continued to build churches, in both historic and modern Armenia, as well as in all corners of the world, often times disregarding other needs and priorities. This was the case in medieval Armenian kingdoms in historic Armenia, Cilicia and beyond up until 1915, then in the diaspora, and now in modern Armenia.

When future generations look back on our 22 year-old Armenia and on the diaspora, they will see the challenges we faced in establishing a new country from the ruins of the Soviet Empire, while at the same time fighting the deadly Karabagh war, dealing with the closed borders and economic blockade by Turkey and Azerbaijan, the disastrous 1989 earthquake, and most critically, the continuing depopulation of Armenia due to a lack of employment and investment opportunities. And they will also see examples of vast church-building activities both in Armenia and the diaspora. In 1997, in the midst of urgent needs to reconstruct Armenia and Karabagh, Armenians found the money to build the St. Gregory Illuminator Cathedral in Yerevan. In 2001, diasporans in Los Angeles started the construction of a huge cathedral, while there was and still remain scarce resources to keep Armenian schools open. In 2011, an oligarch donated all the funds to build the St. Hovhannes Cathedral in Abovyan, while the starving local population had almost emptied the town. Just last month, wealthy Russian Armenians opened a vast new cathedral in Moscow. The Echmiadzin Catholicosate has become a Vatican-like complex continuously expanding with new buildings. The combined total expenditure on these large churches, as well as several other smaller church projects, easily exceeds $200 million. These projects are not funded from revenue-generating sources or regular budgets, but instead, from one-time significant donations from benefactors, mostly from the diaspora. They will not generate any revenue, either, but will create a continuing need for additional donations for upkeep and maintenance.

One wonders if these donations could be used for more worthwhile projects, such as helping Armenians remain in Armenia, or helping Armenians remain Armenian in the diaspora. There seems to be a widely accepted belief that neither the government nor the church is in touch with the concerns and needs of the common people. During a recent private audience with the Catholicos, he was asked what the Armenian Church can do to keep our youth more interested in the church and attached to their Armenian roots. His curt response was, "This should be done at home and at school." The much-anticipated Bishops' Synod, assembled last month for the first time in 600 years, did not produce any tangible resolutions to address the concerns of the common Armenian, be it in Armenia or the diaspora. Most benefactors do not want to invest in Armenia due to a fear that government corruption and required bribes will make their investment useless—and, in so doing, will fail in creating economic benefits for either themselves or the Armenian population. Unless the government takes concrete steps to change the valid perception that investments only end up in the hands of the governing oligarchs, there will not be much participation in the desperately needed economic growth of Armenia. In the meantime, church leaders will continue to preach the tried and tested argument that the most beneficial donation a benefactor can make for himself and his family is giving to the church.

Of course, there are truly worthwhile church-building and restoration projects with strategic and significant benefits for all Armenians. One example is the restoration of the Ghazantchetsots church in Shushi, undertaken immediately after the Karabagh war. During the war, Azeris controlling Shushi used this historic church as an arms depot and military center, from which they continuously bombarded Stepanakert in the valley. They knew that Armenians would never attack or fire on their own church. When Armenian commandos victoriously entered Shushi in May of 1992, they found the church in shambles, burned, desecrated, and full of human excrement. Today, it stands as a symbol of victory against all odds.

The other critical restoration project is the total reconstruction of the Diyarbekir/Dikranagerd Surp Giragos church in Turkey in 2011, the first time a church was restored as a functioning church (and not merely a museum) in historic Armenia after being destroyed in 1915. This project was strategically significant for a number of reasons: First, the restored church is concrete evidence against the denialist state version of history of the government of Turkey, as it demonstrates that there was a large Armenian presence in Anatolia before 1915. Secondly, it immediately became a religious and cultural center, helping the Turkish and Kurdish population of Turkey understand the realities of 1915 through media events, conferences and concerts. Third, and for the first time since 1915, the foundation that restored the church started the process of reclaiming the properties belonging to the church (but confiscated after 1915) with several properties already secured through negotiations and courts. Fourth, the church became a living genocide memorial, attracting tens of thousands of Armenian visitors from the diaspora and Armenia annually, and starting a dialogue while fostering closer relationships with liberated Kurds and Turks who have faced the historical truths of 1915, and now demand their government to do so as well. Last but not least, the most significant outcome of the restoration of this church has been the emergence of "hidden Armenians." Islamized Armenians have started "coming out," visiting and praying in the church, getting baptized, participating in Armenian-language courses, helping build an Armenian museum on church grounds, contributing to the security and administration of the church, demanding acceptance of their real identity by the government, and so on. The church acts like a magnet for these people. More than 100 people visit on average per day, coming from all over Anatolia, and not just Diyarbekir, to try to find their Armenian roots. New initiatives are underway to restore and reclaim other destroyed Armenian churches and monasteries in historic Armenia.

It is my sincere hope that future government and church leaders, as well as future benefactors, will decide more wisely on what projects to invest in, giving higher priority to the needs and wants of the Armenian people compared to their own.

The Islamized Armenians and Us[*]

Reflections on a Groundbreaking Conference in Istanbul

In early November, the Hrant Dink Foundation held a conference on "Islamized Armenians" at the Istanbul Bosphorus University, breaking

---

[*] *Armenian Weekly*, 15 Nov. 2013.

one more taboo in Turkey. Islamized Armenians were hitherto a hidden reality, a secret known by many, but which couldn't be revealed to anyone, whispered behind closed doors but filed in government intelligence offices, and it finally broke free into the public.

The late Hrant Dink would have been elated to see this conference become a reality, eight years after the first conference on "Armenians during the late Ottoman Empire era and the 1915 events" was held at Istanbul Bilgi University, when protesters hurled insults at the conference participants and government ministers labelled them as "traitors stabbing Turks in the back." That conference had also broken a taboo, but Hrant was already a marked man for revealing the identity of the most famous Islamized Armenian—Sabiha Gökçen, Atatürk's adopted daughter and the first female Turkish combat pilot, who was an Armenian orphan named Hatun Sebilciyan.

It is a known fact that in 1915, tens of thousands of Armenian orphans were forcibly Islamized and Turkified; that tens of thousands of Armenian girls and young women were captured by Kurds and Turks as slaves, maids, or wives; that tens of thousands Armenians converted to Islam to escape the deportations and massacres; and that tens of thousands of Armenians found shelter in friendly Kurdish and Alevi villages, but lost their identity. What happened to these survivors, these living victims of the 1915 genocide? Hrant was obsessed with them: "We keep talking about the ones 'gone' in 1915. Let us start talking about the ones who 'remained.'"

These remaining people survived, but mostly in living hells. Remarkably, their children and grandchildren are now "coming out," are no longer hiding their Armenian roots. One of the first was the famous Turkish lawyer Fethiye Çetin, who revealed that her grandmother was Armenian, in her book *My Grandmother*. This was followed by another book edited by Ayşe Gül Altınay and Fethiye Çetin, titled *The Grandchildren*, about dozens of Turkish/Kurdish people describing their Armenian roots, without revealing their real identities. Then came the reconstruction of the Surp Giragos Armenian church in Diyarbekir/Dikranagerd, which became a destination for many hidden Armenians in eastern Turkey. On average, over a hundred people visit the church daily, most of them hidden Armenians. Some come to pray, get baptized, or married, but most just visit to feel Armenian, without converting back to Christianity.

This has created a new identity of Muslim Armenians, in addition to the historical and traditional identity of Christian Armenians. In a country where only Muslim Turks can work for the government, where being non-Muslim is a sufficient excuse for persecution, harassment and attacks, where the word Armenian is used as the biggest insult, it takes real courage for someone to reveal that he is now an Armenian and no longer a Turk/Kurd/Muslim. People can easily lose their jobs, livelihood, or even lives for changing their identity. As an example of the level of racism and discrimination in the country, an ultra-nationalist opposition member of parliament years ago accused Turkish President Abdullah Gul of having Armenian roots in his family from Kayseri. Gul sued her for defamation, and the courts sided with him, ordering her to pay compensation for such an insult.

It is difficult to estimate the number of Islamized Armenians in Turkey, and even more difficult to predict what proportion of them are aware of their Armenian roots, or how many are willing to regain their Armenian identity. Based on independent studies of the 1915 events, one can conclude that more than 100,000 orphans were forcibly Islamized/Turkified, and that another 200,000 Armenians survived by converting to Islam or by finding shelter in friendly Kurdish and Alevi regions. It is therefore conceivable that 300,000 souls survived as Muslims. The population of Turkey has increased seven fold since then; using the same multiple, one can extrapolate that there may be two million people with Armenian roots in Turkey today, originating from the 1915 survivors. There were even more widespread conversions to Islam during the 1894-96 massacres, when entire villages were forcibly Islamized. A couple centuries before, Hamshen Armenians were Islamized in what is now northeast Turkey. The Muslim *Hamshentsis*, numbering about 500,000, speak a dialect based on Armenian, but had never identified themselves as Armenian, until recently. Adding all these forced conversions prior to and during 1915, one can conclude that the number of people with Armenian roots in present-day Turkey reaches several million. (The numbers are difficult to accurately estimate, but in any case, they easily exceed the present population of Armenia.)

The reality is that the secrets of "Armenianness" whispered for three or four generations after 1915 are now becoming loud revelations of new identities. As evidenced in the recent conference, even Hamshen

Armenians have started exploring and reclaiming their long lost roots. During the reconstruction of Surp Giragos church and in my travels in eastern and southeastern Turkey, one out of every three Kurds that I met had an Armenian grandmother in the family. This fact, hidden until recently, is now revealed openly, often leading young generations to reclaim their Armenian identities, but without giving up Islam. One interesting observation is that the hidden Armenians were aware of other hidden ones and all attempted to intermarry, resulting in many couples who ended up having Armenian roots from both parents.

The conference attracted numerous academicians, historians, and journalists from both within and outside Turkey, as well as dozens of presenters of oral history. One of the most dramatic presentations was about Sara, a 15-year-old Armenian girl from Urfa Viranshehir, who was captured by the Turkish strongman of the region, Eyup Aga. Eyup wanted to take Sara as his third wife. When Sara refused, Eyup killed her mother. When Sara refused again, Eyup killed her father. When Eyup threatened to kill Sara's little brother, Sara couldn't resist any more, and married the killer of her parents, on the condition that her brother be spared and she be allowed to keep her name. But her brother was also eventually killed. As she resisted Eyup's advances, she was repeatedly raped and was pregnant 15 times, giving birth to 15 babies, who all died prematurely. Eyup constantly tortured her, even marking a cross in her body with a knife. His family also mistreated her, viewing her as an outcast, and she had a hellish life to the end. At the end of the story, the presenter, a Turkish academician, revealed that Eyup and the family who committed these crimes against Sara was her own family. Her final statement was even more dramatic than the story: "We always hear stories told by the victims. It is now time for the perpetrators to start talking about and owning their crimes."

There are new revelations about how the Turkish government kept tabs on Islamized Armenians. Apparently, the government kept records of every Armenian village or large Armenian clan that was forcibly Islamized in 1915. It was recently discovered that the identification cards of hidden or known Armenians had a special numbering system to secretly identify them. There are anecdotes that a few Turkish candidates for air force pilot positions were turned away even though they qualified after rigorous tests, when government records revealed that they come from Islamized Armenian families.

It is of greater concern to us how the Islamized Armenians are being dealt with by Armenians. It seems that the Istanbul Armenian community and, more critically, the Istanbul Armenian Patriarchate are unable or unwilling to accept the hidden Armenians coming out as Armenians, unless these people accept Christianity, get baptized, and learn to speak Armenian. But it is unrealistic to expect the new Armenians to comply with these requirements. Since Armenians in Turkey are all defined as belonging to the Armenian Church, if the newcomers are rejected by the Patriarchate, they become double outcasts, not only from their previous Muslim Turkish/Kurdish community, but also from the Armenian community, as they cannot get married, baptized, or buried by the church and cannot send their children to Armenian schools. If they have made a conscious decision to identify themselves as Armenian—a risky and dangerous initiative under the present circumstances—they should be readily accepted as Armenians, regardless of whether they stay Muslim or atheist or anything else. Relationships get even more complicated as there are now many families with one branch carrying on life as Muslim Turks/Kurds, another branch as Muslim Armenian, and a third branch as Christian Armenian. The Echmiadzin Church in Armenia is more tolerant, and has issued the following statement: "Common ethnicity, land, language, history, cultural heritage, and religion are general measures in defining a nation. Even if one or more of these measures can be missing due to historic reasons, such as the inability to speak the language, or practice the religion, or the lack of knowledge of cultural and historic heritage, this should not be used to exclude one's Armenian identity." Yet, Charles Aznavour's approach is the most welcoming: "Armenia should embrace the Islamized Armenians and open its doors to them."

After Armenia, Karabagh, and the Armenian Diaspora, there is now an emerging *fourth* Armenian world—the Islamized Armenians of Turkey. Accepting this new reality will help both Turks and Armenians understand the realities and consequences of 1915.

Thoughts on Threshold of Centennial[*]

As we approach 2015, the 100th anniversary of the annihilation of the Armenian presence from their homeland of 4,000 years, we see major activities being planned by both Turkey and Armenians.

When Turkish acquaintances ask me what Armenians, especially the "evil diaspora," are planning to do in 2015, I say they are planning programs to assert the historical facts about the vanishing of Armenians from Ottoman Turkey in 1915. Then I turn around with a question of my own: "What are the Turks doing?" Their short answer is that the Turks will continue to dismiss the "misinformation" that the Armenians are disseminating.

Thus, the Armenians in Armenia and the diaspora are redoubling their efforts to have the genocide recognized worldwide, while the Turks are continuing to pour more money and resources into their official denialist policy both within and outside Turkey. In an attempt to divert global attention from the genocide commemoration, Turkey has decided to promote the 100th anniversary of the World War I Gallipoli campaign to be showcased as an historic event through government-supported activities worldwide and hailed as the "heroic resistance of the Turkish forces against the onslaught of the imperialistic powers at the Dardanelles Strait."

One can easily deduce from these opposing strategies and efforts that the main stumbling block for Turkey and Armenia, as neighbors, in normalizing their relationship and the reconciliation of their respective civil societies is the divergence of both the interpretation and understanding of their shared history. The result is an impasse. By this time next year [2014], I doubt there will be much change and the impasse will go on. The issue will continue to be treated as a political match, with points scored for Turkey if Obama continues saying "*Medz Yeghern*," and points for Armenia if he says "Genocide."

There are geopolitical, military, and economic reasons for the status quo to continue. Armenia may not be influential enough to overcome any of these reasons at present. Be that as it may, I believe Armenians can be

* *Armenian Weekly*, 21 Dec. 2013.

more effective if they re-channel their resources, which are extremely limited in comparison to Turkey, in this struggle.

I see two main areas when Armenians can make some headway on this issue. In my humble opinion, neither one is addressed properly by Armenia and Armenians.

The first target in dealing with the genocide issue is the academic field, which is supposed to arrive at indisputable historic facts after thorough and objective research of a multitude of state archives, documents, communication records, and oral history findings. The struggle in this field regarding the Armenian Genocide can best be summarized as forces of truth versus money and power. On one side there is truth, defended by almost all of the international academia; on the other side, there is the falsification of truth by a handful of scholars generously rewarded with funds provided by the Turkish state.

The second target in dealing with the genocide issue is the general population of Turkey, with the objective of conveying to them the historical truth of 1915 and its consequences, which are still felt today. This truth is best served when delivered to the people of Turkey in Turkish, based on archival material and historic facts—from the 1880s to 1922—directly from Turkish sources and their allies, including the factual consequences of the ongoing cover-up and denial by the state.

Academically, the only organization that spearheads and organizes objective research by independent scholars on this topic is the Zoryan Institute with its subsidiary, the International Institute for Genocide and Human Rights Studies. For the past 30-plus years, it has provided the highest standards of scholarship and objectivity in undertaking multi-disciplinary research and analysis. This includes documentation, lectures, conferences, and publications in seven languages related to human rights and genocide studies. The publications include more than 40 books, some of which are in several languages, and two major periodicals, with one dealing with genocide studies and the other the diaspora.

In addition, the Zoryan Institute provides research assistance to scholars, writers, journalists, filmmakers, government agencies, and other organizations. When Zoryan published Wolfgang Gust's *The Armenian Genocide 1915/16: Documents from the Diplomatic Archives of the German Office* in German, English, and Turkish, prominent Turkish journalist Mehmet Ali Birand could only reflect: "When you read and study these documents, even if this is your first venture into this subject, there is no way you will deny the genocide and disagree with the Armenians."

Even though the Turkish state defines Zoryan as a "propaganda center," several scholars from Turkey have attended the Genocide and Human Rights University Program run by the Zoryan Institute at the University of Toronto, and many of them have become outspoken advocates of historic truth within Turkey and the rest of the world.

To best describe Zoryan's contribution to scholarship is to quote from the "plea" made by the International Scholars of Genocide and Human Rights Studies last year in support of Zoryan's fundraising activities: "For the past 30 years, the Institute has maintained an ambitious program to collect archival documentation, conduct original research, and publish books and periodicals. It also conducts university-level educational programs in the field of genocide and human rights studies, taking a comparative and interdisciplinary approach in its examination of the Jewish Holocaust, the Cambodian Genocide, and the Rwandan Genocide, among others, using the Armenian Genocide as a point of reference. In the process, using the highest academic standards, the Institute has strived to understand the phenomenon of genocide, establish the incontestable, historical truth of the Armenian Genocide, and raise awareness of it among academics and opinion-makers. In the face of the continuing problem of genocide in the 21st century, the Institute is to be commended for its service to the academic community and is recognized by scholars for providing leadership and a support structure in promoting the cause of universal human rights and the prevention of genocide."

Despite its herculean efforts and outstanding results, the Zoryan Institute receives no appreciable financial support or acknowledgment from major Armenian organizations or the state. The institute is supported entirely by private donations. Against it, there exists the full power and unlimited funds of the Turkish state, and more recently the Azerbaijan state, which attempts to lure scholars to rewrite history. As a result, the Turkish State Historic Society reduces the number of 1915 Armenian victims with every new publication; at last count, a few thousand Armenians died of illness and hunger, while the number of Turkish victims of "genocide" perpetrated by the Armenians increases every year and is now more than two million. By the same strategy, the number of Azeri dead in the Khojalu "genocide" keeps increasing with every publication.

Dialogue between two conflicting parties can be meaningful only after both are aware of the truth and the facts. Even though the Turkish state has not allowed the truth to come out until recently, there are now clear signs that the taboos about 1915 are finally being broken and that there is an emerging "common body of knowledge" among Turkish citizens and, more importantly, among the opinion makers. Zoryan contributed immensely to the development of this "common body of knowledge" through conferences, seminars, and the books it helped publish by such authors as Yair Auron, Taner Akçam, Wolfgang Gust, Roger Smith, Vahakn Dadrian, and Rifat Bali.

Given all this, I strongly urge Armenians to support the Zoryan Institute so that it can continue to develop the common body of knowledge to be shared by Armenians and Turks. Hopefully, shared history will help these neighboring peoples reconcile with their pasts, and such reconciliation will help secure a future for generations to come.

I will elaborate on the second target—the population of Turkey—and its challenges in a separate article.

Dialogue Can Lead to Acknowledgment[*]

In a previous article about the approaching 2015 centennial of the Armenian Genocide, I had argued about the necessity of focusing the Armenians' limited resources to support independent academic research, continuing to bring out the truth and facts of 1915 toward establishing a "common body of knowledge" between the Turks and Armenians. In this article, I will elaborate on the necessity to deliver those 1915 facts and truth directly to the Turkish people, will outline some of the obstacles created by the denialist policies of the Turkish state, and finally, will provide a few suggestions for the Turkish state to consider by 2015.

Meaningful dialogue between two conflicting parties can only happen if both parties are aware of the facts and the truth. Even though the Turkish state has not allowed the truth and the facts of 1915 to come out until recently, there are now clear signs that the taboos about 1915 are finally broken and that there is a "common body of knowledge" emerging among the Turkish opinion makers and ordinary citizens. For four generations,

* *The Armenian Mirror Spectator*, 14 Jan. 2014.

the Turkish citizens were brainwashed about 1915 by the state education system and the media. However, Turkish people can no longer be defined as a homogenous, uniform group. Clashes between the Turkish state and the sizable Kurdish/Alevi population, as well as the prosecution and punishment of the "deep state" leaders who ruled Turkey until a few years ago, have become recent factors in questioning the state version of history regarding the 1915 events. A few bright personalities in politics, academia, media and literature, i.e. opinion makers, have advocated increased democratization, freedom of speech and minority rights; moreover, they have acknowledged the truth about 1915 and demanded that the state also do so. There is now a small but fast increasing segment of the population which wants the state to face the past about the 1915 events.

To date, there have been few attempts of dialogue between the Armenian world and this liberalized segment of the Turkish population and opinion makers. Apart from the activities of the Hrant Dink Foundation based in Istanbul, the only contacts by Armenians have been through a few individuals in academia, film, media, music and culture, and organizationally by the Zoryan Institute in the academic field, by the Armenian NGO Civilitas through its recently opened office in Istanbul, and some recent political exchanges between Kurdish political parties and representatives of the Armenian Revolutionary Federation. Armenian academia, NGOs and opinion makers should aim at direct contact with their Turkish counterparts in conveying the truth in Turkish, through jointly organized conferences, seminars, TV programs, films and translated publications. For example, ordinary Turks should find out about the courageous Turkish government officials who resisted the inhumane government decisions to annihilate the Armenian population in 1915. They should learn about the fate of the properties left behind by the annihilated Armenians, including hundreds of thousands of houses, fields, shops, warehouses, factories, mines, churches and schools, all confiscated by the state, Ittihad Terakki leaders or local Muslim notables. They should understand that most of the Atatürk House Museums scattered all over Anatolia belonged to deported or murdered Armenian citizens of the Ottoman state. They should be reminded that the very residence where the Turkish President sits today in Ankara, was once owned by an Armenian family.

GOMIDAS INSTITUTE

Of course, the Turkish state will continue using all its resources to prevent its citizens from finding out the truth. Notwithstanding the boasts of the Turkish Prime Minister Erdoğan that their archives are open and they have nothing to hide, the reality is that their archives are not entirely open and have gone through two major cleanups. The first cleanup and destruction of files was back in 1918, when the Ittihad Terakki leaders escaped from Istanbul in a German warship in order to avoid prosecution as war criminals, carrying several trunkloads of documents with them. At the same time, the main planner of the Armenian deportations and massacres, Special Organization Chief Bahattin Shakir also burned rooms full of documents related to their activities. The second purging was in the 1990s when the Ottoman Archives were reorganized, translated into modern Turkish and digitized. A team of diplomats, historians, retired ambassadors and military officers sifted through millions of documents with the objective of eliminating any incriminating reference to the Armenians. Recent Wikileaks documents indicate that the Ottoman archival documents, initially estimated at 50 million records, turned out to be more like 200 million and therefore, the intended purge could not be carried out effectively. Obviously, several thousand documents escaped scrutiny and a few prominent Turkish scholars like Taner Akçam, Ümit Kurt and Uğur Üngör have been able to produce significant historic facts about the intended annihilation of the Armenians and confiscation of their properties, based only on the Ottoman archives. It was recently revealed that all researchers delving into the Armenian issue in the Ottoman archives were being tracked and monitored. If their work was deemed to be against the state version, there would be harassment and funding repercussions against them and the institutions where they worked and studied. Meanwhile, researchers who produce/falsify/create documents minimizing Armenian losses are encouraged and rewarded. In 2005, Murat Bardakçı, an investigative journalist, published Talaat Pasha's diary revealing that Talaat had kept detailed records about the numbers and destination of the deported Armenians, had tallied the loss of Armenians at 972,000, but had also stated that the total missing could exceed 1.2 million due to unaccounted relocations. During a recent TV talk show about history called Rear Window of History, Bardakçı had invited a history professor from Sakarya University, a state sponsored "expert" on the Armenian issue, where this expert announced that the archives show the Ottoman government took all precautions to care for the 300,000 Armenians temporarily deported "only" from the eastern war front, that "only" a few thousand died from illness, but most of them safely returned home after the war. Bardakçı then confronted him by producing Talaat Pasha's diary and the numbers that Talaat himself had quoted; the expert said he can only work with whatever is available in the state archives. He also announced that Turkish historians have now "proven" that all the genocide allegations are "fiction," based on American Ambassador Morgenthau's book, which was specifically produced as a propaganda tool to drum up support for the United States to enter the war. Even Bardakçı found this expert's comments embarrassing for Turkey, which would result in more ridicule internationally and weaken Turkey's hand further in the eve of 2015.

If Prime Minister Erdoğan really wants to prove that Turkey has nothing to hide in the Armenian issue, all he has to do is order the release of two sets of critical documents – the deportation books and the deeds. first set of documents is the 33 dossiers of the Deportation and Liquidation Commissions formed in 1915-16 in various Ottoman interior provinces, recording, listing, appraising, and holding on deposit the assets of the deported Armenians for their eventual return, but also selling or distributing some of the Armenian assets to Muslim refugees. The whereabouts of these dossiers is a mystery but speculated that they are still intact and kept in the Prime Ministry offices. The second set of documents is the Ottoman land registry and property deeds records. In 2005, when the government attempted to comply with European Union (EU) modernization initiatives by translating and opening up these records to the public, it was prevented from doing so by a stern warning — dated August 26, 2005 — from the National Security Committee of the Turkish Armed Forces, which stated that "The Ottoman records kept at the Land Register and Cadaster Surveys General Directorate offices must be sealed and not available to the public, as they have the potential to be exploited by alleged genocide claims and property claims against the State Charitable Foundation assets. Opening them to general public use is against state interests"…

Recently, it came to light that a former prime minister had come close to taking a positive step toward the Armenian issue. Being a very pragmatic politician, in the early 1990s Turgut Özal had wished the issue to be resolved by ending the Turkish denialist policy, and he had commissioned a study to quantify the amount of compensation needed to be paid to the Armenians worldwide. It is reported that the study did come up with a monetary figure but no further steps were taken, either because the cost would be exorbitant, or because Özal suddenly and mysteriously died in 1993. His sudden death is still subject of speculation today after 20 years, with his body recently exhumed and examined for the presence of poisons. It is said that he was severely criticized by the military and the deep state, not only for this Armenian episode, but more critically, for his desire to end the separatist Kurdish issue by giving concessions to them.

Based on feedback and comments on my past articles, there seems to be a significantly wide readership in Turkey and within their government circles. A recurring theme I hear is that the present government, unlike the previous ones, has taken a lot of positive steps toward the Armenians, and yet, there is no acknowledgment or reciprocating goodwill from the Armenian side. The positive examples cited include the restoration of Aghtamar Holy Cross church (note: still known as Akdamar Museum in Turkey), return of several confiscated properties belonging to the Armenian church and charitable foundations (note: returns still less than 10 percent of properties seized after 1930s, none from before 1915 and none of the private properties), increased freedom of speech with utterance of the term "Armenian Genocide" no longer a punishable offense (note: but still people like Hrant Dink can get killed for uttering it and still the real murderers can remain hidden), and so on. I do acknowledge that these are positive steps in the right direction, but only a few steps toward a mile long journey. Perhaps the mile long journey cannot be completed by 2015, but several concrete and specific steps need to be taken by Turkey in order to achieve some credibility and respectability. Instead of diversionary tactical steps like Foreign Minister Davutoğlu's recent visit to Armenia, which achieved nothing, I will humbly offer a few suggestions for the consideration of my Turkish government acquaintances:

1. Open the border with Armenia without any preconditions, re-name the Alican border crossing as the Hrant Dink Gate, honoring the heroic advocate of dialogue between the two peoples.

Turkish Foreign Minister Ahmet Davutoğlu (*l*)
with author Raffi Bedrosyan (*r*).

2. Grant citizenship to all living descendants of the deported Ottoman Armenian subjects.

3. Clean up the textbooks at all levels of the educational system by eliminating the falsifications, hatemongering and discrimination toward Armenians (and other minorities).

4. Initiate a state program by the Ministry of Culture and Tourism to restore the more than 2,000 destroyed or deteriorating Armenian monasteries and churches, and return them to their rightful owner, the Armenian Church (Istanbul Armenian Patriarchate).

5. Offer a symbolic but meaningful apology to the Armenian people for all the crimes of 1915 by returning Mount Ararat and Ani to Armenia, perhaps as part of a territorial exchange based on equivalent land area.

6. Open up to the public the afore-mentioned documents related to the deportation/liquidation records and the Ottoman property deeds related to the deported Armenians.

7. Allow personal compensation cases by the descendants of Ottoman Armenian subjects related to their confiscated properties to proceed in Turkish and international courts.

8. Offer free transit and duty free port facilities for Armenia at a Black Sea port such as Trabzon and Rize, as partial compensation toward past economic losses of Ottoman Armenians.

Turkish acquaintances in government circles complain that the Armenians' insistence in using the word Genocide is a barrier to any progress toward dialogue about 1915. None of the suggestions above refer to that word, and all of them are do-able by 2015, if there really is goodwill. Once there is knowledge of the facts followed by dialogue about the truth of 1915 among the Turkish opinion makers and ordinary citizens, the far-reaching result would be the creation of voters aware of the truth. Knowledgable voters would then vote in knowledgable parliament members and eventually governments, which would set policies and decisions according to the voters' preferences. I would suggest that decisions taken in the Turkish Parliament respecting the truth of 1915 would be far more effective than any decision taken in the parliaments of third party states.

Sources

* *Vatan* daily newspaper, September 12, 2011, "Bavul dolusu Ermeni belgesi kacirildi" (Trunkloads of Armenian documents were taken out)
* *Zaman* daily newspaper, April 24, 2012, "Özal Yasasaydi Ermeni Sorununu Cozecekti" (If Özal had lived, he would have solved the Armenian issue'
* Internethaber news online, December 12, 2013, "Turkiye'de skandal: Ermeni meselesini calisan ogrenciler fislendi" (Scandal in Turkey: Students researching the Armenian issue are being monitored)
* Murat Bardakçı, *Talaat Pasanin Evrak-i Metrukesi* (Talaat Pasha's Black Book), 2005, Everest Yayinlari (Everest Publishing House)

Hasan Cemal Speaks at Dink Commemoration in Toronto[*]

Toronto, Canada—On Jan. 19, the Toronto Armenian community gathered to commemorate the 7th anniversary of the assassination of Hrant Dink. More than 500 people filled the Armenian General Benevolent Union Centre to capacity, with standing room only. The keynote speaker was renowned Turkish journalist and author Hasan

---

Armenian Weekly, 22 Jan. 2014.

Cemal, who also happens to be the grandson of Djemal Pasha, one of the three leaders of the Committee of Union and Progress (*Ittihat ve Terakki*), which planned and perpetrated the Armenian Genocide in 1915.

Mgrditch Mgrditchian was the master of ceremonies. After a beautiful rendition of *Sari Aghchig* and *Cilicia* by young soprano Lynn Anoush Isnar, Raffi Bedrosyan, one of Hrant's friends, introduced Hasan Cemal. Bedrosyan explained that Hasan Cemal worked for many years (until 1992) as the editor-in-chief of the *Cumhuriyet* daily, the official mouthpiece of the Kemalist state and the defender of the denialist official version of history related to the 1915 events. Hasan Cemal then moved on to *Sabah* newspaper, the newspaper with the largest circulation at the time, as editor (until 1998), and then to *Milliyet* until March 2013, when he had to resign under pressure from Prime Minister Erdoğan for criticizing the anti-democratic policies of the government. In recent years, Hasan Cemal got influenced by the writings of journalist Hrant Dink and historian Taner Akçam, and started questioning the veracity of the state version of history. As a result, he went through a gradual intellectual transformation, until he reached the conclusion that those events were indeed a genocide. In 2008, the year after Hrant Dink was assassinated, he went to Armenia and visited the Genocide Memorial, placing flowers there for Hrant and all the past genocide victims, sharing their pain. In 2012, he wrote a book titled *1915: Armenian Genocide* in Turkish. The book, explaining his personal evolution, became a bestseller.

In his speech, Hasan Cemal stressed the need to separate personal family history from general history. He gave examples as to how he had to distinguish between his grandfather's actions versus his stand against the genocide, and his dramatic meeting in Yerevan with the grandson of one of the planners of Djemal Pasha's assassination in Tbilisi in 1922. Hasan Cemal also explained the long journey he had to go through from having a "captive" mind, based on the state version of history, to an "emancipated" or "liberated" mind, after seeking and finding the facts and truth about the 1915 events. Djemal stated that a small but fast increasing segment of the Turkish civil society has already started to acknowledge the truth about the genocide, and urged the Turkish state also to face its past and acknowledge and apologize for the 1915 events.

After his speech, there was a short discussion session among Hasan Cemal and two Zoryan Institute representatives, president Kurken

Hasan Cemal (l) and author (r).

Sarkissian and Executive Director George Shirinian, moderated by Raffi Bedrosyan, about the significance of building a "common body of knowledge" regarding the historic facts of 1915, in order to be able to have meaningful and constructive dialogue toward reconciliation between Turks and Armenians.

The Toronto commemoration was another proof that Hrant Dink's legacy lives on and gains more momentum every year, both within Turkey and in all four corners of the world, with demands of truth and justice to prevail for the 1.5 million Armenians plus one.

The Four Shades of Turkey, and the Armenians[*]

Like a cell dividing itself into two, then each new cell further dividing into two, Turkey keeps being divided. Although divisions always existed, they remained mostly suppressed, until now. In this article, I will outline the old and new divisions in Turkey, and the Turks' perception of us Armenians.

Beginning in 1923 with the founding of the republic, Turkey was governed by a secular, Kemalist and nationalist ideology, with the single-

_____

* *Armenian Weekly*, 2 April 2014.

minded objective of creating and maintaining a monolithic, single-nation state. Regardless of which party was in power, leftist or rightist, the "deep state"—dominated by the armed forces, big business, big state bureaucracy, media, and academia—directed all affairs behind the scenes. The "deep state" leaders and their backers emerged as the elite of society, aptly named the nationalist White Turks; they inherited and developed a state built on the economic foundations of plundered and confiscated Armenian and Greek wealth. The masses in the provinces were mainly utilized as free bodies for the military elite, or as cheap labor for the industrial elite, and were remembered only at election time. White Turks looked down on the pious Sunni Muslim majority and labeled them *takunyali*, or clog wearers. The disappearance of the Armenians and Greeks from these lands was fiercely denied. The existence of other ethnic people in Turkey, such as the Kurds, was also continuously denied. Turkey is only for Turks, was their motto. As the Armenians and Greeks were already wiped out, the other ethnic groups were told that they were now Turks, or else.

The supremacy of the White Turks ended in 2003 with the election of Prime Minister Recep Tayyip Erdoğan and his moderately Islamic party. Despite attempts by the "deep state" to topple him, Erdoğan outmaneuvered the White Turks, thanks to the religious Sunni Muslims of Anatolia and the recent arrival of underprivileged masses from the provinces to the big cities. The provincial and religious Turks quickly secured and strengthened their grip on power. The influential fundamentalist religious leader Fethullah Gülen, who had been forced to leave Turkey during the previous regimes, cooperated with Erdoğan and his followers quickly filled the cadres of bureaucracy, including key posts in the police, security, judiciary, and academic fields. Hundreds of "deep state" leaders and elite White Turks in the military, media, and academia were arrested and jailed on charges of an attempted coup d'état against the government. Many White Turks began to leave the country. Although less intolerant toward minorities than the White Turks, the attitude of the new leaders toward minorities and the Kurds did not change much.

The alliance between Erdoğan and Gülen ended in late 2013, when Erdoğan felt secure enough to discard Gülen and shut down the numerous supplementary educational facilities he controlled. Many parents in Turkey depended on these facilities for their child's advancement, as the state education system is not sufficient to secure admission to the state universities. These facilities were used as a powerbase by Gülen; they were a major source of income and facilitated recruitment of new followers. Soon after Erdoğan announced his intention to close these facilities, state prosecutors and police controlled by Gülen revealed they had uncovered a major corruption scandal involving four of Erdoğan's ministers and hundreds of millions of dollars in bribes. The scandal was replete with juicy details of money-counting machines and millions stashed in shoeboxes in the ministers' homes. Erdoğan counter-attacked by swiftly removing, replacing, and firing thousands of state prosecutors, judges, and police officers deemed to be followers of the Gülen movement. In the last few weeks, at least 10 taped telephone conversations involving Erdoğan himself have been leaked. In them, Erdoğan directs his son to dispose of hundreds of millions of cash in euros and dollars from their homes; orders several businessmen to pay $100 million each toward buying a media empire that he wants controlled; demands another media owner to fire several journalists; and decides how much certain contractors must pay in return for large contracts.

In the Western world, even a hint of attempted bribery or corruption is sufficient in bringing down governments. But in Turkey, Erdoğan carries on, dismissing the evidence as plots hatched by his one-time ally (and now mortal enemy) Gülen, as well as other virtual enemies, such as "parallel states" within Turkey, and, predictably, external enemies such as Israel, the U.S., the European Union, and the "interest lobby," all jealous of Turkey's fast growth. Erdoğan's latest move is to try to win back the nationalists who were charged and jailed for attempting to topple his own government; as a result, most of the jailed "deep state" leaders have been released, including the former army chief of staff and other commanders; one of the masterminds of the Hrant Dink assassination; the racist lawyer who hounded Hrant Dink for "insulting Turkishness"; the politician who was charged for stating "The Armenian Genocide is a lie" in Switzerland, and with whom the European Court of Human Rights recently sided in the name of freedom of speech; an organized crime leader who arranged several contract killings of anti-nationalists and Kurds; the murderers of a German and two Turkish Protestant missionaries in Malatya; and several other ultra nationalist/racist intellectuals and journalists.

While these divisions have emerged among the Turks of Turkey, the Kurds of Turkey have made major advances toward greater autonomy, language rights, and self-determination—a struggle that began in the 1980s as a guerilla movement and, more recently in the 2000s, has become a political movement. The imprisoned PKK leader Abdullah Ocalan imposed his will on Erdoğan, who conceded to peace talks in exchange for a ceasefire.

Even though the four major divisions within Turkey—the "deep state," the Erdoğan people, the Gülen people, and the Kurds—keep fighting and plotting against one another, they come together and close ranks when it comes to the Armenian issue, past and present. The Turks themselves categorize Armenians into three distinct groups (in a completely misguided manner): the Good, the Bad, and the Poor. The small Armenian community in Turkey is the Good, as it is easily controllable and no longer a threat, possessing neighborly memories of shared dolma or *topik*. They're Good, that is, as long as they don't ask much about the past or present, like Hrant Dink dared to. The Armenian Diaspora is the Bad, with its evil presence in every country poisoning locals against Turks and Turkey, and spreading lies about the "alleged" genocide of 1915. Finally, the Armenians who recently left Armenia to come to Turkey to find bread are the Poor. The Kurds, on the other hand, have more empathy toward the Armenians; however, it is mainly because "the enemy of my enemy is my friend." Although Ocalan came close to acknowledging the genocide, he has empathy only for the Good Armenians in Turkey and continues to define the diaspora as part of the external lobby threat against both Turks and Kurds. While Kurds (barring a few exceptions) acknowledge the sufferings of Armenians in 1915, they cannot bring themselves to acknowledge the active role they played in the genocide, nor open the subject of returning the vast properties seized from Armenians.

Those Armenians who believe in meaningful dialogue with the peoples of Turkey now face the additional challenge of choosing one or more of these groups at the risk of alienating the others. The prospect of any productive result, however, becomes dimmer by the day. Nevertheless, dialogue does continue with the involvement of civil society organizations and intellectuals, and more significantly, through the emerging force of Islamized Armenians of Turkey. Dialogue must and will continue until all four groups start to see that all Armenians, whether in Turkey, the diaspora, or Armenia—and whether good, bad, or poor—were all equally impacted by the genocide and equally demand acknowledgment and restitution.

Erdoğan's Message: Where Do We Go From Here?[*]

On April 23, [2014] Turkish Prime Minister Recep Tayyip Erdoğan sent a message of condolence in eight languages to Armenians worldwide, for their forefathers who lost their lives in 1915. As this was an unprecedented and unexpected gesture by a Turkish statesman, Armenians in Armenia, the diaspora, and within Turkey reacted with a wide range of emotions and opinions. Some dismissed it as a cynical move and a new version of continued denial of the genocide; some saw it as a smart political move and an effective delay tactic to avert the pressure of the centennial of the genocide next year; others optimistically saw it as a change in direction by Turkey in facing its history, hoping for increased dialogue and a resolution of issues; and a few sycophants went as far as to take out newspaper ads thanking the prime minister, or suggesting that he be considered for the Nobel Peace Prize. So, where do we go from here?

One can find many faults with Erdoğan's message. It could be interpreted as one more fitting for the victims of a natural disaster, such as an earthquake or flood, or a man-made accident, such as a train accident, instead of *murdered* victims of a state-planned annihilation of an entire people that has disappeared from its 4,000-year-old historic homeland. One can speculate about the reasons behind such a message: Was it calculated, insincere, or due to pressure by the U.S., so that President Obama would not use the "G" word. But at the end of the day, no matter what the motive, whether genuine or not, one must acknowledge that this is the first time a Turkish leader has said something mildly humane about the Armenian Genocide victims of 1915, instead of complete denial or insults that were the norm for the past 99 years. More significantly, certain terms used in the message are really encouraging, welcome and irreversible, such as acknowledging the historic significance of April 24 for all the Armenians around the world, or acknowledging the inhumane consequences of the "relocation." And therefore, it should be recognized as a small step in the right direction—*provided* that it is followed immediately by real, concrete action and further evidence of a change of direction toward facing history, justice, and restitution. The next 12 months will tell if this is the case or not.

---

[*] *Armenian Weekly*, 6 May 2014.

It is not easy for a statesman to suddenly reverse a nearly century-old course of denial, which included brainwashing its citizens for four generations, and threats against anyone or any state that disagreed with its lies about 1915. But every journey of 10,000 miles starts with a small step. In a previous article I had suggested eight steps that Turkey could take within the next year—immediately and without even acknowledging the genocide—if there truly was goodwill in resolving historical wrongs:

1. Open the border with Armenia without any preconditions. Rename the Alican border-crossing the Hrant Dink Gate in honor of the heroic advocate for dialogue.

2. Grant citizenship to the living descendants of the deported Ottoman-Armenian citizens.

3. Clean up the textbooks at all levels of the educational system by eliminating the falsifications, hate-mongering, and discrimination against the Armenians, and start teaching the correct facts about 1915.

4. Initiate a state program through the Ministry of Culture and Tourism to reconstruct or restore the more than 2,000 destroyed or deteriorating Armenian monasteries and churches, and return them to their rightful owner, the Armenian Church.

5. Offer a symbolic but meaningful apology to the Armenian people for the crimes of 1915 by returning Mount Ararat and Ani to Armenia, perhaps as part of a minor border revision and territorial exchange based on equivalent land area.

6. Open up to the public the archival documents related to the deportation/liquidation records and the Ottoman property deeds related to the deported Armenians.

7. Allow compensation cases concerning descendants of Ottoman-Armenian subjects to proceed in Turkish and international courts.

8. Offer free transit and duty-free port facilities for Armenia at a Black Sea post such as Trabzon and Rize as partial compensation for the economic losses of Ottoman-Armenian subjects.

I am aware that some of these steps have already been taken or been considered by Turkish government officials. Discussions about granting citizenship and restoring a few of the churches and monasteries have started—albeit as "museums," and usually without mentioning their Armenian origins. Opening the border with Armenia without being held

Varak Monastery near Van.

hostage by third countries would be a win-win for both states. A sure sign that Erdoğan's message is sincere could be the elimination of the *names* of the streets, schools, mosques, and neighborhoods named after the Committee of Union and Progress (CUP) leaders Talat, Enver, and Djemal. But we know that there are still Turkish "deep state" leaders (recently released from jail by Erdoğan) who have formed Talat Pasha Committees, or erected statues of such notorius murderers as Topal (Lame) Osman, famous for throwing Armenians overboard from boats into the Black Sea, or even worse, for throwing Pontic Greeks into the boiler rooms of ships through their funnels.

Another indication of Erdoğan's sincerity in changing direction would be to stop the ridiculous publications and conferences by the state-financed Turkish Historic Society. Their latest publication had the number of perished Armenians during the genocide down to 8,000, and all had "died due to illness." Their latest conference in Van in April 2014, where 35 so-called professors presented papers, was attended by only seven people. One of the papers claimed that the 235 intellectuals arrested on April 24, 1915 were all very well treated, well fed and cared for in Ayas and Cankiri, and that all returned to Istanbul within a few months, "without even a tiny scratch on their bodies."

Finally, Erdoğan must understand that there is no need to assemble an international historical commission to prove the veracity of the genocide, as this has already been done for him by scholars worldwide using Ottoman-Turkish and international archives. If the Turkish objective of its historical commission is to prove that Armenians were indeed fomenting rebellion, and thereby to justify the decision of relocation and wholesale massacres, these are already documented and open in Armenian and international archives. And yes, there have been localized revenge massacres of Muslims by Armenian volunteer troops entering Ottoman Armenia with the Russian army in 1916, but after the 1915 genocide had already taken place. He can assemble a commission *within* Turkey, as there are now enough credible Turkish scholars who can overcome the lies spread by the lackeys at the Turkish Historical Society. But he must understand that there are still hidden deportation/liquidation records from the 33 Ottoman provinces, as well as the Ottoman property land registry and deed records, still banned by the Turkish Army Chief of staff. Yes, there is a need for an international commission, not to establish the truths of 1915 but to deal with the *consequences* of the truths and restitution of justice.

Of course, it is essential for Erdoğan and the Turkish state to correctly deal with the trauma and pain of the *murdered*—and not dead—victims of 1915, as he referred to in his message. But the issue is much more than that. There are the bigger issues of massive plunder, transfer of wealth, land, and assets that resulted from the murder of these victims. The president of the Turkish state today resides in the home of the Kasabian family. A well-known Turkish newspaper editor owns the historic Varakavank Monastery near Van, and the entire village where Armenians lived until 1915. The Turkish state today owns the land of more than 4,000 Armenian churches and schools active before 1915. Turkish and Kurdish notables seized—and still possess—hundreds of thousands of houses, shops, stores, farms, orchards, vineyards, factories, warehouses, and mines owned by Armenians before 1915. This massive plunder is not the result of a state conquering a foreign state; it is because a state decided to kill its own citizens and take their assets, followed by a series of legislative acts to legalize the robbery. This issue has nothing to do with whether the murders are defined as "genocide" or not, and this must be addressed by the Turkish state regardless, through revised legislation and a return of the assets to the rightful owners and heirs.

While Erdoğan and Turkey's leaders have a lot of work to do to confront the past, Armenians cannot afford to just meet among themselves or expect third-country politicians to take up their cause for them. As an advocate of direct dialogue with our adversaries, I suggest increased contact with Turks, Kurds, and the new emerging reality of the "hidden Armenians"—toward building trust, understanding, and a common "body of knowledge." Armenian opinion-makers, media, academia, lawyers, artists, filmmakers, engineers, and architects, NGOs and other organizations must make contact with their counterparts in Turkey through conferences, cultural events, media and student exchanges, reconstruction projects, and jointly organized April 24 commemorations within Turkey. Thanks to a number of such initiatives and individuals, the number of opinion-makers and open-minded people who have become aware of the truth has grown dramatically. We are all aware that the problem is within Turkey, but we *must* realize that the solution is within Turkey as well. It is my hope that Erdoğan's message is a real step in the right direction, which will be through the steps described above.

The Genocide of the Pontic Greeks[*]

The annihilation of the non-Turk/non-Muslim peoples from modern Turkey started on April 24, 1915, with the arrest of 250 Armenian intellectuals in Istanbul. Within a few months, 1.5 million Armenians had been wiped out from their historic homeland of 4,000 years in what is now eastern Turkey, as well as from the northern, southern, central, and western parts of Turkey. About 250,000 Assyrians were also massacred in southeastern Turkey during the same period. Then, it was the Pontic Greeks' turn to be eliminated in northern Turkey on the Black Sea coast, sporadically from 1916 onward. The ethnic cleansing of the Pontic Greeks got interrupted when the Ottomans ended up on the losing side of World War I, but their real destruction resumed in a well-organized manner on May 19, 1919. This article will summarize the tragic end of the Pontic Greek civilization in northern Turkey—a series of events less

[*] *Armenian Weekly*, 2 July 2014.

researched and documented than the Armenian Genocide, but equally denied and covered up by the Turkish state.

Pontic Greeks continuously inhabited the southern coast of the Black Sea in northern Anatolia since pre-Byzantine times. The ethnic cleansing of the Pontic Greeks followed the same pattern as the Armenian deportations and massacres: Citing security threats and suspicions of possible cooperation with the Russians, in the spring of 1916 the Ottoman government ordered that all Pontic Greeks be removed 50 kilometers inland from the Black Sea coastal towns. Of course, in the case of the Armenians, the deportation orders were not only in the eastern war zone, but applied to every region in Turkey. The Pontic Greek deportations were carried out by the Special Organization (*Teskilat-i Mahsusa*), the same governmental organization that carried out the Armenian massacres, manned by convicted killers released from prisons. Documents show that the longer the prison term, the higher the rank given by the government to these criminals carrying out their destructive tasks. Naturally, the Greek deportations soon transformed from relocation to robbery to mass murders. But because the Pontic Greeks had observed the fate of Armenians a year earlier, they got their defenses organized and resisted the deportations by taking to the mountains wherever they could. As a result, the deportations and massacres in this "First Phase Massacre" resulted in only 150,000 deaths, eliminating a third of the Pontic population by the end of the war.

The "Second and Real Phase of Massacre" that saw the organized destruction of the Pontic Greeks started in earnest with the arrival of Mustafa Kemal Atatürk in Samsun on May 19, 1919. He met with the well-known mass murderers of the Armenians of the Black Sea region, such as Topal (Lame) Osman and Ipsiz Recep, and secured their cooperation in starting a terror campaign to get rid of the Pontic Greeks from northern Turkey. These two murderers, originally smugglers of illegal goods, had gained notoriety in 1915 when they rounded up Armenian men, women, and children in large boats, took them out to sea, and dumped them overboard to drown, then boasted that the "smelt season will be bountiful this year with lots of food for them." As the Pontic Greek men had taken to the mountains, these two murderers went after the Greek women and children who had remained in the villages. Various methods of mass murder were implemented. It was common to

Hagia Sophia Greek Orthodox church, Trebizond, before the genocide of Pontic Greeks.

take the entire population of villages to nearby caves, seal the entrance of the cave, and burn them alive, or use gas to suffocate them inside. Any male Greeks caught were thrown, alive, into the coal furnaces of steamships through the funnels. Churches became incinerators to burn alive as many Greeks as could be stuffed into the building. The extent of the tortures and massacres the Greeks endured even disturbed the local Muslim population, who petitioned the Ankara government to remove these murderers from the region. Eventually Atatürk brought them to Ankara, where Osman became his personal bodyguard. Yet, when Osman shot a member of parliament for criticizing Atatürk, and then threatened Atatürk himself, he was executed.

There were also the so-called "Liberation Courts" (*Istiklal Mahkemeleri*) set up in cities across the Black Sea region to try Greek rebels. These courts passed arbitrary decisions that almost invariably resulted in death sentences, with no defense or appeals allowed, and hangings carried out immediately. Among the victims of these courts were hundreds of Greek teachers in the American and Greek schools of the region, prominent community leaders, clergymen, and, tragically, all members of the Merzifon Greek high school football team, only because the team was named Pontus Club, which was deemed sufficient reason to label them a rebel terrorist organization. Atatürk then appointed Nurettin Pasha as commander of the Central Army to mop up any resisting Greeks from the entire Black Sea region. This man, also known for his sadistic tendencies, destroyed thousands of defenseless Greek villages. Among his "accomplishments" was the arrest of a Turkish opposition journalist who had criticized Atatürk; Nurettin Pasha then had his soldiers tear the journalist alive limb by limb. He was also at the head of the army units that entered Izmir (Smyrna) in 1922, where he arranged for the lynching of the Greek head of the clergy in the same manner, and then began the Great Fire that destroyed the entire city.

Between May 19, 1919, and the end of 1922, the Pontic Greek population was decimated by 353,000 in the following cities:

Amasya, Giresun, Samsun:	134,078
Tokat:	64,582
Trabzon:	38,434
Niksar:	27,216
Sebinkarahisar:	21,448
Macka:	17,479

There was also a violent campaign to Islamize the Greeks quite a number of them converted to Islam under threats and torture, followed by Turkification. With the 1924 Lausanne Treaty, the few remaining Pontic Greeks were included in the 1,250,000 Anatolian Greeks "exchanged" for Muslims in Greece, thereby completely emptying the Black Sea region from its historic Greek civilization. All the names of the Greek villages and towns were changed into new Turkish names. The Turkish language was forced upon all the converted Greeks, Hamshen Armenians, Laz, and Georgian minorities.

And thus began a century-long brainwashing campaign of single-state, single-nation, and single language policy. The May 19, 1919 date of Atatürk's arrival in Samsun was adopted in 1937as a national holiday celebrating Youth and Sports Day, copying the German Nazis' superior race policies, to demonstrate the athleticism and beauty of the Turkish race. The extent of racism was evident in the statement of then-Justice Minister Mahmut Esat Bozkurt, who said, "Turks are the masters in this country. The remaining peoples have only one right in this country, to be the maids and slaves of the real Turks."

As recently as in 2008, then-Defense Minister Vecdi Gonul echoed the same racist sentiments in Turkey: "If the Greeks had been allowed to exist in the Aegean and Black Sea regions, and the Armenians all over Anatolia, would we be able to have a powerful national state today?" The chief murderer of the Pontic Greeks, Topal (Lame) Osman, is still regarded as a hero by nationalist Turks. His statue was recently erected in Giresun by one of the Eregenekon deep-state leaders, retired general Veli Kucuk, himself responsible for the "mysterious disappearance" of dozens of Kurds, and the assumed mastermind behind the organized assassination of Turkish-Armenian journalist Hrant Dink. Kucuk was arrested and sentenced to life in prison for plotting the overthrow of the Erdoğan government as part of the deep-state trials, but he was recently released from prison by Erdoğan (following the falling out between Erdoğan and the religious leader Fethullah Gülen, whose followers were among the prosecutor team and police forces who had arrested Kucuk).

It has now become clear that the Turkish state's policy to create a single nationalist state with a single religion and language has failed miserably. Within Turkey, Kurds could not be assimilated, and the grandchildren of the hidden Islamized Armenians and Pontic Greeks are starting to "come out" to find their roots. Outside Turkey, the Armenians continue to demand justice and restitution for the 1915 genocide. Assyrians have also started to get organized in various European states to demand their rights. In 1994, the Greek Parliament recognized the Pontic Greek Genocide on the 75th anniversary of the 1919 events. There is now a vast body of common knowledge regarding the true facts of the genocidal events that took place in Turkey from 1915 to 1923, and they can no longer be covered up by the denialist policies of the Turkish state.

Homecoming: Diyarbekir Armenian Language Students Arrive in Armenia[*]

One sunny August morning a bus left Diyarbekir, Turkey, with 50 passengers, and traveled to Yerevan, Armenia via Georgia. At the same time, a man flew from Canada to Yerevan to meet this busload of passengers and lead them on a two- week tour of Armenia.

---

* *Armenian Weekly*, 6 Aug. 2014.

Organizations such as the Gulbenkian Foundation, Hrant Dink Foundation, AGBU, and a few individual Armenians from the U.S. and Canada helped finance the tour. The Armenian minister of diaspora and several senior government officials are scheduled to greet the group.

But what is so special about this group? Why all this attention? They are residents of Diyarbekir, range in age from 18-83, chat in Kurdish or Turkish... Wait, no, they all speak *Armenian*. But there are no Armenians left in Diyarbekir, except for an old couple (and Bayzar *yaya*, the female half of the couple, just passed away two months ago).

So, who *are* these people?

Three years ago, when the biggest Armenian church in the Middle East, Surp Giragos church, was resurrected from its ruins, it served as solid and indisputable evidence of an Armenian presence in historic Armenia before 1915. Some Turks and Kurds, kept in the dark about the facts of 1915, started to question the state version of history, and some initiated the search for the truth. The church also became a living genocide memorial for thousands of Armenians from Armenia and the diaspora visiting the historic homeland. But, more significantly, it became a beacon or a magnet that attracted "hidden Armenians" from various regions near and far. They gathered and met at Surp Giragos. Islamized, Kurdified, or Turkified, they started exchanging family stories and attending cultural events and concerts in growing numbers.

Seeing all this activity come to life, two years ago the church board and the local Diyarbekir Sur municipality decided to offer Armenian-language classes. And now, as a reward for completing the Armenian-language course, the 54 graduates are headed on a tour to Armenia so that they can practice their newly acquired language skills, and develop their understanding of Armenian history and culture.

Almost all of them have some level of "Armenianness" in their family. Some of their families were forcibly converted to Islam in 1915; others have an Armenian grandmother in the family, who was taken in by their Kurdish/Turkish ancestors as a maid, daughter, wife, or worse...

But we don't need to judge or go into the past; rather, we need to focus on the present, on the grandchildren who have now courageously decided to "come out." Some have decided to identify themselves as Christian Armenian, others as Muslim Armenian. Some have changed their Turkish names to Armenian ones, others have still hung on to their names. The

(*Top*) Diyarbekir Armenians on an excursion to Garni in Armenia. (*Below*) An official welcome organized by Sur Municipality on their return to Diyarbekir. Center, standing in dark coat, is Abdullah Demirbas, the mayor of Sur municipality of Diyarbekir.

one common denominator is their desire to learn the Armenian language, history, and culture.

Yet, to truly understand the depth of their courage in "coming out," we must be reminded of the realities in Turkey. Until recently, speaking the Kurdish language was forbidden. Kurds were told they don't exist as a people, that they are mountain Turks who make sounds like "kart kurt" when walking in the snow… The official state policy denied the living existence of Kurds, just like it denied the extermination of the Armenians. These hidden Armenians of Diyarbekir saw their relatives and neighbors lose their jobs, homes, and lives, they saw them arrested, tortured, and "disappeared" by Turkish security forces for speaking Kurdish. And yet, here they are, willing to learn the Armenian language and come out with an identity much more hazardous to their health than the previous Kurdish identity.

In previous articles, I've outlined certain facts about the hidden Armenians of Turkey. In 1915, there were tens of thousands of Armenian orphan boys and girls forcibly Islamized and Turkified, many more captured from the convoys along the deportation routes to the Syrian desert. There were tens of thousands of Armenians who were given protection by a few friendly Kurdish and Alevi tribes, and who eventually got assimilated. There were also quite a few Armenians who converted to Islam to avoid the deportations and massacres in various provinces, at least for a few months in 1915. These people all became the "living victims" of the genocide. Independent studies projecting the Islamized Armenian population numbers, from 1915 to the present, have concluded that the "potential" number of people with Armenian roots in Turkey is in the millions—and more than the present population of Armenia. Of course, it is impossible to predict what percentage of them would be willing or able to "come out" and reclaim their Armenian heritage. But, there is a "back to roots" movement in historic Armenia, even among the Hamshen Armenians in northeast Turkey, who were converted to Islam centuries ago.

A century ago, a 4,000-year-old tree was chopped down, burned, and uprooted in historic Armenia. Spores and seeds from the toppled tree were scattered to all corners of the world, creating the Armenian Diaspora. But some of the *roots* survived, and after staying dormant for a hundred years, tiny seedlings are sprouting again. This trip is a historic first in nurturing those seedlings, a first step perhaps in re-creating an Armenian presence in historic Armenia. It will introduce Armenia to the hidden Armenians, but it will also introduce the hidden Armenians to Armenia.

In addition to the triple realities of Armenians in Armenia, Artsakh, and the diaspora, we now have a fourth reality of emerging hidden Armenians. In the next few days, we will observe many emotional highs and lows while touring Armenia, visiting Echmiadzin, the Genocide Museum, and many historic and cultural sites. We will record their reactions to Armenia, and the reactions of the local Armenians to them.

Poetic Justice: Diyarbekir Armenians Baptized at Echmiadzin[*]

The homecoming trip of the (no more) hidden Armenians from Diyarbekir to Armenia finally began this week, after months of planning, preparation, resolving issues, and seemingly endless three-way long distance discussions from Diyarbekir to Yerevan and Toronto.

And now, the "new" Armenians of Diyarbekir are strolling in the streets and museums of Yerevan, tiptoeing into the various churches scattered all over Armenia. Emotions are near the surface… One moment they burst into dancing in the streets as soon as they hear a playful tune, and the next moment they cry uncontrollably at a scene which may mean nothing to passersby but has reminded them of something, someone – all the way back to 1915.

Yerevan is full of Armenian kids from all over the world as part of the "Ari Dun" program at the invitation of the Ministry of Diaspora, which has also helped organize our itinerary. Government officials arranged to meet the Diyarbekir group on our first day, along with hundreds of the Diaspora kids. The Diyarbekir group was extremely anxious about how they will be greeted. The Armenian officials were equally curious about these Turkish/Kurdish speaking individual—ranging in age from 18 to 83—mostly middle-aged, and representing all socio-economic and education levels. Among them are teachers, students, doctors, housewives, and retired individuals. Some of them are sophisticated urban dwellers; others are going abroad for the first time.

---

* *Armenian Weekly*, 8 Aug. 2014.

I am acting as the translator (from Armenian to Turkish and back), but my task needs to be more than just to relay statements and messages. On the one hand, I have to be able to convey, from Turkish to Armenian, the incredible desire and courage of these individuals in becoming new Armenians; and on the other hand, I have to be able to convey, from Armenian to Turkish, the honest sincerity of welcome of the government officials. But I am happy to report that by the end of the meeting, the previously anxious Diyarbekir Armenians and the previously serious-looking government officials were dancing the Diyarbekir *"halay"* together to Armenian music, while the kids from the Diaspora, Russia, the U.S., France, Iran, and elsewhere, watched these grown-up kids in amazement. A government official says his parents are from Mush, another one says from Sasun, then one of the Diyarbekir Armenians screams "My father is from Sasun, too," and the common stories from Sasun pour forth. They don't need my translation anymore, they have already started comparing Sasun village names and hugging one another...

I had been a bit apprehensive when the Diaspora Ministry representatives told me they had planned two hours of Armenian language lessons each day as part of the itinerary, thinking that our group would be more interested in sightseeing. To my surprise, they all burst into enthusiastic applause and were deeply grateful for the lessons.

When we visited the Madenataran with its manuscript treasures and the village of Oshagan where Mesrob Mashdots, the creator of the Armenian alphabet, is buried, they understood better the mystery of the strange letters that they saw for the first time in their lives just two years ago.

As I reported in previous articles, almost all of the group members have some degree of "Armenianness" in their family, some from one parent, some from both. They have mostly decided to come out as Armenians, but not as Christians—*yet*. Two of them have already been baptized in Diyarbekir's Sourp Giragos church, changing names, identity and religion. Gafur Turkay has become Ohannes Ohanian, his wife Nurcan has become Knar, proudly wearing not one but all three cross necklaces given to her as presents after her baptism. One of the teachers in the group is determined to be baptized at Echmiadzin. The risks he is taking are enormous. He is a primary school teacher in a government school. He may lose his job, circle of friends, or worse; but his mind is made up. In addition, if he is baptized in Echmiadzin instead of back home at Sourp Giragos, he will gain bragging rights over Gafur/Ohannes as being a more complete Christian Armenian... I have arranged for the ceremony beforehand with Bishop Pakrad Galstanian of Echmiadzin, formerly the Canadian Diocese Primate.

We also have a lady who has spent many sleepless nights trying to decide whether she should also get baptized. Her dilemma is even more dangerous. She feels she has an obligation to her long-suffering late father, a hidden Armenian, who had encouraged her to become a Christian Armenian before he passed away. But her devoutly Muslim Kurdish husband has forbidden her from taking this step. The night before our trip to Echmiadzin, she tells me she will not be able to go ahead with the baptism.

In the morning, we are off to Sardarabad, visiting the Victory Museum, understanding the significance and consequences of the 1918 events. As we approach Echmiadzin, the lady with the dilemma walks from the back of the bus to where I am sitting, and tells me her final decision: "My father suffered a lot. I know he is still suffering even though he is dead. I need to do this to end his suffering. If I will suffer as a result of this, I am prepared for it."

So we end up witnessing a double baptism ceremony at Sourp Asdvadzadzin church in Echmiadzin for the "new" Stepan who took his Armenian grandfather's name, and for the new "Anjel" who took her Armenian grandmother's name. I am certain this was the first time in Echmiadzin, or all of Armenia, where the Armenian baptism ceremony was carried out in Armenian along with the Turkish translation word-for-word. At the end, Pakrad *Srpazan* concluded with the statement: "To become a Christian, one needs to be brave, to become both an Armenian and a Christian, one needs to be doubly brave." Everyone had tears in their eyes, including Pakrad *Srpazan*.

Isn't it ironic that these individuals chose to become Armenian on the same day when Turkish Prime Minister and presidential candidate Recep Tayyip Erdoğan stated on national TV: "They [opposition] said I was of Georgian origin. Even uglier, they accused me of being an Armenian, sorry to say"?

Return to the Christian fold : Diyarbekir Armenians choose to
be baptized as members of the Armenian Apostolic church.

And isn't it doubly ironic that if Erdoğan does become President, the
presidential mansion that he will reside in was once owned by an
Armenian family known as the Kasabian family?

Our reporting of the journey through Armenia toward a new life for the
(no more) hidden Armenians will continue.

What's Next for the "Hidden Armenians" of Diyarbekir/ Dikranagerd?[*]

The historic first trip to Armenia of Diyarbekir's "hidden Armenians" is
coming to an end and it is time for us to assess its impact, consequences,
and next steps.

At the end of the first week, we organized a "Dikranagerd Night" at a
beautiful location called the HyeLandz Eco Village in the village of
Keghatir. We invited government officials, academicians, and researchers
following our group, as well as some of the new-found relatives of the
hidden Armenians, whose ancestors had managed to escape to eastern
Armenia after 1915. This reunion between the Islamized Armenians of

---

[*] *Armenian Weekly*, 28 Aug. 2014.

Diyarbekir and their Christian-Armenian relatives was a special one. Needless to say, the dancing and singing kept the whole village awake until the early hours of the morning. During the last few days, the group visited Lake Sevan and there—whether Muslim or Christian—they all reinforced their "Armenianness" by dipping into the holy waters, some just their toes, some their entire bodies... Then they were off to a government camping facility in Dzaghgatsor for a few days, where they had a chance to rest after a whirlwind tour of Armenia, and learn more of the Armenian language, songs, and dances. They all enjoyed the camp, except for the morning gym classes and the "beds from the Stalin era."

On this drive back home to Diyarbekir to resume their lives, perhaps a bit apprehensive about their emerging new identities, I would like to share some of the life stories of these no-more-hidden Armenians. There is enough material for a book or movie for each of the 50 members of the group. Through interviews by the media or Ministry of Diaspora officials, the Armenians of Armenia have started to find out about them. The most interesting responses have been to the question, "When did you realize you had Armenian roots?" Some of them found out they were Armenian when they were already adults, at the deathbed of their parents or grandparents. Some discovered when they were in compulsory military service in the Turkish Army, when their commanders told them they couldn't be trusted because of their "background." Some found out when they were little, when other kids shouted "Armenian" to them in the street or at school; they knew it was a swear word, without knowing its meaning. As they rushed home crying, their parents had to explain that Armenian is not a swear word, but their identity. Some hidden Armenians tried hard to appear as devout Muslims; one even became an imam, a Muslim religious leader, while keeping his identity hidden. However, most hidden Armenians tried to ensure that their children married into other hidden Armenian families. Even the imam gave his daughter to another Islamized Armenian boy, raising questions among his Muslim followers. No matter how much these people tried to hide their Armenian roots, however, it seems that their neighbors or government officials knew about their origins. During disagreements with shopkeepers, businesses, neighboring women or kids at school, the insult of "*gavur*" (infidel) or "devil-rooted Armenian" easily came out, no matter how devout they appeared to be.

One tragicomic story involves three Muslim-Kurdish boys about 8-9 years old; one of them was from a hidden Armenian family, but unaware of his roots at the time. They stole some of those famous Diyarbekir watermelons from the orchard of a hidden Armenian Islamized man. The man caught the three little thieves, but let the two real Muslim-Kurdish boys go and gave a good beating to the hidden Armenian boy. I leave it to the psychologists to ponder the reasons for this man's actions. Years later, this hidden Armenian boy found out about his real identity, and still thinks about this incident.

Another interesting fact that emerged from the interviews is the special place Yerevan Radio has in all Kurdish families' lives, including our hidden Armenians group. As the Kurdish language was banned—and even possessing a Kurdish music tape was a punishable crime in Turkey for several decades—all Kurds tuned in to Yerevan Radio, which broadcast Kurdish news and music for a couple of hours each day. The members of our group all remembered how, when they were growing up, everyone would stop work at their homes or at shops to gather around the radio and hear Yerevan Radio's Kurdish news.

I am confident that the groundbreaking nature of this historic first trip will open the road for other hidden Armenians to follow, but I would like to report on three additional successful outcomes resulting from this trip.

Firstly, two university graduates in our group who wanted to further their graduate studies in Armenia will be able to fulfill their dreams. Through an agreement with Armenian government officials, they will attend Armenian universities with free tuition, mastering the Armenian language during the first year and continuing on in their desired field of study.

Secondly, some members of the group inquired about obtaining Armenian citizenship, perhaps with future plans of retiring in Armenia. As per the existing citizenship requirements, the Armenian government demands documents and proof of Armenian ethnic origin; of course, no such documents exist among our hidden Armenians, except the memories passed on from their parents and grandparents. In discussions with government officials, I proposed the possibility of a baptism document as proof of Armenian origin. I suggested that if a hidden Armenian "comes out" and gets baptized in Armenia—similar to our two members who got baptized in Echmiadzin (see previous article)—then this should be sufficient proof to apply for Armenian citizenship. The proposal was received favorably and will now be discussed in Cabinet, hopefully leading to approval by the government.

Thirdly, learning the Armenian language, history, and culture is essential to re-discovering Armenian roots. The Virtual University run by the AGBU in Yerevan is offering online courses in these subjects. The administrators have agreed to offer these courses for free to all applicants from Turkey. This will have a huge impact on the hidden Armenians of Turkey, wherever they are—in Dersim, Van, Mush, or Diyarbekir—as they can start learning on their own, and in their own homes, even in the absence of organized language courses.

Although this trip was the start of a new reality within the Armenian world, and was received with great enthusiasm by both government officials and the public in Armenia, I must admit that not everyone is on board. There are still quite a few Armenians who disapprove of the time and effort in bringing out the hidden Armenians. Perhaps it is untimely to air our dirty laundry, but I believe the arguments put forth by these disapproving Armenians must be discussed, as some of these people hold important posts within the Armenian Church and in political organizations in the diaspora and in Istanbul. These disapprovers argue that Muslim Armenians are not really Armenian until they convert to Christianity by getting baptized. But then, they argue that they cannot get baptized unless they show proof or documentation of their Armenian origins, until they speak fluent Armenian and "pass tests of being a good Armenian." I believe it is shortsighted and unrealistic to have such requirements for hidden Armenians living in Van or Dersim, who are surrounded by Muslim Turks and Kurds, working in government jobs. The other argument I find incomprehensible is that the emergence of hidden Armenians in large numbers undermine the veracity of the 1915 genocide, and that it is tantamount to strengthening the Turkish case for denial. I have even received comments that Turks will now use the hidden Armenians as proof that the genocide never happened. I should stick to engineering or music, they say, instead of getting involved in these issues. These comments can be dismissed, were it not for the fact that they come from individuals in undeservedly responsible positions in the diaspora and in Istanbul.

Regardless, we will keep on expanding our efforts in Diyarbekir and in other regions of Turkey, pushing the envelope on rules and regulations in order to facilitate the "coming out" of our hidden Armenian brothers and sisters—the grandchildren of the "living" victims of the genocide. There is a Turkish term for these hapless survivors: *kilic artigi*, meaning "remnants of the sword." The attempted murder of a nation and the total confiscation of its wealth took place within Turkey, and as we approach the Centennial, we must realize that its resolution will also take place *within* Turkey. No matter how many events we organize in the Armenian Diaspora or in Armenia, no matter how many third-country parliaments and politicians appear to sympathize with our cause, at the end of the day, the only change will come from within Turkey when the peoples of Turkey realize the truth about 1915 and force their government to stop the denial and deal with the consequences. One of the key components toward this goal will be to re-create an Armenian presence within Turkey. The continuing dialogue between Armenian and Turkish civil societies and opinion makers, combined with the emergence of hidden Armenians within Turkey, are essential toward eliminating both past and present barriers.

I will conclude this series of articles with a tribute to the courage and determination of our hidden Armenians, and a few questions for readers to ponder: How will they be received back in Turkey? How will their families, neighbors, employers, and employees react to their new identity? Just consider Stepan's case, the newly baptized man who works as a teacher at a government school. All of his students are Muslim. He told me he knows there are several kids in his class who come from hidden Armenian Islamized families, but he doesn't know if the kids know about their roots. How will the Muslim kids (or their parents) react to him coming out? How will the hidden Armenian kids (or their parents) react? How will his own kids react?

We are in uncharted waters, but sooner or later, truth and justice will prevail.

Three Fugitives and a Great Crime[*]

Three days after the Marine Minister of Ottoman-Turkey signed the Mudros Ceasefire Treaty aboard the British warship *Agamemnon*, accepting defeat in the First World War, a German submarine picked up three people from three different port locations in Istanbul and spirited them away to

---

[*] *Armenian Weekly*, 3 Nov. 2014.

Ottoman leaders – Talat, Enver and Djemal – who led Ottoman-Turkey into World War I.

Sivastopol in Crimea, and then to Germany. Who were these three persons running away from Istanbul in the middle of the night?

They were the leaders of the Ottoman government—Talat, Enver and Djemal—the triumvirate that led Ottoman-Turkey into World War I, ultimately causing the deaths of millions of Ottoman citizens, the dissolution of the Ottoman Empire, and the deliberate annihilation of the Armenian people from the lands they had inhabited for 4,000 years. Their imperialistic dreams of creating an all Turkic empire called Turan that stretched from Europe to the Caucasus, the Middle East, and into Central Asia—manipulated and encouraged by Germany at the expense of Great Britain and Russia—had failed miserably. Hundreds of thousands of Ottoman Army conscripts had died, and millions of Muslim civilians had become displaced for the sake of this dream. The 1.5 million Armenians regarded as an obstacle to this dream were killed outright or driven to the Syrian desert for a slow death.

Both Turkish and world public opinion had branded Talat, Enver and Djemal as the "Most wanted men and criminals against humanity." German intelligence reports were circulated claiming that these three would be immediately arrested and hanged from street light poles as soon as the Allied occupation forces landed in Istanbul. German leaders who had encouraged the Ottomans to enter the war for their own imperialistic dreams, and who had turned a blind eye to the systematic slaughter of the Armenians during the war, were now afraid that these three would start "singing" upon arrest, would rightly or wrongly blame the Germans for their excesses, and would shift responsibility for the crimes against humanity onto the Germans themselves. Therefore, an escape plan was hatched.

On the night of Nov. 2, 1918, the German boat first picked up Talat, Istanbul Governor Bedri Bey, and five others from the Port of Moda on the Asian shores of Istanbul. The password used to let the Turks come aboard the boat was "Enver." The boat then sailed to Arnavutkoy, on the European side of Istanbul, to pick up Enver and a few other *Ittihat Terakki* Party (or Committee of Union and Progress, CUP) leaders. Following north on the Bosphorus, the boat had a final stop at Istinye for Djemal, before sailing into the Black Sea toward Crimea.

Beginning in May 1919, Talat, Enver and Djemal were tried in absentia by a Turkish military tribunal in Istanbul for "treason, war crimes, and crimes against civilians." On July 5, 1919, the court sentenced all three to be executed. Of course, they were nowhere to be found in Turkey. And it was left to the Armenians to carry out the death sentences through "Operation Nemesis," named after the Goddess of Revenge in Greek mythology.

Talat was executed in Berlin in 1921, Djemal in Tbilisi in 1922, and Enver in Bukhara in 1922. Other *Ittihat Terakki* mass murderers also met justice by Armenian operations, most notably Bahattin Shakir, the leader of the Special Organization (*Teskilat-i Mahsusa*), who organized the implementation of the deportations and mass murders, employing convicted murderers for this purpose, and Cemal Azmi, the governor of Trabzon, who organized the mass drowning of the Armenians of the Black Sea region by shipping them to sea and overturning their boats.

For almost a hundred years, the official history books of the Turkish state have portrayed Britain, Russia, and France as imperialistic powers, with Ottoman-Turkey heroically fighting against them. They have not once mentioned that Ottoman-Turkey was *itself* an imperialistic entity, whose blindly ambitious leaders sent millions of citizens to their deaths without blinking an eye.

The official history books of the Turkish state still portray these three treacherous cowards, who ran away as soon as the war was lost, as national heroes, with their names given to dozens of neighborhoods, schools, streets, and mosques. The official history books still do not mention how much property and assets these three and their followers stole from the Armenians. In fact, the Turkish state passed legislation awarding the houses and assets of murdered Armenians to the families and heirs of these three persons and other executed *Ittihat Terakki* leaders as "blood money"; they continue to receive payments to this day. The denialist policy of the Turkish state was not challenged by the successive brainwashed generations within Turkey. But today, civil society and enlightened citizens of Turkey have started to see the truth and, more importantly, have started to pressure their government to acknowledge the truth, if not out of empathy for the Armenian victims, then for the sake of stopping the embarrassment to themselves as Turkish citizens caused by these blatant lies and denial.

Fethiye Çetin Speaks at 8th Hrant Dink Commemoration in Toronto[*]

On Jan. 18, the Toronto-Armenian community gathered to commemorate the 8th anniversary of the assassination of editor and journalist Hrant Dink, who was murdered in Istanbul on Jan. 19, 2007, in front of the *Agos* newspaper offices.

More than 700 people filled the Armenian Community Center to hear keynote speaker Fethiye Çetin, one of the most prominent lawyers in Turkey. Çetin was Hrant Dink's lawyer while he was alive, and continued to serve as his family's lawyer after his assassination, relentlessly pursuing and investigating the perpetrators of the still-unsolved murder.

I was the master of ceremonies of the event. The commemoration started with a candlelight vigil and a moment of silence remembering Hrant Dink, as well as the latest victims of intolerance toward free press, the murdered journalists of the *Charlie Hebdo* magazine in Paris.

I explained how Hrant Dink became a target of Turkish ultranationalists within the "deep state" that planned his murder, and how officials in the intelligence bureaucracy and state police didn't move a finger to prevent his murder, even though there was overwhelming evidence related to its preparation and implementation. After a beautiful rendition of Gomidas's "*Andouni*" and of "*Anin Desnem ou Mernem*" (words by Hovhannes Shiraz, music by Majag Toshikyan) by young soprano Lynn Anoush Isnar, accompanied by pianist Lena Beylerian, I introduced Fethiye Çetin.

---

[*] *Armenian Weekly*, 20 Jan. 2015.

Fethiye Çetin (*l*) and Raffi Bedrosyan (*r*).

Çetin was born in Maden, Elazig province, and studied law at Ankara University. She is recognized as being the foremost human rights lawyer in Turkey, specializing in minority rights cases. She defended Hrant Dink against charges brought by the state for "insulting Turkishness," only because he dared to speak about the Armenian Genocide. In 2004, Çetin wrote a book, titled *My Grandmother*, revealing her Armenian roots. In it, she explained how her Armenian grandmother was captured as a nine-year-old orphan by a Turkish soldier during the death march of 1915. Although her grandmother was Islamized—and her name changed from Heranoush to Seher—she kept her Armenian roots secret until she was 70 years old, and opened up to her granddaughter, Fethiye Çetin, asking her to find her long-lost brother. After years of searching, Fethiye *did* find her Armenian relatives in New Jersey, but only after her grandmother had passed away.

My Grandmother has been translated into more than a dozen languages. It immediately became a best-seller in Turkey, and opened the floodgates to hundreds of similar stories about hidden, Islamized Armenians. As a result, Fethiye Çetin, in collaboration with Ayşe Gül Altınay, edited another book, called *The Grandchildren*, a compilation of dozens of stories of hidden Armenians. She also initiated a restoration project for destroyed

Armenian fountains in her hometown village of Habap in 2009; several Armenian, Turkish, and Kurdish youth from Turkey, the United States, and France came to Habap to collaborate with local villagers and reconstruct the historic fountains that supplied water to the village.

After Hrant Dink's assassination, Fethiye Çetin represented his family in the murder trials and investigations, which are still unresolved and continue to this day. In 2013, she presented the failure of the judicial system in finding and sentencing the real perpetrators of the Dink murder, as well as the gross negligence and cover-up of state officials, in a book titled, *I Am Ashamed: The Trials of the Hrant Dink Murder Case.*

In a moving speech at the Jan. 18 event, Çetin explained the struggle between individuals' memory and conscience versus state pressure to make people forget past crimes. Below are excerpts from the speech.

***

"My grandmother was about 70 years old when she told me her story, as seen by her as a nine-year-old girl, about the 1915 disaster, the death march, followed by silence, pain, and loneliness. Nearly 60 years had passed after the terror that she experienced, but my grandmother still remembered very clearly her village, her house, all the names of her relatives, including her grandmother, her grandfather, her cousins, even the name of the village official. Despite all the external attempts to make her forget, she remembered everything that she and her family had lived through. It was as if she had kept repeating the story to herself for 60 years, in order not to forget....

"The official state version of history in Turkey is also subject to a similar policy of permanent amnesia regarding the 1915 events. A typical example is a statement given by Sevket Sureyya Aydemir, the author of Mustafa Kemal's biography: 'I believe the fighting and settling of accounts between Turks and Armenians is a page of human history best to be forgotten. Which side was responsible? Who was guilty? I think it is better not to find out answers to these questions and forget these events forever.'...

"But unfortunately, despite all attempts, laws, and pressures to make people forget these events forever, this policy cannot be implemented....

"On the other hand, the state which forces individuals to forget the past keeps all the information, records, documents about the past under its control, in locked safes and rooms, in places beyond the reach of the public, in order to bring them out and use them as discriminatory policies against the minorities, the "leftovers of the sword," the ones defined as 'others.' In other words, on the one hand the state uses every means to make people forget the past, but on the other hand the state never forgets the past and keeps reminding the people about the differences in the minorities. As a result, the forced amnesia policy becomes converted to a policy of continuous remembering....

"With the emergence in recent years of many stories about the past, with biographies, books, films, documentaries, panels, and conferences, one can conclude that the monopoly of the state in controlling the past has come to an end....

"Local memories have started a revival because the great crime was witnessed by all local people. Despite the attempts to wipe out traces of the past, it is impossible for the local memories to be forgotten....

"Remembering and facing the past is now a must for the Turkish people....

"Truth and justice are deadly fears of the perpetrator. The perpetrator attempts to hide the truth with all its might, mechanisms, and institutions. This is why memory is the enemy of the government....

"In my country the most important name of this resisting force is Hrant Dink. Because Hrant Dink, with his stand, kept on reminding them of their past full of crimes, the past which they desperately tried to make people forget. Because Hrant Dink not only kept reminding them of the truth about the past, but everyone that he touched with his words—his readers, his listeners, his followers, people in the street—everyone believed him. They murdered Hrant Dink, because he stood right where the state had drawn the red lines, the taboos that it feared. Hrant Dink became the only visible target for the historical hatred against Armenians, and he stood in the crosshairs of both opposition and government forces....

"The hatred for Armenians also became quite apparent in all the trials and investigations following the murder, as the perpetrator of the crime— the state—ensured that all the state officials would be exempt from any investigation. During these eight years since the murder, the competing forces in the government still use the murder as war material against each other....

"I am one of the closest witnesses of Hrant Dink's murder. I was with him in the court cases throughout the long preparation stage of the murder. My evidence is based on *my* eyewitness account. I presented and continue presenting to the judiciary and prosecution all I know, I see, I think about this murder. But unfortunately, all my efforts so far have ended up in countless binders or in notes attached to desk calendars. They were not included in formal prosecution inquiries, evidence that I pointed out was not investigated, suspects that I pointed out were not questioned....

"The history of this country is full of cases where criminals are not tried, even if tried are not punished, where the perpetrators do everything possible to make society forget the crime. Our history has countless political assassinations and unsolved murders....

"I acted as Hrant Dink's lawyer before his murder, and I am his family's lawyer after the murder. Obviously I do not possess the force and resources of the prosecutor to uncover the real planners and perpetrators of this murder. I don't have intelligence organizations at my control either, which could provide me with clues and information. I base my case only on what I witness, and what I see in the trial documents.

"Yes, our history is full of shameful events, unaccounted crimes, unsolved murders. We inherited this shame from the past, but we are responsible not to pass it on to future generations. I want to pledge, with you as witness, that I will try to bring to account all the shame and present a clean future to the next generations. My promise is a promise to Hrant, that I will continue to seek truth and justice, to the utmost of my abilities and until the end of my life."

***

The Toronto commemoration was more proof that Hrant Dink's legacy lives on and gains more momentum every year, both within Turkey and in all four corners of the world, with demands of truth and justice to prevail for 1.5 million Armenians plus one—for Hrant Dink himself.

Letter: Hrant Dink (1954-1915)*

Dear Editor,

The title is not a misprint.

Hrant Dink was murdered in 1915.

* *Armenian Weekly*, 21 Jan. 2015.

Hrant Dink was murdered because of 1915, because he brought out the truth about 1915.

The same criminals who planned and implemented 1915 also murdered Hrant Dink.

The criminals in 1915 did not only murder people like Hrant Dink— the leaders, the brains and hearts of the Armenian nation—but they followed up by murdering most of the men.

They kidnapped the victims' wives and daughters. They took them as wives, maids, or even worse. They branded them with tattoos, and sold them as slaves in slave markets.

They took the orphaned grandchildren. They placed them in Muslim homes. They Turkified and Islamized them.

They took the victims' assets—houses, shops, valuable possessions— and divided them among themselves. The government legalized this plunder by handing out deeds to the stolen properties.

They did this not only to the leaders, but to hundreds, thousands—no, hundreds of thousands—of families, until one and a half million Armenians were wiped out from their homeland.

This is the truth about 1915; and it is still denied by the Turkish state. The peoples of Turkey are now beginning to discover the truth, but— unfortunately—only after Hrant Dink's murder.

As we commemorate the 8th anniversary of the murder of Hrant Dink, we also commemorate the centennial anniversary of the attempted murder of the Armenian nation.

The Armenians who survived the genocide will continue the struggle until truth and justice prevails.

Sincerely,

Raffi Bedrosyan

Turkey's Tactics of "Oriental Slyness"[*]

Turkey has announced that the annual commemoration of the Gallipoli Dardanelles battles of World War I, which was traditionally held on March 18, will be held on April 24 this year. President Recep Tayyip Erdoğan has invited more than 120 world leaders, including President

[*] *Armenian Weekly*, 24 Feb. 2015.

Serge Sarkisian of Armenia, to attend the Gallipoli ceremonies. The reason for the date change is apparent to all Armenians.

There is a term in Turkish, "*Sark kurnazligi*," which means "Oriental slyness." The term is used to define a person who resorts to cunning to deceive another, but both the deceiver and the deceived know that there is trickery involved, and more cynically, the deceiver does not care if the deceived person is aware of the deceit.

Already, a few state leaders have announced that they will attend, including "Turkey's little brother" Azerbaijan, some African and Muslim states, and notably, Prince Charles.

It is worthwhile to remind these guests, and the entire English-speaking world, of another Turkish scheme involving trickery of dates that happened eight years ago.

The Holy Cross Church and Monastery complex on Aghtamar Island in Lake Van in eastern Turkey had been in ruins since 1915 and, in fact, was being willfully destroyed in the 1950s by the Turkish Army. Only interference by famous Kurdish author Yashar Kemal (whose hidden Armenian roots were recently revealed) prevented the complete destruction of the last remaining church. In the 2000s, the Turkish government decided to restore the church as a museum. The restoration was completed in early 2007, and the government announced the date of the opening of the museum to be April 24, 2007.

The Istanbul Armenian Patriarch of the time, Archbishop Mesrob Mutafyan, forcefully protested that by choosing this date the government was attempting to create political gains using Armenians' pain, and that he would refuse to attend the opening ceremony if this insensitive decision was not revised. The government appeared to appease the patriarch but, continuing to employ tactics of "Oriental slyness," announced that the date would now be April 11, 2007. The government was fully aware that April 11 was equally significant and unacceptable to the Armenians, as in the old calendar, which was in effect in 1915, April 11 was the same date as April 24. In fact, in 1919, the famous Armenian journalist Teotig, himself a survivor of the genocide, had compiled a list and the biographies of the 761 Armenian intellectuals arrested and subsequently murdered, in a booklet called *Houshartsan Abril 11-i* (*Memorial to April 11*).

The first April 24 commemoration took place in 1919, with the opening of a memorial sculpture called "*Abril 11 Houshartsan*," in the

Istanbul Armenian Cemetery in Taksim. In the 1930s, the cemetery was expropriated and converted to the famous Taksim Square, the scene of recent protests against the government. All of these facts, known to both the Armenians in Turkey and the Turkish government, were revealed in an editorial in the *Agos* newspaper that questioned the wisdom of using these dates for the Aghtamar opening, under the headline: "Are you sure? Is this your final answer?" The headline was copied after the often-repeated question heard on the-then popular TV quiz show, "Who wants to be a millionaire?"

The date of that *Agos* editorial, Jan. 19, 2007—the day Hrant Dink was shot dead in front of the *Agos* newspaper offices.

The Aghtamar Museum was opened on March 29, 2007. Patriarch Mutafyan reluctantly attended, and shortly thereafter, he became incapacitated with a still-unexplained debilitating mental disease, and continues to live in a vegetative state. In the meantime, eight years after Dink's murder, the real perpetrators and conspirators of the murder have neither been caught nor tried.

Therefore, it is now appropriate to again ask the Turkish government that sent the Gallipoli invitations for April 24, 2015, and any state leaders who choose to ignore the real significance of this date: "Are you sure? Is this your final answer?"

Dersim Leaders Embrace Armenian Roots, Plan Armenia Trip[*]

Armenian Weekly readers will remember well the historic first journey taken by 50 "hidden Armenians" from Diyarbekir (Dikranagerd) last August to Armenia. These brave individuals were the grandchildren of forcefully Islamized/Turkified/Kurdified Armenians from 1915, who had the determination and guts to return to their roots after the reconstruction of Sourp Giragos church in Diyarbekir, the first Armenian church to be resurrected in Turkey since 1915. As a reward for participating in an Armenian-language course organized by the local Diyarbekir Sur municipality and the Church Foundation, they were taken on an unforgettable journey to Armenia, to better understand their forgotten

---

[*] *Armenian Weekly*, 4 March 2015.

history, culture, and heritage.

I am happy to report that the "coming out" of the hidden Armenians is not restricted to Diyarbekir. Now, it is the turn of the hidden Armenians of Dersim (officially, Tunceli province) in Turkey. Dersim is a vast mountainous region with beautiful valleys, dotted with hundreds of picturesque villages between Erzurum (known as Garin by Armenians) and Erzinjan (known as Yerzinga) in eastern Turkey. Prior to 1915, Alevi Kurds and Armenians populated the region. The Alevi Kurds, who have traditionally been sympathetic to Armenians, did not participate in the 1915 massacre and plunder of Armenians; in fact, they saved tens of thousands of Armenians, either by protecting them against the Ottoman Turkish Army within their own villages, or providing them safe passage toward Russian Armenia.

As a "reward" for protecting the Armenians and for "rebelling" against the new regime, the Alevi Kurds paid dearly 20 years later, in the 1930s, when the Republican Turkish Army indiscriminately killed most of them, including thousands of assimilated, Kurdified Armenians. The army's methods varied from assembling the civilian population—men, women, and children—into caves filled with poisonous gases, to killing them with machine guns.

Fast forward to today, and hidden Armenians are emerging from among the Alevi Kurdish population of the region, reclaiming their Armenian identity, changing their Turkish/Kurdish names to Armenian ones, and beginning to learn Armenian. After overcoming numerous obstacles, and logistical and organizational challenges, an Armenian-language course was launched on Feb. 1, with dozens—young and old—registering for the three times-per-week classes. An Armenian and Alevi cultural association has also been formed, named "Deradost," which stands for Dersim Armenians and Alevis Friendship Society. There is also "Dersiyad," which promotes cooperation and support among Armenians in Dersim, as well as Dersim Armenians in Istanbul and abroad, mostly in Germany.

Similar to the initiative that took Diyarbekir's hidden Armenians to Armenia, a trip is now planned for some of Dersim's hidden Armenians to visit Armenia in late March. But there is an added significance and a historic first in this trip: All 12 of the participants are *elected village officials* of hidden Armenian villages in Dersim. During this trip, they will learn about Armenian history and culture, but, through TV and media, they

The author making a presentation in Los Angeles in October 2015.

will also show the Armenians of Armenia and the diaspora the historic Armenian churches and monuments from their *own* villages, prior to 1915 and now. The trip is sponsored by an individual from Canada, as well as by the Calouste Gulbenkian Foundation, following several e-mails and phone calls between Lisbon, Dersim, Istanbul, Yerevan, and Toronto.

Details about this historic trip and the reflections of the Dersim village officials during their visit to Armenia will be revealed in future articles.

100 Years Later — Genocide Commemoration in Detroit[*]

DETROIT — On April 21, the Detroit United Committee, composed of the Armenian Democratic Liberal Party, Tekeyan Cultural Association, Armenian General Benevolent Union, Knights of Vartan, Daughters of Vartan, Detroit Armenian Women's Club, University of Michigan (Dearborn) Armenian Research Center, and Wayne State University Society of Armenian Students, held an Armenian Genocide centennial commemoration at the AGBU Alex and Marie Manoogian School in Southfield.

Dr. Hosep Torossian, the high school principal, opened the program with remarks in both Armenian and English. He reminded the large audience that the attention of much of the world was on Armenia and the Armenian Genocide, due in large part to the prominence and comments of Pope Francis and Kim Kardashian, both of whose names Dr. Torossian, in his own words, "dared to mention in the same breath," eliciting laughter.

St. John Armenian Church Choir Director Rubik Mailian beautifully rendered the American and Armenian national anthems. He was accompanied by pianist Margaret Lafian.

The emcee for the program was Oakland County Judge Lisa Assadoorian. She presented a moving video by Sen. Debbie Stabenow (D-Mich), and acknowledged the presence of a representative for junior Sen. Gary Peters (D-Mich.). A Proclamation signed by State of Michigan Governor Rick Snyder was read, declaring April 24 Armenian Genocide Remembrance Day. Other state and local political figures had sent their representatives, as well.

---

* *The Armenian Mirror Spectator*, 21 May 2015.

Writer, literary critic, and political commentator Edmond Azadian noted in his remarks that even though there is much discussion these days about the righteous Turks who saved the lives of some Armenian survivors, we should not lose sight of the collective guilt regarding the colossal crime committed against the Armenian people and the responsibility of the Turkish government to properly acknowledge the crime and deal with the issues of territorial and monetary reparations.

As a musical interlude, Yerevan-born cellist Lusine Petrosyan played two well-known folk pieces, Groong and Hov Arek, by Gomidas Vartabed. Manoogian High School Senior Nikole Davtyan read the familiar excerpt from William Saroyan's "The Armenian and the Armenian."

The keynote speaker was Toronto Armenian scientist and activist Raffi Bedrosyan, who has made several trips to historic Armenia, the most recent four days after this event in Detroit, when he played the piano at a hundredth anniversary commemorative concert at the newly restored St. Giragos Armenian church in Diyarbekir. During his slide presentation and lecture, Bedrosyan, who had previously spoken in Detroit about the hidden Islamized Armenians in Turkey, spoke about "The No Longer Islamized Armenians in Turkey." He took his captivated audience along with him through the streets of Diyarbekir, interviewing many who have courageously come forward to reclaim their Armenian identity. He explained that some of these Armenians have chosen to convert to their ancestral faith while others have chosen to immerse themselves in the study of the Armenian language and culture, as a means of reclaiming their heritage, but, at the same time, have elected to remain Muslim.

The program came to an end with a closing prayer by the local clergy, led by the pastor emeritus of St. John Armenian church, Rev. Fr. Diran Papazian, Rev. Fr. Abraham Ohanesian and Rev. Shant Barsoumian.

Sick People: Open Letter to Mr. Erdoğan and Mr. Davutoğlu[*]

The following is the translation of an article which was published in the Turkish Taraf *daily on May 13, 2015. The author Raffi Bedrosyan was involved in organizing the Surp Giragos Diyarbekir/Dikranagerd church*

[*] *Horizon Weekly*, 26 May 2015.

reconstruction project. In September 2012, he gave the first Armenian piano concert in the Surp Giragos church since 1915. The article has received thousands of comments, both positive and negative.

Dear Mr. Erdoğan and Mr. Davutoğlu,

I am writing this open letter to you in response to your statements that if third parties do not interfere, Armenians and Turks would be able to have a more meaningful dialogue. Even though Mr. Davutoğlu now says that Diaspora is full of hatred, anger and vengeance, he had declared in the past that "the Armenian Diaspora is also our Diaspora;" therefore, as a Diaspora Armenian and a Turkish citizen, as well as someone who has spent time and energy on Turkish-Armenian issues, I have decided to share my thoughts.

We Armenians are a sick people, as long as Turkey denies the truths of 1915. We are stuck in 1915, and cannot get rid of the trauma of 1915. But as long as the Turkish state continues to hide and deny the truths of 1915, the Turkish people will remain even sicker. The ones who know the truth but deny and lie about it are sick. The ones who are not aware of the truth because they are brainwashed for four generations over a hundred years are also sick. It is up to you to continue or to end this sickness.

Yes, I admit I am sick. Just like hundreds of thousands of Armenian women, children and elderly men, my grandmother who lived in Bursa was also ordered to be deported in 1915, while pregnant, while her husband was serving in the Ottoman army. She gave birth to a baby boy near Konya, while walking with the rest of the deportation convoy. The baby, who would be my uncle, lasted ten days without food or water. My grandmother placed the dead baby under a rock, and continued walking while being clubbed by the gendarmes, all the way to Syria, over several months. She miraculously survived the ordeal and returned to Bursa after the war, but when she tried to enter her house, she was severely beaten by Muslim Turks who had already taken possession of her house. I wasn't told of these facts until I was eighteen, and no history textbooks in Turkey ever mentioned these facts. When I found out about these facts, I decided to leave Turkey and moved to Canada. The Armenian family, originally from Tokat, with whom I stayed temporarily made me even more sick. The elder Agop Dede, in his eighties, kept saying that he smells urine everyday. He told me that in 1915 while he was about four years old, the murderers of Teskilat-i Mahsusa (Special Organization of the Ottoman state) rounded up the Tokat Armenians. His mother hid him under her skirt, and while she was being beheaded, she urinated on him.

Ever since that day Agop Dede smelled urine every day of his life until his death. Almost every Armenian family in the Diaspora has a story like this from 1915, each one an undeniable historic fact. Almost every Armenian orphan who remained in Turkey and ended up being forcefully Islamized and Turkified as living victims of 1915, has a story like this, more undeniable facts.

I ask you: Did the Armenian women, children and elderly from Bursa, Tokat, or all corners of Anatolia and even Thrace, "stabbed the Ottoman army in the back in the eastern war zone against the Russians." as you keep repeating? Did they join with the "Imperialist states and tried to declare independence"? What kind of threat did these people pose to the state? Until when are you going to deceive your people and parrot the empty rhetoric of "unavoidable losses during war conditions, more Muslims died than the Armenians, no massacres but just a required relocation, our common pain"? When will you face and admit that the Ittihad Terakki government took wrong decisions, ended up losing an empire and caused the death of untold numbers of Muslims, attempted the destruction of the entire Armenian people who lived on their historic homeland for four thousand years, and plundered the entire assets and wealth of the eliminated Armenians? When will you admit and accept these facts? When? Is it the fear of returning the plundered assets that prevents you from accepting the facts? The dead body of the Armenian people is still on the ground in front of you, while you sit on its assets.

If we make a comparison with the present state of affairs, would it be acceptable for the Turkish state to round up, deport and murder all Kurdish women, children and elderly from all over Turkey, just because the army cannot handle the PKK guerrilla movement? This is what the Ottoman state did to the Armenians in 1915. You will either call the murderers as "murderers," or, as you did until now, will you continue to deny the murder and join the murderers, and blame everyone who asks you to face the historic facts as "full of hatred, anger and vengeance," or accuse everyone as "being murderers themselves."

You keep saying "We have opened our archives, let the Armenians also open theirs." You know well this is not true. Let us leave aside the countless foreign state archives, documents, studies by international scholars, and just consider the honest, ethical Turkish scholars who have found enough facts of genocide from the Ottoman archives, which escaped the state attempts of scrutiny and elimination of any incriminating evidence. Aren't you aware of these Turkish publications? And yet, you are the ones who hide the two most critical archives. The 33 dossiers from 33 provinces which documented the names, numbers, dates of deported Armenians, the list of assets that they left behind, are all kept in the Turkish Prime Ministerial Archival Offices, if not already destroyed. The Turkish Army Chief of Staff ordered in 2005 a ban on the translation and publication of Ottoman era property deeds, stating that "this is against state interests." When will you have the courage to open up these documents?

These bans, denials and falsifications shaped the (mis)understanding of the 1915 history by the Turkish people until recently. But the number of people who face historic facts is increasing rapidly in Turkey, especially and unfortunately after Hrant Dink's death. Even more significantly, these people are now starting to pressure the Turkish state to face the historic truths as well. Turks who don't know the historic facts, become sick when they go abroad and face accusations of being liars. Turks who do know the facts but deny them, also become sick when they go abroad, as they are acutely aware that foreigners know the facts and moreover, they know that the Turks are lying. Turks then become isolated, defensive and burdened with this dreadful weight placed on their shoulders. This is an undeserved injustice to the present generations of Turkey. It is your responsibility to lift this weight and eliminate the sickness from your people, instead of being preoccupied with the number of ultra-nationalist votes that you may lose potentially.

I know you are allergic to the use of the word "genocide." But it is still possible to face the historic facts of 1915 and to start dealing with justice and restitution for the Armenian people without using any terms and definitions. What are you waiting for to implement positive measures, without any further buildup of external and internal pressures? I had listed several justice and restitution measures in my previous articles, as well as presented them to the "wise men" that Mr. Davutoğlu had sent recently to open up communication channels with the Diaspora. But it seems that all positive proposals and suggestions on this issue "goes in one ear, and comes out the other," as Mr. Erdoğan recently stated.

Reflections on Turkey's Parliamentary Election[*]

On June 7, Turkish citizens went to the polls to elect 550 members of the Turkish Parliament. What did the election mean for the Armenians of Turkey, of Armenia, and of the diaspora?

First, a few facts and context for the reader: More than 85 percent of the eligible 55 million voters—some 45 million people—voted. Turkey's President Recep Tayyip Erdoğan, who is supposed to be impartial and above party politics by law, relentlessly campaigned every day on behalf of his former party, the Justice and Development Party (AKP), leaving the current prime minister and leader of the party, Ahmet Davutoğlu, mostly out of the limelight. The two opposition parties, the Kemalist/nationalist Republican Party (CHP) and the ultra-nationalist/racist National Movement Party (MHP), tried to attack the governing AKP, but were mostly ineffective. The rising star in the election was the newly formed pro-Kurdish party, the People's Democratic Party (HDP), which ran an extremely effective campaign, organizing not only in Kurdish-populated regions but fielding candidates all over Turkey on a platform of equality, peace, and democracy for all ethnic minorities and the underprivileged. The HDP faced the additional obstacle of needing to go over the barrier of 10 percent of the total votes, failing which they would lose the right to be represented in parliament.

Despite the enormous success of the AKP and Erdoğan in the previous 10 elections—for the considerable economic progress made and the increase in the standards of living and prosperity, the accomplishments in eliminating the interference of the army in politics, and the success of starting a peace process with the Kurdish guerilla movement and ending the daily killing of Turkish soldiers and Kurdish resistance fighters—this election had become a referendum on whether to allow Erdoğan to become a dictator or not.

Erdoğan wanted to increase the powers of the presidential office to be able to govern without much interference and accountability to the elected politicians. He would be able to do that if the AKP elected 330 or more members of parliament. And Erdoğan attacked the weak opposition of the CHP and MHP with utmost contempt for their incompetence, meanwhile ignoring the swelling hatred against him and his cronies after

[*] *Armenian Weekly*, 26 June 2015.

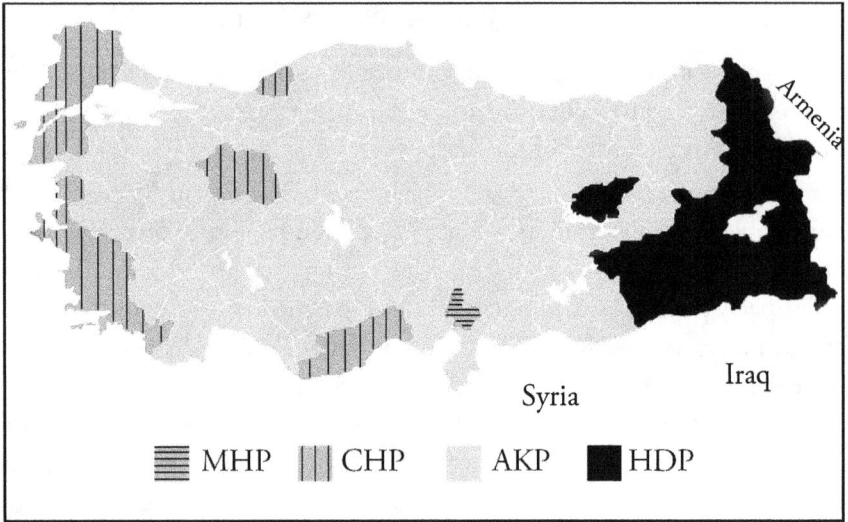

Turkish election results, June 2015.

the discovery of major corruption and bribery scandals, the opulence of a 1,100 room presidential palace that he built for himself, and the revelation of truckloads of arms secretly transferred by Turkish intelligence to ISIS and other forces fighting against the Syrian regime.

The main obstacle against Erdoğan's wish to become a Putin-like president with absolute powers seemed to be the unknown number of HDP voters. If the HDP exceeded the 10 percent barrier, it would elect at least 60 MPs, but if the HDP failed to exceed the 10 percent barrier, all votes cast for the party would be lost—and transferred to elect 60 or more MPs for the AKP. Therefore, President Erdoğan, Prime Minister Davutoğlu, and other AKP leaders attacked the HDP more than the CHP and MHP.

One of the strategies used to discredit HDP was employing the tried and true tactic of hatred against Armenians. It was claimed that the HDP's leaders had made agreements with Diasporan Armenian leaders, promising land and compensation to Armenians. It was claimed that more than 100 HDP candidates were "hidden Armenians." It was claimed that if the HDP came to power, they would kick out all Kurds from eastern and southeastern Turkey and cede those regions to Armenia. Kurds were warned against voting for the HDP, if they wanted to keep their lands. They were ordered to stay away from HDP election campaigns, which were organized by Armenians.

During the election campaigns, seven HDP sympathizers were murdered, more than 500 HDP sympathizers were beaten, burned, and injured, and more than 150 HDP party offices and campaign vehicles were attacked, burned, or bombed.

The results of the election? The AKP elected 256 MPs with 40.86 percent of votes; the CHP elected 132 with 24.95 percent; the MHP elected 80 with 16.29 percent; and the new HDP elected 80 MPs with 13.12 percent of the votes, easily exceeding the 10 percent barrier.

The election results indicate that the AKP could not form a government on its own. Apart from this conclusion, there are now many uncertain scenarios emerging, as to what sort of coalition government can happen, and which parties will go to bed with each other.

The AKP can form a government with either the CHP, MHP or HDP. Failing that—and to the horror of the AKP—the CHP, MHP and HDP can join together and form a government. If that doesn't work either, then there will be early elections. At present, it is too early to tell what sort of policy toward Armenians within and outside Turkey will be adopted, as it will depend on the new coalition partners' composition.

These elections were unprecedented from several aspects. Three Armenian MPs were elected, one each from the HDP, CHP, and AKP. The Armenians of Turkey are now over-represented, with 0.5 percent in the parliament, versus a population proportion of only 0.07 percent. But as Garo Paylan, the newly elected HDP MP, stated, "Rather than the *number* of Armenians in the parliament, it is more important what each of them will *say* in the parliament." The other emerging fact to ponder is the emergence of the HDP as the winner in 16 border provinces. As can be seen in the map, with HDP elected in all of the eastern and most of the southeastern provinces, the Turkish people have now lost contact and borders with Georgia, Armenia, Iran, Iraq, and half of Syria.

The story will continue to unfold.

Project Rebirth: Homecoming of "Hidden Armenians"[*]

Some came by chartered bus from Diyarbekir, Sasun, and Urfa, others by public transport from Dersim through Tbilisi. A few came by rail from

---

[*] *Armenian Weekly*, 11 Aug. 2015.

Artvin in the Hamshen region via Batumi, others drove their own cars from Hopa. The destination for all? Yerevan, Armenia.

Following the success of the historic first trip of 50 "hidden" Islamized Armenians from Diyarbekir, Turkey, to Armenia last August to re-discover their roots, culture, and language, the project was repeated again this year in an expanded fashion.

The trip, now formally named Project REBIRTH: VERADZNOUNT, was part of a wide range of activities supporting Islamized Armenians. This year, 80 selected Islamized Armenians were brought from Turkey to the homeland to participate in the Ari-Tun event organized by the Ministry of Diaspora.

After several months of planning, fundraising, organizing, and negotiating with government officials and hotels in Armenia, the trip was set for the first week of August.

The participants were met in Yerevan by the organizer of the tour, who flew in from Toronto, Canada. The timing of the trip was made to coincide with the Pan-Armenian Games, which brought more than 6,200 Armenian athletes from all over the world to Armenia, including 450 from Turkey, representing the historic Armenian homeland teams from Van, Bitlis, Mush, Dersim, Diyarbekir, and Musa Ler.

This year, more emphasis was placed on having the younger generation participate in the trip; as a result, several children of those who came last year were now part of the group. The age of the participants ranged from 11 to 87. The Islamized Armenians come from all walks of life; they are teachers, lawyers, artists, writers, poets, high school and university students, business people, housewives, and retired pensioners. They may have different perspectives about almost every subject, but they all share one common goal: to search for and find their Armenian roots. Their life stories and quest for their roots are as different as themselves.

They are all descendants of the "living victims" of the 1915 Armenian Genocide—orphaned Armenian boys and girls who were captured, protected, hidden, or bought by Turks and Kurds, and who became Islamized, Turkified and Kurdified.

As the grandchildren of these assimilated orphans, they became aware of their Armenian roots during different stages of their lives. Some found out about their Armenian origins at an early age, while others discovered it in their adulthood, on their parents' or grandparents' deathbed.

During this trip, they eagerly participated in Armenian-language classes every morning, followed by expeditions to significant historic sites during the day, and cultural events in the evenings. Interestingly, the participants from the Hamshen region already spoke a dialect of Armenian and could easily understand or be understood by Armenians in the street.

One of the Armenian cultural events the entire group attended was a concert I gave, performing the works of Komitas, Khatchaturian, Alan Hovhaness, and Edgar Hovanissian. The full-house concert and the activities of the group were followed widely by the Armenian media and TV.

As a result of this trip, the participants will no longer be hidden Armenians when they return to Turkey, as their real identities have been revealed at considerable risk to themselves and their families. They may be discriminated against by their employers, lose their jobs if working in the public sector, lose their Muslim friends, neighbors, and even the rest of their families who prefer to remain Muslim Turks or Kurds. But they are all willing to take the risk.

Throughout the trip, the expectations, short- and long-term goals of Project Rebirth and the needs of the hidden Armenians were discussed. As courageous people willing to take the risk of revealing their Armenian identities, they need support mechanisms related to Armenian-language instruction, increased interaction and exchanges with cultural groups to and from Armenia, and technical and professional help related to restoration projects for abandoned or destroyed Armenian churches, cemeteries, and other monuments in their cities and villages.

More importantly, on a personal level, they may need financial, legal, and social services help for family and employment problems triggered from revealing their Armenian identities.

The Project Rebirth organizers hope to engender a willingness in these new Armenians to learn the Armenian language and history, organize among themselves the planning and implementation of the restoration of Armenian churches and buildings, arrange regular social and cultural activities to encourage others to "come out," and more critically, pass along their desire to return to their Armenian roots to their children and the next generation.

The goals and objectives of Project Rebirth are now well defined, and a few of the short-term goals have already been achieved. One example was the agreement negotiated between the organizer and the Ministry of Diaspora last year to have two university students from Diyarbekir, who had participated in last years' trip, continue their studies in Armenia with free tuition. After a year of intensive Armenian language instruction in Yerevan University, we watched with great pride and satisfaction as one of these students acted as a guide and translator to the participants of this year's trip.

The ultimate goal of Project Rebirth is nothing short of creating an Armenian presence again on historic Armenian lands within Turkey, in terms of people, culture, and architecture.

Although there is support and appreciation by certain influential leaders in Armenia, the significance and potential of Project Rebirth is not yet fully understood by some diasporan leaders and organizations. It is our hope that with increased understanding of the new realities related to the hidden Armenians in Turkey, Armenians within the diaspora and Armenia will be able to undo some of the damages of the past through Project Rebirth.

To Baptize or Not to Baptize the "Hidden Armenians"*

Along with the many high points experienced during the historic Armenia trip of the 80 "hidden Armenians" from Turkey, there were also a few low points. The highs included warm welcomes by both Armenian government officials and common people on the street, emotional triumphs at Sardarabad, feelings of grief at the Genocide Memorial and Museum, new-found friendships, accomplishments like spelling the alphabet during Armenian-language classes, and simply being able to order food in Armenian at a restaurant. However, I want to point out a few of the lows our hidden Armenians encountered—all related to baptism.

From our group, two girls from Dersim and a young man from Diyarbekir wished to be baptized. Unfortunately, at the end of the day, their wish did not come true.

In recent days, the Armenian media—both in the Armenian Diaspora and in Armenia—ran headline news and opinion pieces on this topic. Various individuals gave press conferences; people opined on TV;

---

* *Armenian Weekly*, 14 Aug. 2015.

statements were released by the church, government, diasporan organizations, and political parties; and heated debates on social media argued both for and against the decision to refuse the baptisms.

As the organizer of the group whose three members wished to be baptized, and as the designated godfather—or *"gnkahayr"*—for these baptisms, I would like to provide a first-hand account of what really happened, why it happened, and what we should do to avoid such scandals in the future.

One may recall that during the trip I organized *last* year for the 50 hidden Armenians from Diyarbekir to Armenia, we witnessed the baptisms of a man and a woman in Echmiadzin. The man was a teacher in a public school in Diyarbekir. Because Christians are not allowed to work in the public sector in Turkey—not even as a garbage collector, let alone a teacher—he took a great risk by converting to Christianity. He was prepared for it; and I am happy to report that he is still employed as a teacher. This year, he brought his son to Armenia to extend to the next generation, this process of returning to one's Armenian roots. The woman baptized last year, on the other hand, had an even greater challenge. Her husband, a devout Muslim Kurd, had forbidden her from taking such a step. She nevertheless decided to convert to Christianity to keep her promise to her hidden Armenian father, who had asked her to become a Christian Armenian on his deathbed. I am also pleased to report that she and her husband are still happily married, and are now bravely facing the challenge of how to raise their child together—whether as Armenian, Kurd, Christian, or Muslim.

Therefore, this year, when three members of our group approached me with their wish to be baptized, I thought—perhaps naively—that I could again go ahead and arrange the baptisms for the day we visited Echmiadzin. The two *Dersimtsi* girls would take the names Anahid and Nairi, and the *Dikranagerdtsi* man from Diyarbekir would become Madteos Paramaz. One of the Dersim girls had a brother who was already baptized last year. The *Dikranagerdtsi* man was a distant relative of the family involved in the reconstruction of the Surp Giragos church in Diyarbekir.

Unfortunately, the baptisms weren't allowed to happen either in Echmiadzin, or in the Khor Virab church the next day, or in Surp Hovhannes church in Yerevan the following day. The explanations given to us were as varied as the clerics involved. Some said we should have applied in writing months in advance; our applications would have then been reviewed by a religious council. Others said we should have brought a letter from the Istanbul Acting Patriarch Archbisop Aram Atesyan, granting permission for the baptisms. One cleric suggested that the candidates must visit Armenia at least three times before becoming eligible. An even more preposterous suggestion came from a cleric who wondered why we didn't go to the churches in Turkey, since those wishing to be baptized are all from Turkey, instead of causing headaches for him and his superiors. I didn't bother telling him that although there are churches in Istanbul, no churches are left in historic Armenia except the one we reconstructed in Diyarbekir.

Overall, these clerics seemed to be unprepared for dealing with the baptism requests and had to make endless calls to their superiors for a decision, which either did not come or was ultimately negative. They still lead us on, however, saying that by tomorrow, there might be a positive decision. So, each day—with our hopes high, after buying the required towels, crosses, and headscarves for the girls—we would face renewed disappointment. Even the intervention of the Minister of Diaspora Hranush Hakobyan did not achieve the desired outcome.

An even more upsetting development was the zeal of critics who used this incident to launch misguided attacks. Rather than criticize the decision itself or the persons who made the decision, individuals began appearing at press conferences or on TV, or writing articles in newspapers, attacking the Armenian Church, the Ministry of Diaspora, and the government in general. One organization called the Republic of Western Armenia went as far as issuing fictitious citizenship and identification cards with the baptized names printed on them, and displayed the cards with their fictitious flag, names, and photos at press conferences and on TV. It seems that these people didn't realize (or didn't care) that the two Dersim girls and the Diyarbekir man would be returning to Turkey, that they would be continuing to live among Muslim Turks and Kurds, with their names paraded on a fictitious republic's citizenship cards. Do they have the right to jeopardize the lives of these already endangered persons? For that matter, do any of these opinion makers, who pass along all sorts of judgment in the media, care about the emotions of these three young people who had made such a personal decision as changing their faith, their religion?

The hidden Armenians have no control over their ethnic roots or their genetic identity—they were given no choice. They were born as Armenians, even though the fact that they are Armenians was not revealed to them until later in life. Some of them have now made a conscious decision to return to their ethnic roots. But changing one's *religion* by converting to Christianity is an entirely different matter. No one is born with a religion—Christian or Muslim. Religion is not a genetic identity but a faith acquired by personal choice and through family. If someone has made the decision to become Christian through baptism, there should be no individual, no institution, and no force to prevent that from happening—especially in the case of the hidden Armenians, who are taking a risk by first revealing their Armenian identity, and then by converting to Christianity.

If the reason for these increasingly difficult barriers to prevent baptisms is fear of abuse, there should be ways of dealing with them quickly and without delay. Sure, there could be some Muslim Turks or Kurds just pretending to be hidden Armenians. There could be others who have no intention of becoming Christian Armenian and who are getting baptized to gain some sort of advantage, such as employment or a way out of Turkey and into Europe or the Americas. However, these exceptions should not lead to draconian rules and regulations for all those who genuinely want to become Christian. Moreover, why do we have godfathers? The role of the godfather is to assure the Armenian Church that the person being baptized is eligible and worthy of baptism, and there should be no excuse or delay by the clerics for further investigation.

The objective of Project Rebirth is to help the hidden Armenians think, feel, and act as Armenians. Our work will continue regardless of the barriers placed before us by certain people. Whether these hidden Armenians become Christian or not, they have decided to return to their Armenian roots, and we will continue to encourage them. It would be ideal if the Armenian Church would also fulfill its duty in encouraging them to become Christian Armenians. But if not, it is still alright. After all, Armenians were Armenians for centuries before they adopted Christianity.

The Implications of Turkey's Renewed War on the Kurds[*]

One hundred years ago, the leaders of the Ottoman government were paranoid that Armenians' demand for reform, improved legislation, civil rights, and protection of life and property in the historic Armenian provinces would lead to Armenian independence, and thus the breakup of the empire. Their response to eliminate the Armenian problem was to attempt the elimination of the Armenians themselves. The civilian Armenian population that disappeared from the state was about 10 percent of the total population.

One hundred years later, Turkey's leaders are paranoid that the demands of another minority population—for education in their own language, self-rule, and local autonomy—will lead to independence and the breakup of the state. However, it is not easy to eliminate the Kurdish problem by eliminating the Kurds, as they make up one-third of the population in Turkey; they also form the majority of the population in the eastern and southeastern provinces. Instead, the government has employed tactics to break the will of the general Kurdish population by "cleansing the region from Kurdish militants," isolating them town by town, street by street, and house by house.

The result has been the huge suffering and loss of the civilian population. For the past several weeks, there have been ongoing curfews imposed in seven southeastern provinces. Electricity, water, and essential services have been cut off. One or two bakeries have been allowed to stay open, but people get shot when they venture out of their homes to get bread—the police and the troops shoot anyone who ventures out into the streets. Civilian losses are in the hundreds if not thousands, and include women, children, and the elderly.

The state and the state-controlled media do not report these civilian killings, or merely report them as "killed terrorists." In fact, the government uses the rather cryptic phrase "terrorists made ineffective" when referring to these killings. Among the civilians shot as terrorists are a five-month-old baby, pregnant women, and an 80-year-old elder. The bodies of civilians shot in the streets lie there for several days, as it is impossible to remove them under the barrage of gunfire from the police and army troops. The bodies of those shot in their houses cannot be

---

[*] *Armenian Weekly*, 7 Jan. 2016.

removed for burial, as people cannot leave their homes; the dead bodies are kept in freezers hooked to generators or wrapped in nylon bags. The morgues at the hospitals are so full that there are reports of hospital kitchen freezers being used to store the bodies, with the stench spreading through the building.

One of the worse areas of suffering is the historic central municipality of Sur in Diyarbekir, where the recently reconstructed Armenian Surp Giragos church is located. This municipality is recognized as a cultural heritage site, with many historic buildings, churches, and mosques. It is now mostly in ruins. Most of the buildings have been destroyed by rockets and cannon fire from army tanks. The Surp Giragos church has escaped relatively unscathed with only broken windows and some bullet holes. But the Armenian Catholic church had its doors broken down and some internal damage. The most important mosque in Sur, the historic Kursunlu Mosque—originally the St. Theodoros or Toros Armenian church, converted to a mosque in the 16th century—has been completely burnt down.

The population of Sur has declined from 24,000 to only 2,000 in the past month. None of the shops and restaurants remain open in the lively, bustling center of Diyarbekir, now completely deserted. Several shops that were recently returned to the ownership of the Surp Giragos church after successful negotiations and court cases are now shuttered, with loss of revenue to the church. Ironically, the government has just announced that the bullet-ridden and burned historic buildings of Sur will all be expropriated and demolished, to be replaced by modern housing to be constructed by the government's urban renewal agency.

Why are these events critical to the Armenians?

Firstly, there are untold numbers of "hidden Armenians" among the suffering Kurdish civilian population in these eastern and southeastern provinces. Whatever hell their grandparents went through 100 years ago, these hidden, Islamized Armenians are suffering a similar fate now. The ones who recently "came out" and revealed their Armenian identities are perhaps suffering even more.

Secondly, the hatred toward Armenians among the Turkish population, and especially in the Turkish security forces, has come out in the open during these blockades and attacks on the Kurdish population. The brainwashing, discrimination, and hatred against Armenians in the media,

(*Top*) Pro-government graffiti in Diyarbekir"– Ermeni Picleri" (Armenian bastards). (*Bottom*) Surp Giragos after it was ransacked in the summer of 2015 and its aftermath.

education system, and in government circles are apparent in the announcements from the Turkish police loudspeakers that taunt the Kurdish public and militants with pronouncements like: "You are all Armenians, you are all Armenian bastards," or "You will all die, seeds of Armenians."

Thirdly, and more ominously, the possibility of a proxy war between Armenia and Azerbaijan is increasing greatly, and is linked to these events. The war on the Kurds in Turkey is connected to preventing Kurdish moves for autonomy in Syria and Iraq. Increasing evidence of connections, cooperation, or—at a minimum—complicity between Turkey and ISIS has resulted in increasingly dangerous steps being taken by the Turkish leaders to cover up the evidence. Journalists who uncovered evidence of arms flowing from Turkey to ISIS have been jailed or even killed. Russian, Norwegian, and international evidence of oil flowing from ISIS to Turkey resulted in a downed Russian jet. One of the retaliatory moves by Russia was the installation of the most advanced antiaircraft weaponry in Armenia, with instructions to shoot down any Turkish jet that crosses the Turkish-Armenian border. And the potential for war involving several countries in the region keeps increasing.

Canadian Man Fights to Return Expropriated Armenian Church in Turkey[*]

Raffi Bedrosyan is a man on a mission.

The Toronto-based civil engineer and pianist is gearing up for a fight to restore the ownership of St. Giragos Armenian church in the city of Diyarbakir, southeastern Turkey, after it was expropriated by the Turkish government last week along with other properties in the city's historic Sur district.

Over the last few months, Sur has been the scene of heavy fighting between Kurdish militants affiliated with the PKK, which is considered a terrorist organization by Turkey and several other countries, including Canada, and Turkish security forces backed by armour and air power.

The fighting has destroyed or damaged large parts of the historic district. And under the pretext that it needs to repair and protect these

---

[*] Levon Sevunts, Radio Canada International, 1 April 2016.

historic structures the government in Ankara decided to expropriate large swaths of the old city, including the St. Giragos church, which had sustained only minor damage, "a few broken windows and bullet holes in the walls," Bedrosyan said.

Bedrosyan, who was born in Turkey to Armenian parents, has a very personal connection to the church.

"St. Giragos church in Diyarbakir, or Dikranagert, the Armenian word of the city, is the largest Armenian church in the Middle East," said Bedrosyan speaking from his office in Toronto. "It dates back to the 14th century and with several expansions it served the large Armenian community of 100,000 in Diyarbakir until 1915."

Then, as the Armenian population of the city was wiped out during the 1915 Armenian genocide, the church was also destroyed, Bedrosyan said.

The bell tower was taken down for being higher than neighbouring mosque minarets and the rest of the church fell into disrepair and collapsed by early 2000s, he said.

A few years ago, Bedrosyan joined a group of fellow Armenians, who formed a charitable foundation to restore the church to its original glory.

"With worldwide fundraising from Diaspora Armenians, as well as from Istanbul Armenians, the church was reconstructed in 2011," Bedrosyan said.

Last year, Bedrosyan performed a concert in the packed church to mark the 100th anniversary of the genocide, which Turkey officially refuses to recognize.

More Than a Place of Worship

In the short time since its restoration St. Giragos had become a spiritual centre, drawing Armenian pilgrims from all over the world, as well as a cultural centre for the remnants of the Armenian community in Diyarbakir, and a genocide memorial, a monumental reminder of the city's once thriving Armenian community, Bedrosyan said.

"But more significantly it has become a meeting place for the "hidden," Islamicised Armenians in the region who are the grandchildren of the forcefully Islamicised Armenian orphans from 1915," Bedrosyan said. "Thanks to this church they showed the courage to research and find their Armenian roots again; quite a few of them got baptised in this church and started taking Armenian classes, which we had organized."

Many of these people are now very frustrated and angry, Bedrosyan said.

"People are shocked right now, plus they just survived almost like a civil war," Bedrosyan said. "There are several people without a place to live any more, they are thrown out from their apartments and houses, which are now burned down and bombed out, but this church expropriation is like the last straw."

Finding Legal Avenues

Bedrosyan says he is trying to find out what legal means there are to contest the legislation in courts. There is work to be done within Turkey through the lawyers of the Armenian Patriarchate of Istanbul, which along with the charitable foundation owns the church and a few other properties that were confiscated along with it, Bedrosyan said.

Outside Turkey, Berdosyan and his associates are consulting lawyers to launch lawsuits against the Turkish government.

"I was instrumental in fundraising from Diaspora Armenians and in almost every country: the U.S., Canada, most of the EU countries there are Armenians who donated money towards this reconstruction and now all these people are completely upset and shocked, and all that work, and money, and efforts are now gone to waste by this legalized robbery," Bedrosyan said.

Armenian organizations in Canada and the United States are lobbying their respective governments up to the level of President Barak Obama to get involved in this issue, Bedrosyan said.

"And the American embassy in Turkey is very closely following this case," Bedrosyan said. "Everybody is waiting for some sort of explanation and basis for this decision by the Turkish parliament."

Bedrosyan said he has also contacted the Turkish embassy in Ottawa to get some explanation.

"They have so far not provided any explanation other than referring me to announcements by certain members of parliament whose explanations are quite childish," Bedrosyan said.

Contacted to comment on the expropriation on Friday, Turkey's ambassador in Canada Selçuk Unal said his government has pledged at the highest level to restore all the properties that can be repaired and build new housing where buildings have been damaged beyond repair.

"But for that they need to expropriate a couple of buildings, maybe more than that, so there will be new buildings to be built in the vicinity and (they) will be returned to the persons who have owned the original places," Unal said.

Bedrosyan says he doesn't buy that argument.

"In order to replace a few windows, which were broken in this church, you don't need to expropriate the church," Bedrosyan said.

There have also been assurances by a local MP from the governing AKP party of President Recep Tayyip Erdoğan, Turkey's minister of culture who visited Diyarbakir with two other cabinet ministers on Thursday that there will be no expropriations of churches or mosques, Unal said.

"And today the prime minister (Ahmet Davutoğlu) was visiting Diyarbakir province," Unal said. "He made a public speech, assuring everybody that whatever is destroyed will be restored within a new property development package and he also stressed that property rights and tittles will be strictly upheld during any possible reconstruction efforts."

Despite all these assurances, the fact remains that the St. Giragos church along with a couple of other properties belonging to the church, are on the official list of expropriated properties published by the government, Bedrosyan said.

And if political pressure to stop the expropriation within and outside Turkey doesn't work, he and his supporters are ready for a lengthy legal battle, Bedrosyan said.

"This act is against human rights, the property rights or every other right that I can think of, which is supposedly safeguarded by the Turkish constitution, EU laws that Turkey is bound by, so there will be lengthy lawsuits."

The Plight of Hidden or Islamized Armenians in Turkey[*]

What a difference a year makes…

It was August of last year, when Project Rebirth organized trips to Armenia for a large group of hidden Islamized Armenians from Diyarbekir, Urfa, Dersim, Sason, Van, and the Hamshen regions of Turkey, to help them find their roots, language, culture, and history.

---

[*] *Armenian Weekly*, 18 Nov. 2016.

It seems like decades ago, but it was last April, that a piano concert took place at the recently reconstructed Surp Giragos church in Diyarbekir, to commemorate the Armenian Genocide Centennial—a concert attended by more than a thousand hidden Armenians.

The regular monthly breakfast meetings of the hidden Armenians of Diyarbekir at Surp Giragos church have now become a distant memory. The Armenian language classes so enthusiastically attended by Islamized Armenians in Dersim and Diyarbekir have long been suspended.

As the organizer of the trips to Armenia, it was gratifying for me to receive emails from some of these *no-longer* hidden Armenians.

"Before I went to Armenia I was a Kurd, and I returned as an Armenian," read one. "For years I fought for the rights of Kurds before I found out I was an Armenian at the deathbed of my father. Now I want to go fight in Artsakh (Nagorno-Karabagh/NKR)," read another.

It was doubly gratifying to see youngsters from Diyarbekir attending university in Yerevan, already speaking Armenian and acting as guides to tourists. It was also a pleasant surprise to find out that the last trip to Armenia resulted in a marriage between a hidden Armenian from Hamshen and a hidden Armenian from Diyarbekir, who wouldn't even have known about each other's existence before last year.

In ever growing numbers, the hidden Armenians had started making contact with one another within Turkey, establishing links with people in Armenia and Diaspora.

And now? The past year has been a living hell for the hidden Armenians of Turkey. The civil war between the Kurdish resistance guerrillas and the Turkish army has resulted in massive destruction in southeastern and eastern Turkey. Most of the buildings in the region have been bombed or burnt by the army and police forces, followed by complete demolition and razing of the damaged buildings, creating vast open areas in many urban centers, with only a few mosques, police stations, or government buildings left standing.

Entire neighborhoods have disappeared, reduced to rubble. The Surp Giragos church in Diyarbekir has escaped the fighting relatively intact structurally, with only broken windows and a large hole in one of the exterior walls. But the Turkish security forces have used it as an army base, desecrating the church, burning some of the pews as firewood, with

The author performing at Surp Giragos church.

garbage and smell of urine everywhere. The attached gift and souvenir shop is destroyed.

Several stores and houses in the adjacent blocks to the church, which were originally owned by the church and only recently returned to church ownership after years of negotiations, have now been demolished by the government, along with many of the historic narrow streets and buildings leading to the church.

At present, the church stands in the middle of a vast open area. But worst of all, in March 2016, the Turkish government passed legislation, expropriating the church and all of the properties belonging to it. The church is now closed to public. The Armenian church foundation has taken the expropriation to Turkish courts, and in the case of an unsuccessful outcome at these courts, the intention is to take the matter to the European Court of Human Rights.

More than a million people have been displaced in the region, forced to flee to safer areas. Thousands of people have been killed or injured, including children and elderly, some burnt alive in the basements of apartment buildings while being bombed by the government forces. Thousands more have been fired from their jobs, arrested and jailed for "supporting terrorist Kurdish organizations," especially intellectuals, teachers, lawyers, and journalists.

The democratically elected Kurdish mayors of most towns and cities in the region have been removed from their posts, arrested and jailed. The co-leaders of the Peoples' Democratic Party (HDP), as well as several members of parliament, have also been arrested and jailed.

Following the failed coup attempt against President Erdoğan in July, dictatorial powers and the state of emergency in Turkey have resulted in silencing of all opposition, media, intellectuals, and opinion makers.

The situation is worrisome and continues to get worse in Turkey, especially in the southeastern regions, with military operations within Turkey as well as across the border within Iraq and Syria. Although Turkey has pledged to fight against ISIS, it seems that their main fight is against Kurdish forces within Turkey, Iraq, and Syria. The Turkish army and police forces taunt the Kurdish guerillas with the ultimate insult, calling them "Armenian bastards."

Our hidden Islamized Armenians living in the region suffer the same fate as the rest of the population, perhaps even worse. They are discriminated against, no matter where they go. The Kurds discriminate against them for not being "real" Kurds. The Turks discriminate and harass them even more, as they are brainwashed to hate and fear Armenians as perpetrators of genocide. If the hidden Islamized Armenians choose to go to Istanbul, they are discriminated against by the Armenians there. Until they satisfy the unreasonably strict requirements of the Istanbul Armenian Patriarchate and get baptized as Christians, they are not received well by the Armenian community.

Naturally, the efforts of Project Rebirth to help the hidden Islamized Armenians find their Armenian roots, culture, and language by organizing Armenian language classes in places like Diyarbekir and Dersim, as well as planning trips for them to Armenia, are now on hold.

Instead, the efforts are now geared toward helping the hidden Armenians relocate away from the war zones into safe areas, and arranging lawyers for people who are arrested, jailed, or unfairly dismissed from work.

There have been major setbacks this year, with great human suffering and material losses. We have lost control, for now, of Surp Giragos church in Diyarbekir, which was beautifully reconstructed after years of painstaking effort, sacrifice, and hard work. But we must remind ourselves that it has already served its main objective—the re-awakening of the hidden Islamized Armenians. This church has acted as a magnet, bringing together once hidden Armenians—the grandchildren of the living victims and orphans of the Armenian Genocide—who continue surviving and living on our own ancestral lands, albeit under very difficult conditions.

Programs Featuring Cem Özdemir Draw More than 1,000 in Canada[*]

MONTREAL and TORONTO — Altogether more than 1,200 people attended events in Montreal and Toronto commemorating the tenth anniversary of the assassination of Turkish-Armenian journalist Hrant Dink, and featuring Cem Ozdemir, the co-chair of the Green Party in Germany, and a member of parliament there who was the main force behind the resolution which that body passed recognizing the Armenian Genocide.

Among those attending were Armenian Ambassador to Canada Armen Yeganyan, the German Consul Generals of Toronto and Montreal, Russian Consul General of Montreal, Armenian Consul at the Armenian Embassy, several members of parliament, and significantly, the Premier of Ontario Province Kathleen Wynn, who gave a passionate speech about Hrant Dink. Dink's widow, Rakel, sent a special video message to both audiences thanking the organizers and Özdemir.

Zoryan Institute Outreach Coordinator Megan Reid explained the relationship between Hrant Dink and the Zoryan Institute toward the objective of creating a "common body of knowledge" of historic facts about the 1915 events, and introduced Raffi Bedrosyan, the moderator and the propeller of both events.

RB stated that with these events we do not only commemorate Hrant Dink, but we reaffirm our commitment to continue Hrant's mission for reconciliation between Armenian and Turkish peoples through dialogue. But dialogue can only happen when based on historic facts and truths. As soon as Hrant started revealing facts, such as Sabiha Gökçen (known as Atatürk's adopted daughter, first Turkish female military pilot, a hero whose name is given to Istanbul's second airport) to be in fact an

---

[*] *The Armenian Mirror Spectator*, 26 Jan. 2017.

Raffi Bedrosyan (*l*) and Cem Özdemir (*r*) at Hrant Dink memorial in Toronto, 2017.

Armenian girl orphaned during the 1915 Armenian Genocide, he became a target, subject to endless threats, insults and charges of "insulting Turkishness," ultimately ending in his murder.

The murder was perpetrated by the deep state and the state security forces just watched or even encouraged and then covered up the murder and the perpetrators. Video clips which became available only recently, ten years after the murder, were presented to the audience, that show several state military intelligence officers based in the assassin's hometown of Trabzon, who were aware of the assassination to be carried out, and had travelled to Istanbul to observe the murder. Based on historical context presentation prepared by the Zoryan Institute, Bedrosyan also talked about the significance of the book *Armenian Genocide: Evidence from the German Office Archives*, edited by German scholar Wolfgang Gust, which was financed, researched, published in German, English and Turkish in collaboration with the Zoryan Institute of Toronto. The book was distributed to many opinion makers in German and Turkish governments, media and academia, and deeply influenced Özdemir and his colleagues who prepared the German parliament resolution recognizing the Armenian Genocide and acknowledging Germany's responsibility in not preventing it. Immediately after the passing of the resolution, Turkish president Recep Tayyip Erdoğan castigated Cem Özdemir and wondered: "What sort of Turk is he? His blood must be tested in a lab." Other Turkish government leaders then followed by hurling the ultimate insult at Özdemir, by calling him an Armenian.

Bedrosyan then introduced Özdemir, whose parents came to Germany from Turkey in the 1960s as guest workers. Özdemir explained Dink's profound influence on him and stated that if it were not for him, the Turkish population would not have known any of the truth about the 1915 events. Thanks to Hrant, Dink, he said, the Turkish people started to understand the truth and to question the state version of history. After sharing his experiences in the preparation of the resolution bill, he stated that German Parliament's recognition of the genocide resolution is much more significant than the parliamentary resolutions of other countries, because Germany accepted its guilt as an ally of Turkey and wanted to set an example for Turkey also to accept its own responsibility about the genocide.

A Diasporan Minister of Diaspora: A Proposal[*]

When the Government of Armenia decided to establish the Ministry of Diaspora in 2008, the objective was to form a partnership between the Armenian state and Armenians in the Diaspora and to help strengthen the ties between Armenia and Armenians abroad, by preserving the Armenian national identity in the Diaspora and the historic homeland. This was to be accomplished by developing multiple pan-Armenian initiatives in educational, professional, entrepreneurial, cultural, social, and sports fields, as well as by combining the talents, skills, resources and capital of both Diaspora and Armenia Armenians. Thanks to the strong personality and leadership of the first and only Minister of Diaspora, Hranush Hakobyan, the Armenia-Diaspora partnership has been founded on a solid base, with many success stories.

But there are also many failures, particularly in the areas of Diaspora investment. When Karen Karapetyan, the Prime Minister of Armenia, sent an appeal recently to the Diaspora Armenians to strengthen their ties

---

[*] *Armenian Weekly*, 8 March 2017.

and commitment to Armenia, the response from several Diaspora organizations and activists within Armenia was mostly negative, citing several examples of failed initiatives due to corruption and bribery. Some even blamed the Armenian government for thinking of Diaspora just as a "cow to be milked" (*'gtan gov'*).

So, where do we go from here? Is there room for improvement? Are there better alternative ways of growing the Armenia-Diaspora partnership? Are there different ways of solving recurring issues related to mutual trust, confidence or cooperation between the partners? With the impending elections in Armenia next month, I believe it is appropriate to re-assess the form of governance for the Ministry of Diaspora.

Despite all the good intentions, goodwill, and accomplishments of the Ministry of Diaspora, there are serious problems between Diaspora Armenians and Armenia. The initial enthusiasm of the first few years is long gone, when Diaspora Armenians were much more willing to visit, live, work and play, and more significantly, invest in Armenia. There is now a general lack of trust and discontent by the Diaspora Armenians toward Armenian government leaders. When it comes to the issue of investing in Armenia, there is a widespread conclusion that investments mostly disappear due to bribery and corruption. When it comes to the issue of governing Armenia, there is heavy criticism of the Armenian government leaders. Growing protests by a multitude of Diaspora intellectuals, celebrities, and artists against the Armenian government leaders is a testament to that.

Armenian government leaders, as well as Armenians living in Armenia, may very well tell the protesting Diaspora intelligentsia: "If you want to make a difference, you better move to Armenia, come and live and vote in Armenia, instead of just complaining from abroad." However, I suggest the Diaspora Armenians would have a much more defensible argument if they focus on improving the relationships between Diaspora and Armenia. The very reason for the establishment of the Ministry of Diaspora *is* the Diaspora Armenians.

There is an absolute need to reverse the vicious cycle of mistrust, and as a first step, I suggest that the Minister of Diaspora be a Diasporan Armenian. Along with the additional suggestions given below, there should be confidence—building measures taken by the new government, in order to encourage Diasporan investment into Armenia again. If the government is successful in creating credibility and a level playing field for investors from abroad, the source of potential foreign investment would not only be limited to Diaspora Armenians, but would also attract international investors as well, without the need for appeals from the Prime Minister.

I would like to add the following points.

1.   The Armenian government does not and will not take seriously the Diaspora intelligentsia protesting against poor governance. However, it would seriously consider any proposal that would improve relationships and flow of investment from Diaspora to Armenia.

2.   The Diaspora organizations and, more importantly, Diaspora Armenians as individuals and investors, would have more control, trust and confidence if the "one window" into and from Armenia is an effective Diasporan, with all the facilitations and dealings handled transparently by the Diaspora Ministry, at least until the perception of mistrust has been eliminated.

3.   As the Diaspora is not a homogenous body and spread in communities worldwide with quite distinct resources, capabilities, and characteristics, it is suggested to have six deputy ministers to be responsible for Armenian Diaspora in Europe, Russia, North America, South America, Middle East and Far East/Australia. These deputy ministers would coordinate all activities related to investment, repatriation, cultural, educational, and social exchanges closely with the staff of Armenian Embassies in the countries where Armenian Diaspora communities exist. Two examples of already successful implementers in this regard are the Armenian Ambassadors in Canada and Austria.

4.   As an alternative source of funding the Diaspora Ministry activities and to lessen the burden on the Armenian government budget, the Diaspora Ministry could be financed entirely by Diaspora contributions. As an example of the resources required, for a million Diaspora Armenians, even a $10 annual dues co uld result in an annual budget of $10 million for Ministry staff and activities, much higher

than the present finances of the Ministry. This alternative proposal would also trigger a healthy competition among the various political, cultural, and religious Diaspora organizations in membership drives.

5. Appropriate Diasporan Minister (and deputy ministers) of Diaspora could be selected by the President and government of Armenia, chosen from candidates nominated by Diasporan organizations and public at large. The details for nomination and selection of the candidates can be adapted from a variety of tried and tested processes elsewhere, with obvious priority given to non-partisan, trustworthy and capable Diasporan individuals. Diaspora relations of Israel and India would act as successful role models.

The primary purpose of this article is to open up the subject for discussion by government leaders in Armenia as well as among Diasporan community leaders, political, religious, cultural organizations, and interested individuals. The problems have been discussed and argued for many years without any solutions, and it is my hope that by soliciting comments and constructive criticism of this proposal, we can perhaps strive toward a workable, achievable and fair solution to improve the Armenia-Diaspora partnership, for the mutual benefit of all Armenians in Armenia, Artsakh (Nagorno-Karabagh), and the Diaspora.

Turkey vs. Europe: Any Lessons?[*]

Last week, for the first time in the history of the Turkish Republic, one of its ministers was declared *persona non grata*—an undesirable alien—and was deported from the Netherlands, a state which is a NATO ally of Turkey. Again for the first time, the Turkish Foreign Minister was told not to visit Rotterdam in Netherlands, and his flight landing permit was cancelled after he ignored the Dutch orders not to come.

The previous week, the same Turkish Foreign Minister's plans to address Turkish-German dual citizens in various rental halls in several German cities were cancelled, and he could only speak from the balcony

---

* *Armenian Weekly*, 16 March 2017.

of a Turkish Consulate residence to a few gathered in the garden under the rain. This week, Denmark cancelled the visit of the Turkish Prime Minister. Switzerland cancelled the visit of other Turkish ministers. Austria proposed to have a European Union (EU) ban on visits of any Turkish politicians to Europe.

Why is this unprecedented humiliation and embarrassment happening to Turkey? What did Turkey do to deserve this? How is Turkey, Turkish government leaders, and Turkish people reacting to this humiliation? What are the lessons to be learned by Turkey, and more importantly, how is it relevant to Armenia? This article will attempt to shed light on these questions.

Turkey is getting ready to vote Yes or No on April 16 for a referendum to change the constitution so that all governmental, legislative, and judicial powers can be concentrated in one person—President Recep Tayyip Erdoğan. Erdoğan had already started exercising most of these powers under a state of emergency, declared after the failed military coup against him on July 15, 2016. And now, it is time for Erdoğan to legitimize these de facto dictatorial powers by entrenching them in the revised constitution.

Erdoğan fully blames the failed coup on his erstwhile ally Fethullah Gülen, an Islamic cleric who lives in exile in Pennsylvania. Once close allies against the previous secular regimes, the Islamic leaders had a falling out a few years ago, and everything wrong happening in Turkey now is blamed on Gülen and his followers.

The witch hunt to identify and punish followers of Gülen has created great turmoil among Turks in all levels of society—the army, academia, government bureaucracy, media, and business world. Add to this the ongoing war between the government forces and the Kurdish militants in the east and southeast, the human toll is unprecedented.

Since the July 2016 failed coup, 128,625 people have been fired from their jobs, including state officials, teachers, bureaucrats, security forces, academics, lawyers, and journalists. There are 94,224 people of various professions, arrested and jailed under state of emergency powers. 2,099 schools and dormitories and 15 universities have been shut down. 7,316 academics, including many top professors have lost their jobs, resulting in many faculties of still open universities to be closed, with hundreds of thousands of university students left in limbo. 4,070 judges and prosecutors are dismissed, some of them jailed, ironically, in the same prisons as criminals that they had convicted previously. 149 media outlets, television stations, and newspapers have been shut down, allowing only pro-Erdoğan media to exist, and even then, undesirable headlines still result in the dismissal of editors. And finally, 162 journalists have been jailed, highest number in the world.

The human toll resulting from the war on Kurds is even more grim. A recent United Nations investigative report estimated that at least 2,000 Kurdish civilians have been killed since 2015. There are an estimated 50,000 injured and more than 500,000 citizens left homeless after Turkish army tanks bombed and burnt several towns in the southeast. The bombardment of hundreds of apartment buildings was followed by the demolishing and bulldozing of the rubble, sometimes still containing burnt bones and body parts. Since 2016, 13 Members of Parliament belonging to the pro-Kurdish Peoples' Democratic Party (HDP) have been arrested and jailed, including the two co-chairs, after their political immunity was removed by dictatorial legislation. The democratically elected Kurdish mayors of 35 municipalities in the east and southeast are removed from their posts and jailed, replaced by Turkish bureaucrats appointed from Ankara.

Against this truly anti-democratic backdrop, Erdoğan and his ministers planned to visit Europe to convince the three million Turks living in various EU states to vote Yes in the referendum, in order to give more dictatorial powers to the President. It should be pointed out that EU legislation prohibits political rallies of non-EU persons. What is even more interesting, Turkish legislation, passed in 2008, also prohibits Turkish politicians from holding political rallies outside Turkey. Ironically, this legislation was proposed by Erdoğan's party itself, in order to give it an advantage over other Turkish parties. At that time, Erdoğan was still allies with Gülen and could use Gülen's vast network in Europe and U.S. to carry out propaganda rallies. But now, the situation has changed. The Yes and No votes are almost even and Erdoğan desperately needs the support of Turks in Europe in order to win the referendum. So, to hell with any EU or Turkish laws…

It seems the European leaders decided to show some backbone and refrain from participating in Erdoğan's mission to become a dictator. Hence, the cancellations of halls, flights, and meetings.

Turkish government reaction to these rejections? Blaming German Chancellor Angela Merkel, and Dutch Prime Minister Rutte as Nazis, accusing them of preventing freedom of speech and freedom of movement.

Erdoğan stated that if he is not allowed to speak in Germany, he will still come to Germany and "turn the world upside down." The Foreign Minister bellowed that "Nothing and no one can stop him from coming to Holland regardless of what the Dutch say." In addition to insulting the German and Dutch leaders as Nazis, they also accused the mayor of Rotterdam as an Islamophobe, who happens to be a well-liked Muslim, originally from Morocco.

As a state that has committed and still denies genocide of its minorities, Armenians, Assyrians, Greeks, Alevis. and Kurds, the Turkish government officials accused the EU leaders as followers of Nazism.

Turkish public reaction to these rejections? The rabble rousing mobs took to the streets to protest against the Dutch, by burning French and Russian flags (the flags are all the same colors, they look alike, so who cares, right?). They also piled up many oranges and repeatedly stabbed them with knives, because orange is the color of the Dutch. One "hero" climbed the flagpole of the Dutch Consulate in Istanbul and replaced the Dutch flag with a Turkish one. A member of Istanbul Municipal Council threatened to slaughter his cow imported from Holland, if the Dutch don't apologize within two days. One unfortunate Norwegian journalist got beaten up by mistake, as the mob thought he was speaking Dutch. But these are normal occurrences in Turkey. A couple of years ago, when the Turks heard that the Chinese government oppressed their cousins, the Uygur Turks, Turks had started beating up many Korean tourists in Istanbul by mistake. They look alike, so who cares... right?

Lessons to be learned? Based on history repeating itself, it is highly unlikely that Turkish authorities will ever learn how to behave democratically. They will either see themselves as poor victims, unfairly and anti-democratically treated by the Europeans who refused them freedom of speech, or they will bully, threaten, and insult by demanding apologies, ban of flights or sanctions against Netherlands and other EU states, completely ignoring the fact that Turkey is totally dependent on the EU states for tourism, investments, and trade. They did the same bullying and bravado against the Russians after downing a Russian plane in Syria, which resulted in the total crippling of the Turkish economy due to Russian trade and tourism bans. At the end, the Turkish government capitulated by profusely apologizing to Putin and agreeing to Russian terms—especially regarding Syria—before normal relations could resume. The same routine will happen again with EU.

There is, however, a lesson to be learned by the U.S. in these episodes. Rather than giving in to all the demands of an anti-democratic state which acts like a spoiled child, the U.S. should start behaving more responsibly, fairly, and firmly against Turkey. It is scandalous that Mike Flynn, the recently fired nominee for the National Security Advisor post in the Trump Administration, had collected $530,000 for lobbying services that benefitted the Turkish government. Lobbying for what? Is that money wasted now?

And lastly, lessons for Armenia and Armenians? We have to be well informed about the Turks' weaknesses and strengths. We have to learn from their mistakes. For a nation of ten million people with a tiny country sandwiched between two belligerent adversary states, we cannot afford to be as divided as the Turks, as anti-democratic, or as ignorant as them… But perhaps most importantly, we cannot afford to be as mistake-prone as them.

The Hidden Lives of Islamized Armenians Living in Plain Sight in Turkey[*]

WATERTOWN — For more than an hour and a half on Friday, April 20, speaker Raffi Bedrosyan rattled off stories and statistics about "hidden" Armenians in Turkey today, accompanied by slides, keeping the audience at St. James Armenian church's Keljik Hall entranced.

Bedrosyan spoke at a program sponsored jointly by the Tekeyan Cultural Association and St. James Armenian church. He had come to Boston to be the keynote speaker at the Massachusetts State House annual Armenian Genocide commemoration, which had taken place earlier in the day.

_____

[*] *The Armenian Mirror-Spectacor*, 17 March 2017.

Bedrosyan started on the subject by saying, "My late friend, Hrant Dink, kept telling me they kept talking about the dead and the gone, but it's time to speak of the living."

Bedrosyan said regretfully that of his three close friends in Turkey, two, Hrant Dink and Tahir Elçi, were killed, while a third, Osman Kavala, is in prison. Elçi was a prominent Kurdish human rights attorney whom the Turkish military killed in 2015 while he was speaking about Kurdish rights at a press conference. Kavala is a proponent of Genocide recognition and Kurdish rights.

Bedrosyan said that the Armenian population globally comprises four sources: Armenia, Artsakh, the diaspora and Turkey. In the latter, he estimates, there are about two million Armenians who either know and keep quiet about their identity or who are still unaware they are at least part Armenian.

Tracing back the story, he showed slides of "lucky" orphans who survived the Armenian Genocide and were forcibly Turkified and Islamized in the many state-run orphanages.

"They were given Turkish names, circumcised, and Turkified," he explained. "Thousands of boys that were physically fit were trained in military schools and became soldiers. Some were taken to the front to fight against the Armenian Republic" in 1918, in a particularly ironic and cruel gesture.

The girls did not make it into orphanages often; they sometimes endured an even crueler fate: being sold as slaves. While the slave markets in the Ottoman Empire had been abolished and closed down in 1908, by 1915 the practice restarted. Armenian girls sold for the price of a lamb; however, girls from wealthier families were worth more as the buyer also got the girl's property as often they were the sole survivors of their families.

Among the most famous of the Armenian girls adopted was Sabiha Gökçen, the daughter of Mustafa Kemal Atatürk, the founder of the modern Turkish Republic. Gökçen is a historic character in her own right, including for being the first female military pilot in Turkey, and her name graces the Ankara airport. Hrant Dink, the assassinated journalist, was the one who exposed the story about her heritage. Bedrosyan said Dink might as well have signed his own death certificate when he exposed Gökçen's Armenian heritage.

194

"Hrant Dink was persecuted, prosecuted and finally assassinated" as a result of the story, Bedrosyan said.

Dink's lawyer, Fetiye Çetin, also had Armenian roots. She wrote about it in her groundbreaking book, *My Grandmother*. Her grandmother, a kerchiefed and pious Muslim woman to all appearances, had told her the truth about being Armenian when Fetiye was 25. She also told her granddaughter about a surviving sister whom the lawyer eventually traced to New Jersey, unfortunately after the sister's death.

Lost Churches

One of the striking elements of Bedrosyan's talk was the simple diagrams and heartbreaking photos that illustrated his words. A particular one was a map of the Ottoman Empire before 1915 and now which showed the number of the Armenian Churches there. Before 1915 there were 3,000 churches and 1,000 schools throughout the empire, with more than 300 churches alone in the vicinity of Lake Van.

"All were converted or destroyed," he said, either turned to mosques in the best-case scenarios, or barracks, stables and in one case even, a house of prostitution.

The largest church of all was Surp Giragos in Diyarbekir/Dikranagerd. Not long after its construction before the Genocide, the massive church's bell tower was shot off by a cannon as it was taller than the tallest minaret in the town. After the Armenian population of Dikranagerd disappeared, the church continued its steep slide into a decline.

The church had continued to fall into decline and in 2011, during a brief period of freedom by the government, Bedrosyan and a few others banded together to restore the decrepit church back to its former glory. Millions of dollars were raised and in October 2011, the church opened with a massive service and concert, during which Bedrosyan played. More than 4,000 came, Bedrosyan said, with many among them hidden Armenians. Until February 2016 the church held services twice a year at Easter and Christmas, with the participation of an ever-growing number of Armenians from Turkey visiting. However, with the increased agitation by Kurds against their mistreatment by the government, the armed forces trained their weapons on Diyarbekir, reducing much of the region into rubble, with the church another casualty.

Now, the church which was so lovingly restored and provided happy celebrations to so many has reverted back to ruins. While Bedrosyan said the structure is still sound, the interior of the church has been gutted, with the pews upended and put in front of the windows and strewn garbage and the smell of urine everywhere.

Hidden Armenians and Project Rebirth

Finding out you are Armenian in Turkey is not always easy. It is a country where the word "Armenian" is still hurled as an insult and where a Muslim Turkish heritage is needed to for civil service jobs. Still, many hidden Armenians have embraced their heritage.

It is precisely this group that Bedrosyan has taken under his wing. He started Project Rebirth, which helps Armenians who either recently or earlier found out they are Armenian on one or both sides, to explore what their ethnicity means.

"These people still show courage at the risk of losing their jobs, with some even risking losing their families," Bedrosyan said. Among them are doctors, engineers, lawyers and teachers.

He showed many slides of the groups he has taken to Armenia with the support of the Diaspora Ministry in Armenia for the past several years, with several opting to get Christened in Echmiadzin.

(The Istanbul Patriarchate forbade any more conversions in Echmiadzin, suggesting that it, not Echmiadzin, had control over its subjects.)

He praised the reception the group got in Armenia not only from everyday folks but from the government and the church.

Among those was one man named Selim, who was very interested in finding out about his Armenian heritage, was so immersed in his identity that the following year he greeted the Rebirth group as a tour guide.

Another two visitors converted to Christianity and faced a lot of difficulties because of this decision. One, a woman, was married to a devout Muslim man and worried about her marriage but said she felt she had to do that to satisfy the deathbed wish of her father.

All these cases, Bedrosyan said, raise interesting questions: "Who is an Armenian? Do you have to be Christian to be an Armenian?"

He also showed videos from Armenian TV covering the group's visits to Armenia.

During an enthusiastic question-and-answer after the talk, Bedrosyan spoke about the online registry briefly put out by the government. Because of the extreme interest of people, the site collapsed. However, it created a lot of difficulty, including for some hard-core Armenian haters who found out to their dismay and subsequent depression that they were Armenian.

Bedrosyan said that based on official Turkish calculations that there were at least 200,000 Armenian orphans left after 1915, with at least another 100,000 people who converted to Islam to save themselves from death, there are more than two million people with Armenian ethnicity in Turkey today.

Starting in the past couple of years, after the repression by the government began in Turkey, instead of trips to Armenia, Project Rebirth uses its funds to help the hidden Armenians.

These hidden Armenians are different from Hamshens, who live in the northeast of Turkey. They are treated as if a separate ethnic group, though of course, they are Armenians who were converted to Islam and isolated to form an insular community, some as early as after the destruction of Ani. In fact, he said, the Hamshens do not realize that the language they speak is Armenian as the official line is that they speak a dialect of central Asian Turkish. Bedrosyan said with an amused expression that he was debating with one Hamshen man, in Armenian, that the language the latter was speaking was not Armenian. Others were shocked many years back when the trial of Levon Ekmekjian, who was the sole survivor of an ASALA attack at the Ankara airport in 1981, was broadcast live and he acted as his own attorney and spoke in Armenian. Many Hamshen were shocked, thinking Ekmekjian was one of them.

Bedrosyan was introduced by Aram Arkun, the executive director of the Tekeyan Cultural Association. Arkun, whose father hailed from Turkey, added some anecdotes of his own about Turkification.

What's Next for Turkey?[*]

The April 16 referendum in Turkey—to revise the constitution and grant expanded powers to President Recep Tayyip Erdoğan—passed by a slim

* *Armenian Weekly*, 17 April 2017.

margin, as 51.3 percent of voters said "Yes" amid claims of significant illegal voting procedures.

Opposition parties have stated that the winning margin of 1.1 million votes was only achieved by the action of government election officials, allowing up to 2.5 million non-registered invalid "Yes" votes.

The election campaign itself was already deemed to be vastly unfair and uneven, with zero coverage and airtime allowed by the state controlled media and TV stations for the pro-Kurdish party, whose co-chairmen were in jail along with 13 other elected parliamentarians and thousands of party members for "supporting terrorism."

Despite the crackdown on all propaganda of "No" supporters, the population of major cities, coastal regions, the Kurdish regions in the east and southeast, and generally urbanized and educated people, voted "No." But the central regions of the country, generally less educated, rural people and the pro- Islamic masses, as well as thousands of Syrian Sunni refugees carried the day, with some help from the voting officials.

Nevertheless, by hook or crook, Erdoğan—who now will have all executive, legislative, and judiciary powers in his control after abolishing the Prime Minister's office and greatly reducing the role of the parliament—has already declared a victory. This concentration of power in one person has already been declared as the "death of democracy in Turkey" by European statesmen, who are now firmly convinced Turkey should never join the European Union.

In any case, trying to get into European Union is no longer an objective for Erdoğan. He has called the European leaders Nazis and Crusaders because they prevented his ministers from campaigning to Turkish workers living in Europe.

One of Erdoğan's top priorities now is to bring back the death penalty, pushing Turkey further away from European norms. He wants the death penalty in order to execute the perpetrators of the failed coup of 2016. His need to avenge is apparent in every speech that he has made since that event, and put in effect in the continuing purge of hundreds of thousands of people fired from their jobs or tens of thousands of people put in jail, for suspicion of sympathizing with the alleged coup leader, exiled preacher Fethullah Gülen.

Although Erdoğan supporters blindly voted to place dictatorial powers in his hand, one wonders what will happen when Erdoğan starts losing his grip on power. The steady economic growth from the earlier days of his government, which resulted in higher living standards for the masses helping his popularity, has now halted, with massive losses in tourism, manufacturing, export, and trade. Record numbers are unemployed and deemed "unemployable" as either Gülen or Kurdish movement supporters. There are grumblings and potential splintering groups forming even in Erdoğan's own ruling party.

In the short term, Erdoğan seems invincible, but consider these scenarios for the longer term—sooner or later, when he loses an election, his all powerful post may be occupied by an anti-Erdoğan individual. Perhaps not probable now, but an elected president may be a secular Kemalist, who will go after Erdoğan, and all he stands for, especially if he is empowered with the death penalty. Perhaps even less probable, an elected president may be a pro-Kurdish politician, who will have the powers to grant local autonomy to the Kurdish regions, even paving the path toward Kurdish independence.

And perhaps the least probable scenario: an elected president may be a hidden Islamized Armenian politician, who may single-handedly decide to start facing historical truths and stop the denial of the Armenian Genocide with all its consequences.

Never say never in politics…

Oil, Gold, and Bribes: A Ticking Turkish Time Bomb[*]

In a small courtroom in Manhattan, New York, there is a legal drama playing out, which may have serious consequences for the U.S., Turkey and Iran, but more critically for Turkish President Recep Tayyip Erdoğan. This court case is a ticking time bomb, which may explode in President Erdoğan's face, despite all his clandestine efforts to diffuse it.

Reza Zarrab, a 33-year-old Turkish citizen of Iranian descent, was arrested in Miami on March 17, 2016, as soon as he got off a plane. He stated that he had come to the U.S. with his wife and daughter to see Disney World. But the three charges against him were serious— conspiring to evade U.S. sanctions against Iran, money laundering and bank fraud. He was promptly transferred to a New York jail, where he

---

* *Armenian Weekly*, 5 May 2018.

currently sits. And the connection to President Erdoğan? Read on, as this is an international thriller in the making.

For several years, the U.S. had slapped sanctions on Iran to contain Iran's nuclear ambitions. The U.S. had imposed strict controls on all international banks and corporations, banning them from doing any business with Iran. Therefore, Iran faced great difficulty getting paid for its oil exports. A couple of Iranian businessmen, Babek Zenjani in Tehran and Reza Zarrab in Istanbul, stepped up to circumvent the sanctions. Oil payments would be made to companies and banks in Turkey, huge amounts of gold would be bought with those funds, and then the gold would be exported from Turkey to Iran, directly or perhaps with a few stops in Dubai, United Arab Emirates, and other places in between. This scheme, although very simple, required huge amounts of money and gold transferred on a daily basis, which would undoubtedly attract the unwanted attention of government officials. That problem would be addressed by generous bribes, commissions, and police protection. When you are moving billions of dollars daily, a few hundred million dollars to government officials is just the cost of doing business.

So, with the system set up in Iran and Turkey, Reza Zarrab quickly became a "gold trading" tycoon in Turkey, making headlines with large donations to religious charities linked to Erdoğan as a philanthropist, marrying a popular pop star singer, and buying several mansions along the Bosphorus. Erdoğan's government also bestowed Turkish citizenship on him with a special decree. There were a few mishaps in the scheme, such as 1.5 metric tons of gold seized in the cargo of an airplane in Istanbul by a "misguided" or "uninformed" customs official, who was promptly suspended and sent to "exile" in the interior of Turkey.

But the scheme blew up and came out in the open on Dec. 17, 2013, when Turkish police, or rather, a certain section of Turkish police not loyal to Erdoğan, arrested Reza Zarrab and the sons of three cabinet ministers, along with a few bank leaders. They had indisputable evidence including wiretaps, videos, telephone conversations, and documents proving the large amounts of bribes passed on from Zarrab to the ministers and bank officials. The evidence also included money counting machines in living rooms, several million dollars in shoeboxes, expensive gifts, and money being delivered to the ministers' homes in suit bags. All the dirty laundry came out.

One of the most interesting telephone conversations released by the investigators and reported by several media outlets was between Erdoğan and his son, when Erdoğan instructs his son to get rid of all cash in the house, after he hears about the raids to his ministers' houses. His son's response after several hours of frantic work reveals that despite all his attempts to distribute the cash at home to colleagues, relatives, or associates, there is still some thirty million euros left at home. Despite the evidence, Erdoğan did manage to escape the investigation unscathed, fired the three ministers, and also fired all the police officials and prosecutors involved in this operation, claiming that this was a conspiracy and coup attempt by the followers of Fethullah Gülen, the Muslim fundamentalist preacher living in exile in Pennsylvania. Most of the police officials and prosecutors are now in jail, and a few lucky ones have fled the country.

Reza Zarrab was released from prison in two months, in Feb. 2014. His defense was very simple: "If you don't release me immediately, I start talking."

It is not known why Zarrab chose to come to the U.S. Perhaps he decided to seek protection there, albeit in jail, instead of facing attempts to silence him in Turkey. Meanwhile, his partner in Iran, Babek Zenjani, was arrested and sentenced to death for defrauding the Iranian Oil Ministry for four billion dollars.

The Zarrab affair gets even more interesting in the U.S. The man who brought the charges against Zarrab was Preet Bharara, the U.S. attorney for the Southern District of New York—a star attorney who made his name as a fearless prosecutor of Wall Street wrongdoers. Erdoğan's concern about the Zarrab case was evident when he asked former Vice President Joe Biden to intervene. But luckily for him, just as the case against Zarrab started moving, the new president Trump fired Bharara, along with hundreds of other Obama appointees.

Zarrab has hired nearly 20 elite white-collar criminal lawyers to defend him. The last two hired lawyers are especially noteworthy, Rudi Giuliani, former New York Mayor and U.S. Attorney, and Michael B. Mukasey, the former U.S. Attorney General, who have promptly met top Turkish government officials. The presiding U.S. District Judge Richard Berman has asked defense lawyers to explain Giuliani and Mukasey's role in the case, and to disclose if the government of Turkey is paying their fees. Prosecutors claimed that the hiring of Giuliani and Mukasey might present a conflict of interest because their firms also represent some of the banks alleged to be victims in Zarrab's case. Prosecutors also said that Giuliani and Mukasey were hired to try to reach a political settlement in the case.

In another twist, Mukasey's son, Marc, has been widely speculated as a candidate to become the New York U.S. Attorney under Trump, to replace Preet Bharara. The Zarrab case will be one of the agenda items when Erdoğan meets Trump in the next few weeks.

This thriller involving power, bribery, corruption, oil, and gold will come to an end soon, but it is highly doubtful that justice will be served…

When Even the Dead Cannot Rest in Peace: Turkey's Intolerance toward the "Other"*

Just when one thinks the level of hatred and intolerance in Turkey toward minorities cannot get any worse, something shocking happens that surpasses even the worst incidents of the past.

Aysel Tuğluk, formerly a human rights activist, is a Member of Parliament for the province of Van in Turkey from the pro-Kurdish Peoples' Democratic Party (HDP). Along with the two co-leaders of the party and 11 other fellow deputies, she was arrested and has been kept in jail without any trial since Dec. 2016, based on charges of "supporting a terrorist organization."

Tuğluk's 78-year-old mother, Hatun Tuğluk, of Alevi descent and originally from Dersim, passed away this week. As per her will, she was to be buried in an Ankara cemetery. With special permission of the jail authorities, Tuğluk was temporarily released from jail to attend her mother's funeral and burial.

Just as her mother's coffin was buried in the cemetery, a group of 30 fanatical ultranationalists showed up at the grave site with a tractor, chanting slogans such as "These are Turkish lands, these are not Armenian lands," "Burial of Alevis, Armenians, and Kurds is not allowed here," "Seeds of Armenian not allowed in a Turkish cemetery," and more ominously, "If you don't remove this coffin, we will shred it to pieces."

Soon the mob increased to 100 people, and they started throwing stones at the mourners, including Tuğluk. Although many police officers

* *Armenian Weekly,* 18 Sept. 2018.

were present, they simply watched the mob without interfering. In fact, several attackers seemed to know the officers and addressed them by name.

In the end, Tuğluk had no choice but to remove her mother's coffin from the grave and decided to have her transported to Dersim for burial there. The prison authorities refused to allow Aysel to travel to Dersim, as the funeral permission was only for Ankara. So, while Aysel's mother's body traveled to Dersim, Aysel went back into jail.

The level of intolerance and hatred displayed during this incident is shocking. It is a generally accepted fact that any living person defined as "other"—that is, non-Turk, non-Sunni Muslim—will be subject to discrimination, insults, and even physical attacks in Turkey, but this incident showed that the scope of attacks now includes dead people.

There is no question that the attack was organized and planned, with the mob arriving just in time equipped with a tractor and prepared slogans, and obviously condoned by the state or deep state. The governor of Ankara minimized the incident as a provocation by a few drunken people, and the pro-government media covered the incident merely as "tension during a burial."

In 1915, the main "others" were the Armenians, who were almost wiped out through genocide, resulting in a huge transfer of wealth, lands, and property to the government, as well as through government-sanctioned plunderers and attackers.

In 1955, again on a September night, it was the turn of the Greek "others." Ultranationalist mobs attacked the houses, shops, and churches of the Greek minority in Istanbul, as revenge for the alleged bombing of Kemal Atatürk's house-museum in Thessaloniki, Greece. All 73 Greek churches in Istanbul were burned, more than 5,000 properties were demolished, hundreds of Greeks were murdered, several hundred Greek women were raped, and two Greek priests were forcibly circumcised. Greek cemeteries were also attacked and newly buried bodies removed in search of gold teeth.

Years later, it was revealed that it was Turkish government intelligence forces themselves who planted the bomb at Kemal Atatürk's house, organized and transported the attacking mobs in trucks, as well as supplied them with wooden clubs, all one standard size. Most of the Greek "others" left Turkey after that incident.

So now, the main "others" left in Turkey are the Kurds and the Alevis. However, 100 years of brainwashing preached in schools and mosques still keeps the hatred alive against the Armenians. Today, attacks or insults against Kurds and Alevis must also include the swear word "Armenian." When government forces fought against the Kurdish militants in Diyarbekir for the past two years, they wrote on the walls of bombed out buildings or taunted the Kurds with loudspeakers, calling them "Armenian bastards, seeds of Armenians."

Perhaps Hatun Tuğluk from Dersim did have Armenian roots, perhaps not. But that is not the issue for the ultranationalists, as long as they can direct their hatred of the Armenian toward all the remaining "others."

For a few years, until about two years ago, the Turkish government preached respect for democracy and human rights, tolerance, and equality for minorities and all "others," especially promoting peace and ending the war with the Kurds. The slogan "Turkey for Turks" was almost replaced with "Turkey for all citizens" for a few short years. Now, however, Turkey's defining slogan seems to have become "Turkey only for Turks… who support President Erdoğan."

The Untold Stories of Turkey: An Armenian Island on the Bosphorus[*]

What makes Istanbul beautiful is the Bosphorus, dividing the city between Europe and Asia. And what makes the Bosphorus beautiful is a series of architecturally magnificent palaces, mansions and mosques.

Most of these architectural masterpieces on both sides of the Bosphorus are created by one Armenian family of architects: the Balyans. This article will explain the little-known history of the only island in the Bosphorus and its connection to the Armenians, specifically to the Balyans.

Some three generations of Balyans served the Ottoman Sultans in the 18th and 19th centuries, building a multitude of palaces, mosques, barracks, schools, and clock towers for the Ottomans. The Balyans also built churches, schools, and mansions for Armenian communities all over the Empire, but mostly in Istanbul, and specifically along the Bosphorus.

---

[*] *Armenian Weekly*, 3 Oct. 2017.

Among the most notable Bosphorus works by the Balyans are the Palace, Mosque, and Clock Tower of Dolmabahce; Beylerbeyi Palace; Ciragan Palace (now a luxury hotel); Kuleli Military School (used as an orphanage by the British army after WWI to gather thousands of Armenian orphans rescued from Turkish and Kurdish homes); Ortakoy Mosque; Kucuksu Palace; and several other mansions. The Turkish Tourism Ministry and official guides refrained from identifying the architects of these buildings as the Armenian Balyans until the 2000s and instead mentioned an Italian architect called "Baliani."

While the Ottoman Sultans ordered the Balyans to build one palace after another, they started to pile up enormous amounts of debt and had to declare bankruptcy in 1876. The Chief Architect of the Empire, Sarkis Balyan, was owed large sums of money as well, and Sultan Abdulhamid decided to give Balyan the only island in the Bosphorus as compensation against his debt. The island was just a formation of rocks across from the village of Kurucesme, right in the middle of the Bosphorus.

Sarkis Balyan decided to build a summerhouse on these rocks to enjoy with the love of his life, his wife Makruhi Dadyan, the daughter of another famed Armenian family in the service of the Ottoman Empire as suppliers of gunpowder and armaments. Unfortunately, Makruhi died young soon after, because of tuberculosis, and Sarkis started living in seclusion on the island.

The island became known as Sarkis Bey Island, a meeting point for Sarkis Balyan's intellectual and artistic friends. One of his guests was famed Armenian-Russian painter Ivan Hovhannes Aivazovski, who always stayed on this island whenever he visited Istanbul. Some of his famous seascape paintings were created there.

Sarkis Balyan passed away in 1889, and, unfortunately, the island was not maintained by his heirs. The government took over the island and started using it as a coal depot for the steamships crossing the Bosphorus. In 1940, the heirs of Balyan were successful in having the island returned to their ownership, but they ended up selling the island in 1957 to Galatasaray Sports Club, one of the most prominent sporting institutions in Turkey. The island was renamed Galatasaray Island and expanded with swimming pools and sports facilities. In 2006, it was leased to a private entity for further expansion with several restaurants, as a high society entertainment center. In 2017, much of the expanded facility was demolished by the pro-Islamic government; at present, there are proposals to build a mosque on the original Sarkis Bey Island.

The Bosphorus is connected to Armenians in many other ways. Robert College, the oldest American college outside the United States, was founded in 1863 on the European shores of Bosphorus by Christopher Robert, a wealthy philanthropist, along with missionary Cyrus Hamlin.

Hamlin had learned Armenian to communicate with the first students of the boarding school: Armenian boys. The school expanded rapidly and became a leading educational institution in Istanbul, eventually adding a university with many faculties. Until WWI, most of the students were minorities—Armenians, Greeks, Bulgarians, and Jews. Unfortunately, the Armenian Genocide claimed several Armenian graduates of Robert College, along with the rest of Armenian intellectuals. Prominent Armenian journalist Teotig (Teodoros Lapchinjian), who compiled a list of the Armenian intellectual victims in his 1919 book "Memorial to April 24," mentions at least 10 Robert College graduates murdered by execution or massacre.

I will conclude with a personal anecdote. I was also a high school student at Robert College. Our Phys Ed teacher was Abbas Sakarya, the first Turkish wrestling champion who had won international gold medals, the first accredited gymnastics coach, the first founder of a swimming academy, and an all-around sports legend in Turkey. He was a very strict, severe man who never cracked a smile.

Robert College held annual Bosphorus Crossing swim races from the Asian to the European side. The width of the Bosphorus Strait is about a mile, but with the treacherous currents one has to swim double or triple that distance during the crossing. Along with dozens of other university and high school students, I also participated in the race and ended coming in second among the high school students. Mr. Sakarya congratulated me and, along with a rare smile, whispered into my ear: "Abris," in Armenian ("bravo").

At the time, I thought he might have used that word as a complement because he knew I was Armenian. But, years later, near his death at age 97, I found out that this Turkish legendary sportsman and teacher was in fact a hidden Armenian from Bursa—and an orphan of the Genocide.

There are many secret and untold stories about Armenians in Turkey. Turks may not know or may not want to know them, but they must be told.

Genocide Denied, Armenians Denied: Rejecting the Very Existence of Armenians in Turkey[*]

Last week, while criticizing Israel and the United States on President Trump's recent recognition of Jerusalem as Israel's capital, Turkish President Recep Tayyip Erdoğan stated with great conviction, "There has never been any genocide, holocaust, massacre, ethnic cleansing, or torture in our [Turkish] history."

He said this without even batting an eye…

This wholesale denial of historic facts regarding the treatment of minorities by the state is nothing new, but with each act of denial, history keeps repeating itself with sickening regularity—the massacres of Armenians were followed by the massacres of Greeks, Assyrians, Alevis, and Kurds.

This article will focus not on the denial of genocide, but on the denial of the very existence of the Armenians and the many contributions they have made in the country.

In a previous article ("The Untold Stories of Turkey: An Armenian Island on the Bosphorus"), I had touched upon how a single family of Armenian architects, the Balyans, had shaped the skyline of Istanbul, particularly along the Bosphorus, with their creations of palaces, mansions, military barracks, and mosques. Although revered and respected as Royal Architects during Ottoman reign, their Armenian identity was denied by the Republic of Turkey and they were referred to as the Italian Balianis by official tour guides until the early 2000s.

Even more famous than the Balyan family, an architect living in the 16th century, Mimar (architect) Sinan (1489-1588), has left his mark all over the Ottoman Empire. He built 92 mosques, 55 schools, 36 palaces, 48 hamams (bathhouses), three hospitals, 20 inns, 10 bridges, six water channels, and hundreds of other government buildings—almost all of them still standing after five centuries. His masterpieces are the

---

[*] *Armenian Weekly*, 18 Dec. 2017.

Over the years, there has been an effort to deny the very existence of the Armenians and their contributions to Turkey.

Suleymaniye Mosque in Istanbul and Selimiye Mosque in Edirne, which are both registered UNESCO World Heritage sites.

The average Turk knows Mimar Sinan as the "Great Turkish Architect Sinan," and his name is given to fine arts and architecture universities. But little is known about the fact that he was an Armenian from the Agirnas village of Kayseri province, seized from his parents as a boy, Islamized, circumcised, and raised as a soldier and subsequently as an architect by the state. When he died at the ripe age of 99, he was buried near Suleymaniye Mosque.

During the 1930s, the Turkish state was dominated by racist intellectuals who claimed that the Turkish race was superior to all other races and that there was a definable set of Turkish race characteristics in the shape of skulls and other features. To prove their point and to demonstrate that historically intelligent Turks match their defined racial characteristics, these so-called anthropology experts decided to exhume the remains of Architect Sinan, a most prominent Turk from the past. Unfortunately, Sinan's skull did not match these experts' theoretical Turkish skull dimensions, and as a result the skull was kept hidden. To this day, the whereabouts of the skull is still unknown, and Sinan's body lies in his grave without a head.

Again in the 1930s, when President Mustafa Kemal decided to introduce the Latin alphabet and modernize the Turkish language, he turned to professor Hagop (Agop) Martayan, a prominent linguist, to head the Turkish Language Council. As a reward for his services to the Turkish language, Kemal gave him a new surname, Dilaçar, meaning "language opener" [i.e., one who bestows language]. In return, Martayan proposed the surname "Atatürk" to Kemal, which was eventually adopted by Parliament.

When Martayan passed away in 1979, the Turkish media announced his name as A. Dilaçar, without ever mentioning his Armenian identity. In fact, some newspapers further distorted his name, calling him Adil Acar. After Mustafa Kemal became Atatürk, he needed to create a new signature, and he called upon another Armenian, master calligrapher Vahram Çerçiyan (Jerjian). Çerçiyan's Atatürk signature was adopted in 1934, and it appears on everything from Turkish banknotes to parliamentary records. Today, nearly nobody in Turkey remembers Çerçiyan.

In 1932, the Turkish government commissioned a prominent Armenian musicologist and conductor, Edgar Manas, to create the harmony and orchestration for the Turkish national anthem based on a melody by a Turkish musician. Today, nobody remembers Edgar Manas in Turkey, even though his composition of the national anthem is sung every week in schools, stadiums, and Parliament.

In Turkish cinema, movie stars Adile Naşit, Toto Karaca, Vahi Öz, Sami Hazinses, and Kenan Pars are known all over Turkey, after making millions laugh or cry in their films over the years. But very few Turks know or acknowledge that these stars are all Armenian. They all had unique reasons for hiding their Armenian identities, and many of their true roots were revealed only after they passed away. Adile Nasit was Adile Keskiner (1930-1987), Toto Karaca was Irma Felegyan (1912-1992), Vahi Öz was Vahe Ozinyan (1911-1969), Sami Hazinses was Samuel Agop Ulucyan (1925-2002), and Kenan Pars was Kirkor Cezveciyan (1920-2008).

The first opera in Turkey was staged in 1874 in Istanbul by an Armenian; it was composed, conducted, and produced by Dikran Çuhacıyan (Tchoukhajian) (1837-1898). Turkish sources deny this and cite Turkish singers for much later dates. The first theater production in Istanbul was staged six years earlier, in 1868, again by an Armenian, by the name of Agop (Hagop) Vartovyan (1840-1902), also known as Güllü Agop and Yakub. Though it is safe to call Vartovyan the founder of modern Turkish theater, most Turkish sources deny this fact.

The first athletes representing Ottoman Turkey on the international stage were two Armenians and a Greek at the 1912 Olympic Games in Stockholm. The Armenians were Vahram Papazyan and Mgrditch Migiryan, both competing in track and field. Most Turkish sources deny this and cite Turkish athletes at later dates.

Examples of Armenian contributions, innovations, or accomplishments, denied or forgotten in Turkey, can be seen in nearly every imaginable field of arts, science, business, finance, banking, engineering, and publishing in Ottoman or Republican Turkey. One of the best sources to comprehend the role of Armenians in Turkey is an incredibly detailed series of four books called "Western Armenians Throughout History" (*Tarih Boyunca Batı Ermenileri*), in Turkish, authored by Professor Parsegh Tuglaciyan (1933-2016), better known as Pars Tuğlacı.

Tuglaciyan is the author of the first Turkish encyclopedia, called the "Ocean Encyclopedia Dictionary," and several other books. However, perhaps his lifetime achievement is this four volume history of Armenians, based on hundreds of thousands of meticulously researched documents. Each volume totals about 900 pages, covering the periods of 289-1850 (Vol. 1), 1850-1890 (Vol. 2), 1890-1923 (Vol. 3), and 1923-1966 (Vol. 4). His last volume was published in 2009 in Istanbul.

Unfortunately, after being diagnosed with Alzheimer's disease, he was not able to publish the fifth volume, which would have covered the period of 1966-2010.

The most dramatic and indisputable evidence of the Armenian Genocide is in Tuglaciyan's third volume (1890-1923), which reveals thousands of documents showing Armenian achievements in nearly every field imaginable, including within the Ottoman government. Until the mid-1910s, Armenians were prominent in all levels of the Ottoman foreign ministry and embassies, indispensable in state enterprises and the central bank, and highly influential in the fields of business, art, science, academic institutions in Istanbul as well as all the Ottoman provinces. The dramatic disappearance of all these Armenian names in 1915 is evidence enough of the Armenian Genocide.

When I once asked Professor Tuglaciyan how he was allowed to publish such a critical book in Turkey, he simply stated: "I am just presenting state documents showing promotions or rewards of Armenians in state bureaucracy, achievements of Armenians in arts, sciences, and business, promotional ads of Armenian enterprises or cultural events. They all existed before 1915, but no more after 1915. Who can dispute that?"

In conclusion, I urge all Armenian scholars in Armenia and the Diaspora to consider translating Professor Tuglaciyan's hidden treasure to English and Armenian for future generations to better understand what we had, what we lost, and—perhaps most important—why we lost it.

Returning to the Roots: Stories of Hidden Armenians*

Over the years, I have met many hidden Armenians from different regions of Turkey. Each one has a unique story that can become an article or even a book on its own. Some stories can be shared; most cannot. Some are funny; most are sad.

Recently, many hidden Armenians decided to return to their roots, culture, and language after they discovered their Armenian origins and the forced Islamization/Turkification/Kurdification of their grandparents, who were orphans and the living victims of the Armenian Genocide.

In 2014 and 2015, I organized trips for dozens of them from Turkey to Armenia, in cooperation with Armenia's Ministry of the Diaspora. In past articles, I have shared the stories of some of these "no longer hidden" Armenians. In this article, I will tell some stories of the "still hidden" Armenians, names withheld for obvious reasons.

Let me start with a memory from my days in the Turkish army. Although I was already living in Canada at the time, I had to return to complete my compulsory military service in the Turkish army in order to be able to travel back to Turkey to take care of my elderly parents. On top of the drills and other military activities during the day, the conscripts were required to attend lectures in the evening. One of the subjects was "Who are the enemies of Turkey?" After discussing the assorted bad deeds of all the "enemy" neighboring countries, such as Soviet Russia, Iran, Iraq, Syria, Bulgaria, and Greece, the instructor would inevitably conclude that

* *Armenian Weekly*, 2 Jan. 2018.

the worst enemy were the Armenians, since they had massacred the Turks in 1915 and were still after Turkish diplomats.

After these lectures, a few fellow conscripts with Turkish or Kurdish names, especially from the eastern provinces, would approach me and confess that their grandmothers were Armenian, or that they lived in a house left behind by Armenians, or that their village was Armenian before 1915 but had converted to Islam.

When I started writing articles about the hidden Armenians and the Surp Giragos church reconstruction project in Diyarbekir (Dikranagerd), an elderly Armenian lady from the United States made contact with me. She was an orphan of 1915 and had found her way to the U.S. Her brother, however, had to remain in Turkey and was eventually Islamized and Turkified. This brother prospered and became a successful builder in Turkey, with cement plants in many provinces. After some research, I tracked his grandson in Turkey, a man in his early thirties, who had carried on the family construction business, building luxury condos in Istanbul. He was aware of his Armenian past, but obviously unable to reveal it publicly for fear of losing his wife, business, and status as a successful Turkish builder. He eventually made contact with his grandfather's Armenian sister in the U.S. and visited her.

"My grandfather's sister had one request when I traveled to the U.S. to see her, to lie in bed with her, just as she had done with her brother when they were little, so that she can smell the scent of her brother," he explained to me. And that is just what they did—an 85-year-old Armenian woman hugging in bed with a Turkish condo builder in his thirties that she just met, in order to remember her long-lost family.

There are many stories of orphans torn apart from their loved ones in 1915. Some were brought to orphanages under the control of the victorious Allies after WWI, eventually finding their way to the Armenian Diaspora or Soviet Armenia, while others were placed in Turkish orphanages, becoming Muslim Turks or Kurds. We witnessed a few happy reunions on our trips, as once-hidden Armenians found their long-lost relatives in Armenia for the first time. We brought together a 65-year-old hidden Armenian from Diyarbekir with his cousin, a 70-year-old villager from Armavir region. One didn't speak Armenian, the other didn't speak Turkish, but they held hands and hugged each other continuously for three hours during a dinner.

Hamshen (or Hemshin) is the name given to people living in the eastern Black Sea coastal region of Turkey. There is strong evidence that they are Armenians who have migrated to this region after Seljuk Turks captured the city of Ani in the eleventh century, followed by more waves of Armenians settling in the region in later times. Soon after, in the 16th century, the region was conquered by the Ottoman Turks, and the Armenians were eventually forced to convert to Islam. Most of them did convert, but interestingly enough they kept the Armenian language, and continue to keep it until today. And although they still speak a dialect of Armenian, with constant indoctrination from the government they have been made to believe that their ancestors migrated from Central Asia and their language was a branch of Central Asian Turkish.

Until recently, most Hamshen people had a strong nationalistic—even racist—allegiance to Turkey. In conversation with a Hamshen woman, I was amazed to hear the following: "Yes Hay chem. Yes Turk em" ("I am not Armenian. I am a Turk.")—in Armenian!

Since the early 2000s, Hamshentsis (Hamshen people) have started to search for their real, Armenian roots. Here is the story told by an elderly Hamshentsi about how people in the region first got a clue that what they spoke was Armenian and not a Central Asian Turkic language. In 1982, Armenian Secret Army for the Liberation of Armenia (ASALA) commandos carried out an unsuccessful attack at the Ankara airport. All were killed, except Levon Ekmekjian, who was captured, tortured, and then put on trial. His trial was aired live on Turkish television, and Ekmekjian gave his testimony in Armenian, which was then translated to Turkish. People all over Turkey, including the Hamshentsis, were glued to the television watching the trial. The Hamshen people were surprised to discover that Levon spoke their own language. Many of them wondered if he was a Hamshentsi, and eventually realized that their language is Armenian, like his.

As a postscript to this story, the trial was just a formality, and Ekmekjian was executed in Jan. 1983, buried in an unmarked grave until 2016, when the heroic Turkish human rights lawyer Eren Keskin succeeded in having Levon's remains transferred to France, to reunite with his family.

On a happier note, one of the hidden Armenians from Hamshen who traveled to Armenia with me met a hidden Armenian woman from Diyarbekir, and they are now married.

In the mid-1990s, I joined the Hayastan All Armenia Fund as a volunteer participant in reconstruction projects. One of the projects was the reconstruction of the Spitak church, which was damaged during the 1988 earthquake, financed from an account in Switzerland administered by lawyers on behalf of an anonymous donor—who turned out to be the hidden Armenian grandmother of a very wealthy, high-profile Turkish family.

In 2013, I was fortunate enough to accomplish one of my bucket-list items by climbing Mount Ararat with my son Daron. The starting point for the expedition was a town named Doğubayazıt—the former Daroynk of medieval Armenia, now populated entirely by Kurds, except for Turkish security forces. One of the roads is built with the contents of the Armenian cemetery, with Armenian-scripted gravestones and bones still visible on the road shoulders. The grandmother of one of the Kurdish mountain guides was Armenian, and he fondly remembered how she prayed five times a day as a Muslim, while keeping a cross and Bible under her pillow. The guide had 18 brothers and sisters, most of them married to other Kurds with Armenian grandmothers in their families, and each brother and sister had at least five children themselves. He wished his children would go to a university on the other side of the mountain, in Armenia, instead of a Turkish university.

Hidden Armenians have complicated lives, full of emotional turmoil and psychological scars. They are shunned by Muslim Turks and Kurds—and also by most members of the Armenian community in Istanbul and the Armenian Patriarchate.

When the grandchildren of forcibly Islamized Armenian orphans find the courage to come out and return to their Armenian roots and identity despite all the risks, discrimination, and abuse they will receive in their neighborhood, workplace, and even their own families, they must be encouraged, not rejected. Sure, there may be opportunistic pretenders with Armenian claims for personal gain who should be investigated and scrutinized, but I have come to realize that through my network of hidden Armenians and their links it is surprisingly easy to uncover them. For example, when someone claiming to be Dersimtsi Armenian approached a cleric here in Toronto, I was able to determine the truth about him after some questioning and investigation in his Dersim village. When I took hidden Armenians to Armenia and some of them wanted to become Christian by baptism, it was easy to determine through family ties back in Diyarbekir whether they really had Armenian roots. The obstruction of some clerics preventing them from becoming Christian Armenian is unreasonable, however, when a trustworthy Armenian godfather (gnkahayr) is vouching for the truth.

Being born an Armenian is not a choice, and if someone chooses to return to his/her roots after discovering his/her Armenian origin, no cleric or government official has the right to prevent that. Whether someone adopts a new religion is a choice that comes later. There are many differing viewpoints on the subject of who can "become an Armenian." Of course, there is freedom of thought and expression, but if someone in power or influence makes a decision that infringes on another's freedom, that is simply unacceptable.

"Gna Merir, Yekur Sirem": Artsakh War Veteran, Outspoken Activist Sarkis Hatspanian Dies at 55[*]

Artsakh War veteran, political commentator, and political activist Sarkis Hatspanian passed away on Jan. 20 in Lyon, France. He was only 55.

Born in Adiyaman in southeastern Turkey (former Cilicia), he had left for France in 1980 to avoid persecution of the military dictatorship in Turkey. In 1990, he moved to Armenia to join the Artsakh War effort. Sarkis participated in the liberation of the Karvajar (Kalbajar) region, which unites Artsakh and Armenia. A photo of him with an elderly woman became a symbol of the war.

A photo of Hatspanian with an elderly woman became a symbol of the war. The photo had two stories—one very real, the other a complete lie.

The real story was as reported by a French journalist who accompanied the Armenian forces during the campaign, depicting Sarkis with an 80-year-old Azeri woman, Shaikha Hanum. She was left behind, along with other elderly Azeri women and children in the Karvajar district, when all the able-bodied Azeris had fled ahead of the advancing Armenian forces.

[*] *Armenian Weekly*, 22 Jan. 2018.

Sarkis Hatspanian during the Karabagh War, 1990.

Her son was a police commander in the district. Sarkis was in charge of taking care of the Azeri civilians, and eventually providing safe passage for them to Gandzak (Kirovabad). Armenians took such good care of the civilians that Shaikha Hanum stated she loved Sarkis more than his cowardly son who had abandoned her. On the same day that this story and photo was published in France, a fake story was posted in the Turkish daily *Milliyet* using the same photo. Sarkis was described as an Azeri soldier rescuing his Azeri grandmother from the Armenian enemy.

After the war, he became politically active and a fierce critic of corruption in Armenia, particularly of the oligarchs who had stakes in the government and in the Armenian Church, expressing his views eloquently and articulately during frequent television appearances. Sarkis and I met and became fast friends when I took groups of hidden Armenians from Turkey to Armenia. He was fascinated by this new Armenian reality. He would follow our tour itinerary and meet us at museums and churches that we visited, becoming a volunteer guide, counselor, mentor, and lifelong friend to our "once hidden" Armenians.

When he was struck by cancer this past summer, he had to move to Lyon to receive the required treatment in a race against time. He needed a place to stay during the treatments and was in dire financial need. Our numerous pleas for some financial assistance from heads of Armenian organizations, influential or politically active Armenians in France or Europe, unfortunately fell on deaf ears. Ultimately, a fundraising campaign was organized in Canada to send emergency funds to Sarkis and family, with a few anonymous donors from Turkey also contributing. He passed away disappointed and dejected by the apathy of his fellow Armenians.

And now, as soon as he passed away, the accolades and eulogies by Armenian Diaspora leaders rise to the sky for the "Artsakh war hero." We have a saying in Armenian: "Gna merir, yekur sirem" ("Once you die, then you're loved"). Perhaps this attitude is unique to Armenians, because I cannot find such a cruel yet poignant proverb in any other language.

I remember a similar situation with my other hero friend, Hrant Dink. He was disliked and heavily criticized by most Diaspora Armenian leaders for his readiness for dialogue with Turks. We were chatting after the first Ottoman Armenian conference held in Istanbul Bilgi University in Sept. 2005, where he and other speakers were pelted with eggs, tomatoes, and coins. I had suggested that perhaps a similar conference can be organized somewhere in U.S. or Europe, by inviting both Turkish and Armenian historians. He smiled bitterly: "Raffi, you would have more problems with the Diaspora than I have here with the Turks." Unfortunately, Hrant became a unanimously accepted hero only after he was shot dead.

In the last few months of their lives, both Sarkis and Hrant felt alone and abandoned in their struggles, one fighting the ever-increasing cancer eating at him from the inside, and the other fighting the ever-increasing death threats eating at him from the outside.

I hope Armenians can adopt a new proverb by reversing the order of the four words: "Yekur sirem, gna merir" ("Let me love you, then you may die.")

The Failed Istanbul Armenian Patriarchate[*]

The never-ending manipulations and power games at the Istanbul Patriarchate took a turn for the worse this past week.

In 2008, the Istanbul Patriarch, Archbishop Mesrob Mutafyan, was diagnosed with dementia—a disease that has incapacitated him and effectively put him into a vegetative state. The cleric next in line at the

* *Armenian Weekly*, 12 Feb. 2018.

Patriarchate, Archbishop Aram Ateshian, was appointed the Acting Patriarch at that time, with the expectation that unless Patriarch Mutafyan miraculously recovered, elections would be held to decide a successor.

For the past nine years, Acting Patriarch Ateshian had resisted all attempts of the Istanbul Armenian community, other Patriarchate clerics, and even the Echmiadzin Catholicos, to hold the elections. Finally, in March 2017, Ateshian relented to the Religious Council of the Patriarchate's request to start the election process. Archbishop Karekin Bekdjian of the Diocese of Germany was elected Locum Tenens—a caretaker cleric—until the election of a new Patriarch to replace the ailing Patriarch Mutafyan and the Acting Patriarch Ateshian.

Both Ateshian and Bekdjian were supposed to be candidates in the elections, along with four other eligible clerics. But now, following a meeting with Turkey's Minister of the Interior and a letter received from the Istanbul Governor, the Religious Council of the Istanbul Patriarchate has declared that there will be no elections and that Archbishop Ateshian will continue serving as Acting Patriarch until Patriarch Mutafyan dies.

Archbishop Bekdjian has since resigned and is on his way back to Germany.

How is all this possible? Ateshian is favored by the government of Turkey, which, from day-one, considered the election process and the selection of the Locum Tenens null and void, even though the process for the community to freely elect their religious leaders is clearly spelled out in the legal authority of the Istanbul Patriarchate and the Lausanne Treaty defining the legal rights of the minorities in Turkey.

The Turkish government—and the country's authoritarian President Recep Tayyip Erdoğan—interprets the laws as it pleases. And, in Turkey, that "interpretation" is all that counts.

Archbishop Ateshian once proclaimed that he was proud to call President Erdoğan his brother. Ateshian was also a fierce critic of Germany's passing of an Armenian Genocide resolution in June 2016. The Archbishop even wished Erdoğan success in starting the Afrin invasion in Syria, which has killed numerious Kurdish (and some Armenian) civilians. It is natural that the Turkish government will interfere to the benefit of an Armenian religious leader so much in line with its priorities.

There have been two occasions during which I had the chance to communicate directly with Archbishop Ateshian. The first instance was when I planned to perform a piano concert at the then-newly reconstructed Surp Giragos Armenian church in Diyarbekir, during the Centennial Commemoration of the Armenian Genocide in April 2015. As part of the concert program, in addition to my performance of Armenian composers, I had proposed to invite a well-known Armenian and a Kurdish opera singer to present songs of Komitas, a noted victim of the Armenian Genocide. Archbishop Ateshian opposed the idea of the concert in "his church" and suggested that I hold the concert somewhere else in Diyarbekir. At the end, the concert did take place in the church, in the presence of more than 1,000 attendees, including elected officials, local Kurds and Turks, and—perhaps most significantly—hundreds of hidden Armenians. Instead of the two singers, I ended up playing the Komitas works in the church myself—so meaningful and symbolic, 100 years after the Armenian Genocide.

The other occasion was when my friends and I approached the Archbishop about the thousands of abandoned Armenian churches in Turkey. For a few years in the early 2010s, there was a window of opportunity by an apparently liberalized Turkish government to allow for the return and reconstruction of Armenian churches. The reconstruction of Surp Giragos church is one example, even though the situation has dramatically worsened in the past two years. However, at that time, there was some willingness by the government to return or restore the churches as our cultural heritage in Anatolia. We even had discussions with government officials on specific churches in Van, Sivas, and Malatya. Unfortunately, Archbishop Ateshian turned down these attempts. "I cannot even take care of the Armenian Churches in Istanbul, what do I need to have more churches in Anatolia?" he said.

I am not sure whether to call this line of thinking shortsightedness or toeing the line of the state. But my intention is not to blame Ateshian or the Turkish government, which sees him as its man. I would like to focus on the attitude of the Istanbul Armenian community, and more specifically its non-religious leaders, who are the elected leaders of dozens of charitable organizations attached to the Istanbul Armenian Churches, schools, and hospitals.

The charitable organizations are all supposed to be under the control of the Istanbul Patriarchate and act in unison. The wealthier foundations, which own large assets, are supposed to help the less fortunate ones. Unfortunately, this rarely happens, and as long as there is no interference from the Patriarchate, most of the leaders, with a few exceptions, treat the charitable organizations as their own personal empires without much consideration for the overall benefit of the community.

The community itself is deeply divided, apathetic, and/or unable to voice any protest, except for a few progressive groups—including the Nor Zartonk movement—and some young intellectuals and activists gathered around the *Agos* newspaper.

After what happened this past week at the Patriarchate, one would expect the community to organize and take some protest actions against the unilateral takeover by Ateshian. A possible protest could be boycotting the religious services conducted by the Archbishop and instead attending church services at other local Armenian churches.

Of course, the church in which he presided over Mass this past Sunday was completely full. There was only one Armenian lawyer among the crowd who dared to protest—she sang aloud the prayer "Der Voghormia" out of turn. According to *Agos*, she was removed from the church upon instructions from Archbishop Ateshian, arrested by Turkish authorities, and taken to a police station. She was released after being held in detention for about an hour.

As the saying goes, people get the leaders they deserve. While we lament and complain and protest against the unfair treatment of Armenians by other nations, we should also recognize our own weaknesses and do something about them.

Armenian Turks and Other Tragic Stories of Roots[*]

Last month, the Turkish government released a website where Turkish citizens can look up their ancestral roots all the way back until the mid-1850s. There are hundreds of stories in printed and social media, which sent shockwaves in Turkey and beyond, about several Turks who discovered that they had Albanian, Arabic, Pontic Greek, and—worst of

* *Armenian Weekly*, 19 March 2018.

all—Armenian roots. There have even been reports that some members of an ultra-nationalistic and racist Turkish party were ostracized and thrown out of their ranks, went into depression, and even committed suicide upon discovering their Armenian family roots.

Whether these stories are true or exaggerated, the subject of one's roots is critical—and in some cases, deadly— in Turkey. The late Hrant Dink was continuously persecuted, prosecuted for "insulting Turkishness," and eventually assassinated after revealing that Kemal Atatürk's adopted daughter and first female military pilot in Turkey, Sabiha Gökçen, was in fact an Armenian girl orphaned during the Armenian Genocide. In another case, a former President of Turkey had sued an opposition Member of Parliament for "accusing and insulting" him by stating that "he came from an Armenian family in Kayseri."

And yet, in a country where calling someone Armenian is the biggest insult, there are numerous documented and undocumented stories about prominent Turks having Armenian roots, including a past president, another former president's wife, and several opposition politicians. In one of the documented stories, the family of a past opposition leader—an ultra-nationalistic Turk—was actually converted to Islam from an Armenian family in the Black sea region, whose Armenian descendants now live in Canada.

When this official genealogy website was made public, I immediately wondered how the hidden Armenians' (Armenians and their descendants, who were forced to convert during the Armenian Genocide) roots were recorded and a quick survey revealed that absolutely none of them were recorded as Armenian. Their family history started only with their adopted Muslim Turkish names. Although there is past evidence that the government kept detailed records of converted Armenians among Turks and Kurds, these records are not made public and are not revealed in this new website. Interestingly, it became evident that many Armenians killed, lost, and deported during the genocide are still marked as being "alive" on the website. Many Armenian families who knew the tragic fate of their grandmothers or grandfathers born all the way back in 1850s, are now finding out that these people are still miraculously alive, according to the doctored records of the website.

I wish here, to relate two interesting—and little known—stories of roots.

A weathly Armenian family lived in a village of Malatya in the 1880s. The region was terrorized and harassed by Kurdish tribesmen, who regularly raided Armenian villages. Eventually, Armenians started organizing defense forces by banding together fedayees (freedom fighters) to protect the Armenian villages. An Armenian fedayee leader once approached the head of this wealthy Armenian family and asked for money to buy weapons and horses. The wealthy Armenian said that he would decide in two days whether to comply with this request or not. After two days, the fedayee returned and the wealthy Armenian refused to give any money. The fedayee promptly shoots the man. The widow of the killed Armenian man fled with her newborn son to Izmir, where she converted to Islam and raised her son with utter hatred toward Armenians. That boy grew up to be Ismet İnönü (1884-1973), the second President of Turkey after Kemal Atatürk—and perhaps one of the worst enemy of the Armenians and other minorities in Turkey, after the Ittihadist (Young Turk) leaders.

İnönü brought forth legislation called the "Wealth Tax" in 1942 (Varlik Vergisi), ostensibly to help Turkey cope with the war economy, but with the intent of ruining the minorities. The taxes were assessed based on ethnic origin—the level of taxation with respect to total capital was 232 percent for Armenians, 184 percent for Jews, 159 percent for Greeks, and only a mere 4.9 percent for the Turks. The payment deadline was 15 days and anyone who could not pay was arrested and sent to the eastern provinces to work as laborers in stone quarries, building roads or tunnels. This was, in effect, a wealth transfer from the minorities to Turks.

Many Armenians, after selling all their assets at dirt cheap prices, went bankrupt and still could not raise the required amounts and ended up at labor camps and dying there. In 1964, İnönü further oppressed the Greeks, when he deported 45,000 of them who had dual Greek and Turkish citizenship during the Cyprus crisis. They were given ten days to leave behind all their properties, assets, and belongings to leave the country with the allowed $20 and 20 kg (45 lbs) of possessions. The story of Ismet İnönü's Armenian roots was corroborated by prominent historian Prof. Pars Tuglaci (Parsegh Tuglaciyan) (1933-2016), a family friend of İnönü.

Ali Kemal was a prominent liberal Ottoman journalist and editor of the *Ikdam* newspaper in the 1910s. He was also a member of the opposition Liberal Union (Itilaf) party and severe critic of the ruling Ittihad Terakki party. He fiercely criticizes the ruling party for entering the war, and for committing "war crimes and massacres" against its own Armenian citizens. His editorials and brilliant political speeches defending the Armenians are so vehement, that the pro-Ittihadist media dubbed him "Artin Kemal" (Artin is an Armenian name, short for Harutiun).

After the war, when Ottoman Turkey was defeated and the Ittihadist leaders fled the country, the Sultan appointed a new government and Kemal briefly became Minister of Interior. Kemal relentlessly demanded prosecution and punishment of the Ittihadist leaders. While he continued his attacks on the Ittihad leaders and defends the Armenians' rights, he decided to send his British wife and children to England for safety. Unfortunately, the tide turned against Kemal when the resistance started by Kemal Atatürk in Ankara gained power and swept the Sultan and the Istanbul government away. Kemal got caught in the barber shop of Tokatliyan Hotel in Istanbul . While being taken to Ankara for trial, one of Atatürk's commanders, "Red" Nureddin Pasha (dubbed "Red" for his red beard as well as his bloody cruelty) ordered his soldiers to lynch Kemal, who was torn apart limb by limb while still alive.

Kemal's family settled in Britain and his great grandson eventually became the Mayor of London, and current Foreign Minister of Great Britain, Boris Johnson. As a master diplomat, Johnson continuously tells Turkish President Erdoğan that UK will do everything possible to get Turkey into the European Union, but at the same time, advocates Brexit by arguing that if Turkey enters EU, Britain would be flooded by Turkish immigrants.

If it weren't for stories of tragic roots, politics would be fun.

Artsakh Karabagh – First Memories[*]

My first trip to Armenia was not really to Armenia, but to Artsakh, known internationally as Nagorno Karabagh, right after the war with the Azeris ended in 1993 with victory for the Armenians. The united goodwill,

[*] *Asbarez*, 20 July 2018.

cooperation, sacrifice and courage of Armenian leaders, peoples of Armenia, Artsakh and Diaspora had made the miraculous victory possible in those early days, followed by enthusiastic rebuilding and reconstruction projects. Unfortunately the winning spirit was replaced over the years by selfish greed, power grab, corruption and bribery by the leaders, while bringing disillusionment, disappointment, frustration and poverty to the people. It is my hope that the leaders and people of independent Armenia and Artsakh as well as the Diaspora learn from the lessons and memories of the first quarter century, build on the good deeds and avoid the bad ones.

I remember the Hayastan All Armenian Fund or "Himnatram" was just formed then to provide desperately needed funds and know-how to construct civil infrastructure such as highways, water distribution networks, gas pipelines, schools and hospitals, either destroyed during the recent war or left in ruins during decades of neglect. As a civil engineer specializing in public works infrastructure in Toronto, I volunteered to go to Karabagh and help the Himnatram engineers in implementing these essential projects. I informed the Armenian Ambassador to Canada: "The leader of Himnatram is Mrs. Manoushag Petrosyan, the leader of Karabagh is Leonid Petrosyan (assassinated along with other politicians in the Armenian Parliament in 1999), the leader of Armenia is Levon Ter-Petrossian, and since my name is also Petrosyan, I have no choice but to volunteer and go to Armenia and Karabagh." Therefore, I boarded the Tupolev jet of Armenian Airlines in Paris and landed in Yerevan around 3 a.m. one night. Himnatram engineers picked me up at the airport, and we traveled in pitch dark from the airport to a downtown hotel, with electricity and streetlights off. There were several gas tanker trucks parked along the road, selling gas by container, as gas stations didn't function. In the morning, I saw beautiful Mount Ararat and beautiful Yerevan for the first time, but also the makeshift pipe chimneys sticking out from all apartment windows and the thousands of chopped down trees all over the city for heating and cooking purposes.

We started our long journey to Karabagh, six people including two young soldiers going to the front, all crammed into a small Niva. We stopped for breakfast by the Arpa River in Yegheknadzor, not with tea or coffee but with the obligatory mulberry vodka, "tuti oghi" in Armenian. As we left Goris and entered Karabagh through the Lachin corridor, we could see the violence of the war all around us, the burnt houses as well as

Ghazantchetsots Cathedral, Shushi.

hundreds of destroyed Azeri tanks strewn on the side of the road. One of the Himnatram engineers who knew the heroic commander Monte Melkonian explained how Monte changed the course of the war when he told the Armenian fighters: "Why do you destroy the gift of the Turks (Azeris) to us?" After that, the Armenians changed tactics to preserve the captured Azeri tanks instead of destroying them, and won the war against the Azeris by using Azeri tanks. To understand the realities of the war and the enormity of the victory, one should visit two sites in Shushi, Karabagh. The beautiful white church in Shushi, Ghazantchetsots church, was used as an arms depot by the Azeris on the assumption that Armenians would not fire on their own church. The Azeris controlled Shoushi, which is situated on high cliffs literally on top of Stepanakert, enabling the Azeris to target and rain hundreds of rockets on any Stepanakert building that they wished to destroy. But Armenian commandos accomplished the impossible, climbed the almost vertical cliffs at Jdrduz near Shoushi in one night, and gained control of Shoushi, which paved the way to victory.

I worked for a while on the highway construction project joining Armenia to Karabagh, known as the Goris-Stepanakert Highway, which became a lifeline and replaced an almost unpassable mountain road reducing the trip from Yerevan to Stepanakert from 11 hours to 5 hours. During the war, even this road was blocked and the only connection between Armenia and Artsakh was via helicopters, bringing supplies, medicine, arms into Artsakh, and returning with wounded soldiers back into Armenia. I then moved on to the water supply and water distribution project for Stepanakert, capital of Karabagh. Before fleeing, Azeris had destroyed all the plans for existing infrastructure, making it even more difficult for our contractors. Without knowing the location of underground gas, electric or telephone ducts, it was slow and dangerous work to dig the streets for new water pipes. Almost everyone I met in Karabagh had participated in the war or had lost a family member to the war. The main contractor, Felix, told me his story. He was sitting with his friend on the front steps of his contractor's office one day, to smoke cigarettes. He couldn't find matches and went inside to get some. Just then, an Azeri Grad missile landed at his friend's feet, blowing him to pieces. Seeing this, Felix just grabbed a Kalashnikov, stopped being a contractor and became a soldier. From the highest government official to the lowest construction labourer, every person regarded these construction projects as a patriotic mission. Donations poured in to Himnatram, from the Diaspora as well as from within Armenia and Artsakh, large and small, even from a beggar on a Yerevan street.

I learnt a lot about land mines on this first Karabagh trip. They are one of the most cruel and sinister inventions. Years after the war ended, children playing in the countryside would blow up, or a farmer working in the field, or a grazing cow. Some mines are weight sensitive, which will not detonate when several cars pass over it, but will blow up if a heavier bus or truck rolls by. Some mines have counter mechanisms, designed to blow up after a certain number of passes over them. Other mines are designed to blow up even at the slightest touch. On a rural road, we had a close encounter. The road had a huge failure creating a pothole the size of a car, filled with water like a pond, virtually impossible to pass. We had no choice but leave the road and find a way through the forest nearby. As we started weaving a passage through the trees, we suddenly came by a car blown up by a mine in the forest... When planning the route of water supply or gas pipelines in the mountains or countryside, I learnt that we had to walk behind one another in a single line, with the most experienced engineer familiar with the area or the mine tracker in front. In the western world, a sign of respect is to give way to someone and tell him/her: "Please, after you," whereas in Artsakh, a sign of respect or care is: "Please, walk behind me".... I doubt if any engineering contract in the western world has a tender item making the contractor responsible to detect and clear land mines along the project route.

We went to northern Artsakh near Sarsang Reservoir, to provide preliminary engineering and cost estimate for another water project. The flowers were budding in the beautiful spring weather, and we picked up some of them. The village leader and his three year old grandson greeted us. When the little boy, Armen, saw the flowers in our hands, he started calling "Baba, baba," leading us and his grandfather in a certain direction. Curiously, we followed him and his grandfather... until we reached a home-made cemetery with a tombstone covered by flowers. In tears, the grandfather explained that his son, Armen's father, was recently martyred in the war, and every day the grandfather and Armen would bring flowers to the grave. The grandfather had two sheep, and he offered to slaughter one of them for us so that we can have dinner together, basically offering half of his entire assets as a donation or present to us for bringing water to his village...

We also went into Aghdam with my Himnatram engineer buddies, Azerbaijan's third largest city before the war. In a calculated way to keep Karabagh Armenians isolated, Azeris had not built any roads within Karabagh and one had to go through Aghdam, in order to travel from north to south Karabagh. As we know, Armenians have now built an economically and militarily critical north-south highway within Artsakh joining most cities and villages to one another, as well as a second lifeline link between Armenia and Artsakh through Kelbajar. Aghdam was evacuated in panic by the Azeris due to the superior military tactics of the Armenians, even though Armenians were outnumbered both in men and equipment. There were even restaurant menus intact in Aghdam for the day of the rout. The city had become an open air building materials supply centre for the Karabagh Armenians, a virtual Home Depot... Armenians would come and pick up housing materials, furniture, even pots and pans from the abandoned city. With some of the army commanders and contractors, I helped transport pipes, electric poles, even hydro transmission towers to the Armenian side. But when one of the contractors proposed to use the precast concrete girders from a recently blown up bridge as the sides of a water reservoir, I had to object... Perhaps this was the first time in Armenians' history that instead of being plundered, Armenians had become plunderers.

In one of our travels, we brought a wealthy Armenian lady from California with us to Aghdam. She was in her eighties and in a wheelchair, but very feisty and determined to see Karabagh, as she had donated substantial sums to Himnatram. We stopped at the Aghdam mosque as some of the engineers wanted to climb the minaret to see the entire city from up above. This lady told us that she also wanted to go into the mosque. Our objections that it may be unsafe or difficult to take her in a wheelchair were to no avail, and she insisted that we carry her into the mosque. We had no choice but to comply. Once inside, she knelt, lifted her skirt, and urinated. And she said: "Now I can die in peace." She told us her story, that she was an orphan of the 1915 Armenian Genocide, and most of her family was put to the sword by the Turks who had then urinated on the dead Armenians...

Armenians of Armenia and Artsakh have paid and continue paying a high price for Karabagh/Artsakh but it is worth it, for many survival reasons – strategic, military, economic, and last but not least, historic.

Hostages as State Policy[*]

In August 2018, US President Trump angrily announced that sanctions will be implemented against Turkey, and personally against the Turkish ministers of interior and justice. What was the reason for Trump's fury? The refusal to release Andrew Brunson, a US evangelical pastor arrested and jailed over two years ago, on still unproven charges of aiding terrorist organizations in Turkey and aiding the failed coup attempt against President Erdoğan in June 2016. The alleged mastermind of the failed coup attempt is Fethullah Gülen, a Turkish cleric who lives in exile in Pennsylvania. Erdoğan has repeatedly demanded his extradition from the US. In the absence of any real evidence, the Americans have not complied with the Turkish demands for Gülen's return, and therefore, Turkey resorted to an age old tactic of hostage taking to achieve its objectives. The arrest and jailing of pastor Brunson, as well as several Turkish employees of

[*] *Armenian Weekly*, 4 Oct. 2018.

the American Embassy in Turkey were meant to pressure the US to exchange them for Gülen. President Erdoğan was even quoted a few months ago to have stated: "You give me my cleric, I give you your pastor."

The use of hostages is a normal state of affairs in Turkish politics. Other recent examples include the arrest of a German journalist of Turkish descent, used as a hostage to secure the return of several Turkish military officers who had sought asylum in Germany. A similar demand for the return of Turkish military officers who fled to Greece was made by Turkey by taking hostage a Greek soldier who allegedly crossed the Greek-Turkish border.

The Greek, Armenian and Jewish minorities living in Turkey have been treated as hostages by the Turkish state throughout history. The religious and community leaders of these three minorities are pressured to declare their allegiance to the government, despite openly discriminatory conditions, unfair legislations, denials of historic facts, and so on. The pressure on the hostage minorities is maximized during crisis times. The most recent example is again related to the Pastor Brunson affair. Just as Trump demanded the release of the pastor, for no apparent reason, out of the blue, all the minority religious leaders including the Armenian Acting Patriarch, the Greek Patriarch, the Jewish Chief Rabbi were paraded with one of the presidential aides of Erdoğan; they signed a declaration that "minorities live happily in Turkey, completely free to practice their religious and citizenship rights without any pressure." It was obvious that the declaration that minorities are not under pressure was obtained by pressure applied by the state on the minority leaders who had to comply – or else… Sometimes, the state does not even have to exert any pressure and, as a classic case of Stockholm Syndrome, some minority leaders like the chairman of an Istanbul Armenian hospital foundation, voluntarily profess their love for their Turkish masters or parrot the state version of history.

This pattern keeps repeating itself in Turkey. During the Cyprus crisis in the 1960s and 1970s, the Greek Patriarch in Istanbul was obliged to condemn the Greeks and praise the Turkish invasion of Cyprus. When the German Parliament recognized the Armenian Genocide and acknowledged its responsibility, the Istanbul Armenian Acting Patriarch condemned the decision and defended the Turkish version of history. When Israel takes any steps against Palestinians or Muslims in general, the Jewish minority in Turkey pays for it with attacks and vandalism against

Jewish synagogues, shops and homes. When Greece is perceived to treat its Muslim citizens unfavorably, the Greek minority in Istanbul is punished by the state as retribution.

Sometimes one hostage community is used against another hostage community. When Armenians worldwide started to push for Armenian Genocide recognition in the parliament of several states, the Jewish minority leaders in Istanbul were pressured to actively engage Jewish parliamentarians and influential political leaders in those countries to stop genocide recognition legislation. Jewish minority leaders in Istanbul were "persuaded" by the Turkish state to convince the Jewish lobby in the US to counteract Armenian and Greek lobbies.

But the most obvious and painful hostage incident in Turkish history relates to the perpetrators of the Armenian Genocide. When World War I ended with the defeat of Ottoman Turkey in 1918, the victorious Allies started occupying Istanbul and other regions of Turkey. In cooperation with the occupying British forces, the new Ottoman government went after the Ittihad Terakki leaders for war crimes, crimes against humanity, and for wholesale massacre of its own Armenian citizens. Turkish and British police started rounding up dozens of Ittihad Terakki leaders and commanders, at least the ones who had not fled yet. Trials ensued in Istanbul and most of the wartime Ittihad Terakki leaders, including Talat, Enver and Djemal who had already fled, were sentenced to death in absentia. Two lesser officials who were sentenced to death were executed by hanging in Beyazid Square in Istanbul in April 1919. Turkish public opinion was dead set against these hangings; concerned with increased protests against them, the British decided to transport all the jailed Ittihad Terakki leaders to the British colony island of Malta in the Mediterranean and continue the trials there. Almost 150 Turkish leaders were interned in Malta. Almost all of them were actively involved in the massacres and deportations of Armenians from various regions of Anatolia. Some of them had amassed great fortunes with stolen property, possessions and lands left behind by murdered or deported Armenians.

In the meantime, the Turkish resistance movement led by Mustafa Kemal in Anatolia started to gain momentum against the Istanbul government, which was regarded as a puppet regime friendly to the occupying Allied forces. Mustafa Kemal and the newly formed government in Ankara demanded the release of the Malta prisoners. The

Allied forces had sent British Colonel Rawlinson to Turkey to assess the situation in Eastern Anatolia, ahead of the Sevres Peace Treaty negotiations. Rawlinson had met with Mustafa Kemal, other Turkish commanders and community leaders. He was married to the niece of Lord Curzon, who was the British Prime Minister and chief decision maker at the peace treaty negotiations. Declaring that Rawlinson is a "valuable catch," Mustafa Kemal promptly decided to arrest Colonel Rawlinson in order to force the British to release the Ittihad Terakki leaders jailed in Malta. After several rounds of negotiations, the British resolve to hold on to the Malta prisoners started to weaken. The hostage taking tactic of Mustafa Kemal succeeded, as Lord Curzon finally declared that "one Briton is worth more than a shipload of Turks.'" An exchange of prisoners was agreed and Colonel Rawlinson, along with 20 other British prisoners of war, was exchanged for the 121 Turkish prisoners of Malta at the port of Inebolu on the Black Sea in October 1921. The freed Ittihad Terakki leaders were never tried for their war crimes nor their roles in the Armenian Genocide. In fact, most of them assumed leading positions in the new republican government as ministers and members of parliament. The state policy of hostages, denial of historic injustices and racist ultra nationalistic hatred of minorities inherited from Ittihad Terakki leaders continue today.

About the Author: Raffi Bedrosyan is a civil engineer, writer and concert pianist, living in Toronto, Canada. He donated proceeds from his CDs and concerts in North America and Europe toward the construction of school, highway, and water infrastructure projects in Armenia and Karabagh, in which he also participated as civil engineer. He helped organize the reconstruction of Surp Giragos Diyarbekir/Dikranagerd church, the first reconstruction and return of property project in Turkey. His many articles in English, Armenian and Turkish media deal with Turkish-Armenian issues, Islamized hidden Armenians and history of thousands of Armenian churches left behind in Turkey after 1915. He gave the first Armenian piano concert in the Surp Giragos church since 1915, most recently at the 2015 Genocide Centenary Commemoration. He is the founder of Project Rebirth, which helps Islamized Armenians return to their original Armenian roots, language, and culture. He has appeared as keynote speaker in numerous international conferences related to human rights, genocide studies and Armenian issues.

GOMIDAS INSTITUTE PUBLICATIONS

For more information visit *www.gomidas.org*. For news and special offers follow us on FaceBook or join our mailing list.